W9-CFO-294

*Jewish
Memories*

Jewish Memories

Lucette Valensi and Nathan Wachtel

translated from the French by Barbara Harshav

*University of California Press
Berkeley
Los Angeles
Oxford*

from the Collection Archives
edited by Pierre Nora
and Jacques Revel

University of California Press
Berkeley and Los Angeles, California

University of California Press
Oxford, England

Published in French under the title *Memoires Juives*
© Editions Gallimard-Julliard, 1986

Valensi, Lucette.
[Mémoires juives. English]
Jewish memories / Lucette Valensi and
Nathan Wachtel; translated from the
French by Barbara Harshav.
p.   cm.
Contents: Translation of: Mémoires juives.
Includes bibliographical references.
ISBN 0-520-06637-5
1. Jews—France—Biography.   2. Holocaust,
Jewish (1939–1945)—France—Personal narratives.
3. Immigrants—France—Biography.   4. Oral
history.   I. Wachtel, Nathan.   II. Title.
DS135.F89V3413   1990
909'.04924082'0922—dc20
[B]
90-11183
CIP

Printed in the United States of America
1   2   3   4   5   6   7   8   9

Contents

Listen . . .   AT THE END of the 1970s, the authors undertook to interview and collect the life stories of Jews living in France but born in other distant lands. "Your history is important," we told them. "The society you belonged to no longer exists. It passed away without leaving any archives and you were witness to an eventful period. Tell us about it."

In the following pages we will hear these voices. They come to us from Paris and its suburbs, from Strasbourg or Clermont-Ferrand. These are the voices of average, ordinary people. One woman was a seamstress, another a cleaning lady, several simply spent their lives taking care of their families. There were businessmen—one was also a poet and art collector—and physicians, a bookkeeper, a watchmaker, some leatherworkers, and several tailors. Some were rich people who frequented casinos and spas, well-read people who spoke like books, and some were poor people who never learned how to read.

These voices come from far away,[1] for all these people spent their childhood, their youth, and sometimes most of their adult life thousands of miles away, in such cities as Alexandria in Egypt, Casablanca in Morocco, Kalisz in Poland, or Berlin in Germany. Two thirds of the people we interviewed were born between the end of the nineteenth century and the beginning of World War I; most of the remaining were born in the inter-

1. Philippe Joutard, *Ces voix qui viennent du passé* (Paris: Hachette, 1983).

I

war period. All are Jewish, each in his or her own way, and for that reason, had to leave their homeland.

The fifty or so biographies reported in this book do not form a statistical sample of the Jewish population living in France. More than five hundred thousand people of various conditions constitute the Jewish community in France today. They come from communities that were in turn diverse and counted several million people before the second war. Needless to say, it would have been impossible to provide any statistical sample of such a population.

Nor do these fifty or so biographies constitute all the narrative we recorded. For when the time came to write down the stories we were told, a kind of dialogue emerged between characters who had never met one another. Without knowing it, our interlocutors broached subjects that another had raised, they responded to one another, and echoed one another. All we had to do was to orchestrate that chorus, giving up a number of biographies we had collected, and cutting large fragments of those we retained.

While not statistically representative, these individual fates are nonetheless typical. Each person made choices in his/her life within a set of social and historical constraints. Each one, retracing his/her past, used the words, the tones and shades of the culture he (or she) belonged to. Each of them, speaking of him (her)self, spoke of "us" and "ours." This might be partially because of the way in which we framed our initial questions. The stories we were told speak of experiences that remained engraved in memory, but not of *all* memorable experiences. If we had called their attention to other aspects of their lives—love, work, this or that revolution in Europe or in the Near East— other memories would have emerged and would have woven different narratives. From the start, our question put memory at the junction of individual and collective destiny. Yet when Suzanne T., a woman born in Algeria, wrote her life story by herself, without being interviewed orally, she evoked the same sequences of the larger history and the same crucial moments of her existence as other women whom we interrogated. Similarly, a group of women questioned about family practices in

Algeria in the past, and in France today, referred to the same episodes in their own lives. Thus individual memory made itself multiple, as if each protagonist was posted as a sentinel receiving the passwords of former generations and transmitting them to those who follow.[2]

When we started collecting these life stories, we thought we would thereby take part in the shaping of a collective memory and would also play the part of the sentinel transmitting the passwords. Indeed, the French version of the book followed paths similar to those of the wandering people it presents, and became itself part of shared memories. Passing from hand to hand, it provoked unexpected reunions between individuals and between generations. We must tell the story of one of these unlikely encounters.

In the course of scholarly and friendly exchanges with our Polish colleagues—then part of the opposition movement and working under very adverse conditions—we gave a copy of our book to a prominent historian in Warsaw, who in turn loaned it to one of his colleagues, Anna Z. She then discovered with astonishment that one of the characters in the book, Charles H., was born in Nysko, the shtetl where her own parents had lived. Born after the war, Anna Z. was the daughter of one of the last survivors of this shtetl, a place she had known only in her earliest childhood. When she returned to the village after her parents' death, not a single Jew remained, and nobody could tell her what Nysko had been like in the old days.

Yet here it was in the pages of a small book. A few months later, Anna Z. had an opportunity to come to Paris for a brief visit on a study grant. She came to us and asked, hesitantly, if she could meet Charles H. She did indeed meet him on the very next day. And this is how, on a winter day in 1988, Charles and Anna spent hours together, with tears in their eyes, evoking the village they had known. What seemed so unusual in their meeting—so Charles H. later told us—was that they owed it to a book; that without it, they would have missed each other and what each of them gave the other. What they shared in common

2. We borrow this metaphor from Walter Benjamin, *Mythe et violence*, trans. Maurice de Gandillac (Paris, 1971), p. 98.

was the memory of the place, of its landscape, even though they had known it at different times. Charles was born in that shtetl forty years before Anna. He had left in 1928, without ever meeting Anna's parents. Yet they both remembered the river that had carried Charles's grandfather's wooden rafts, the same wooden rafts Anna had contemplated as a child. What Charles brought to Anna was a past she had lost, and the memory of all the generations of Jews the shtetl had known until the *Shoah* interrupted their flow. For years, Anna tried to recall the time when the shtetl was full of Jews but was met with a silent absence of memory. She found it again in Paris—guided by a few lines of a small book—in the memories, the pictures, the words and emotions of a man who had left so many years before. Her trip to Paris had turned into a journey into the past.

The narratives that follow present both fragments of an oral history of the period their narrators lived through and fragments of an ethnology of their communities. Yet these fragments have been selected according to a logic that is neither that of the historian nor of the ethnologist. In studying a particular period, the professional historian is no longer the chronicler of his prince, his church, or his nation. Today, addressing a specific issue, the historian locates and organizes facts in such a way as to answer the questions he has raised. His goal is to understand and to make things intelligible. The ethnologist, for his part, observes and orders social practices that make sense for the society that produces them, since culture, a symbolic construct of collective experience, is a major condition of the existence and reproduction of any social unit. What distinguishes their approach from that of people who recall their past is that both the historian and the ethnologist aspire more or less explicitly to thoroughness and objectivity. Situated outside the game they observe, *they* seek to seize it from as many angles as possible. Perceiving themselves as above the game, they believe they can see it better even than the players—although they rely on them to supply the material of their intellectual construct. To remember, however, requires a personal involvement in the drama. *I* is the necessary subject of the action, the one who maintains and cultivates the sense of the past. His subjective narrative is nourished on emotions, unlike the rational construct of the professional scholar. Certainly, like the construct of the historian or the ethnologist, his is a narrative, that is, a fiction, and not the direct and immediate transcription of the lived experience. But something different is at stake in this construct. To draw your self-portrait is to expose your identity. And in the same way that childhood memories shape the identity of the adult individual, so memory does with collective identity. Recounted "by heart," as the saying goes, the narratives we have gathered are the vehicles of a collective memory for which good and bad events of the past have meaning precisely because they form part of a shared experience.[3]

But it might be an illusion to imagine the scholar in a position of neutrality, outside and above the object he constructs and the results he formulates. Each stage of a quest grips the scholar to the core, and no one returns untouched after completing a project. As for us, in any case, we knew we would not be external and objective. As unobtrusive as we tried to be in the course of the interviews, *inter-views* they were, and it was, by our very first question, we who set memory in motion. We wanted this complicity and empathy that bound us to the narrators. Indeed, when we failed to establish this bond, the discourse was inevitably conventional and studied—it rang false. A defensive

3. We have not attempted to confront the narratives collected with history and ethnology books except, in rare cases, to facilitate the understanding of the texts reported here. Hence, the bibliography to be found in some of the notes is deliberately brief. Nor have we indicated the correspondences between the narratives gathered and other expressions of collective memory. In Jewish societies that are only slightly secularized, the religious tradition takes the place of collective memory to a large extent. The secularization of these societies has not given scientific history the advantage over holy history but has rather scaled collective memory which is expressed today by theater, film, novels, painting, music, or so-called Jewish humor. Choosing to remain within a single genre, we shall only note here and there the echoes our narratives find in other published autobiographical texts (narratives or novels). For a discussion of such autobiographies published within the last two decades, see Lucette Valensi, "From Sacred History to Historical Memory and Back: The Jewish Past," pp. 283–305 and Nathan Wachtel, "Remember and Never Forget," pp. 307–335, in *History and Anthropology*, vol. 2, part 2 (1986). On the more general problem of the relations between memory and history in the Jewish experience, see Y. H. Yerushalmi, *Zakhor, Jewish History and Jewish Memory* (Seattle: University of Washington Press, 1982).

and evasive mode blocked communication and suppressed the narrative. In introducing ourselves, without even saying so explicitly, we proposed, accepted, and concluded a contract with our interlocutors, according to which they expected us to listen to their words in order to put them into the pages of a book, since it was our profession to write books.

We generally interviewed people in their own homes. Sometimes, at their request, meetings took place in the bustle of a café or in the presence of friends and relations invited for the occasion. Julien, whom Marx would have characterized as a "professional conspirator" and who has been knocking around since he was eighteen, never received us in his home. Instead, he spent many a long night with us in the Parisian streets around Montparnasse. Elie B., who wanted to emphasize his activities as a man of letters in his long multifaceted career, invited us to a literary café in the Latin Quarter. Hence, from the choice of the venue for our interviews, we could get a sense of the character they wanted to put on stage or to will to posterity. Most often, however, we were invited to enter into the intimacy of their domestic world. In these interiors, there were almost no visible signs of the place of origin. One physician collected nineteenth-century illuminated marriage contracts (*ketubbot*); another had brought objects from Tunisia—some North African, some not—that could have been bought in an antique shop. But generally, objects from their past were not to be found.

The first traces of the past to resurface were words, the wave of words that poured out once contact was established. Then came images, as the characters who populated the narratives now reappeared in family photos. They were images of joy, since it is the nature of such documents to preserve only happy events and leisure moments. Sometimes, from a life turned upside down by the war, all that remained were one or two photos, which then assumed the value of relics. In which case, it was precisely as an act of piety that people wanted to talk: "You see," says Georges F., whose family was exterminated in the camps, "my children don't even know my mother's name." Her name was Esther. By telling us about his childhood, then, he was atoning for oblivion as one atones for a sin, and recalling to life those he had lost.

The ultimate reminders came in the form of sweet-smelling pastries. Almost without fail, important rituals and noteworthy events were associated in the memory with a particular food whose preparation was described and whose recipe was given. Soon enough, those memories would materialize before our eyes, like Proust's madeleines, in the form of cookies and cakes. Preparing to paste together again the pieces of their past, our interlocutors had remade the forgotten gestures, and entrusted to the oven the task of exhaling the lost perfumes. By offering us these pastries, they could better make us share the associations of ideas and images their preparation had called forth and communicate directly to us the taste of yesterday's life.

Words, images, and tastes have made us participate in the destinies whose history we have gathered. Since the beginning of our enterprise, several of the voices we are going to hear have died. Toward those who are now gone we assume the same obligation that they felt toward their own dead. Here we stand at our sentry posts giving the password. *Listen.*[4]

ACKNOWLEDGMENTS

We want to thank Raymonde Adda, Henri Benzakki, Joëlle Bahloul, Arlette Chourna, Claudine Guittoneau, Claudine Herzlich, Alex Kurc, Nine Moatti, Véronique Nahum-Grappe, Gérard Namer, Suzy Sitbon, Jean-Claude Sitruk, and Monica Tiffenberg for the inteviews they conducted for us—with or without us—and which they have given us permission to use. Even when we have not reported them in this book, these texts nourished our reflection and influenced the choice of those we have kept. We also profited from the comparison of our experi-

---

4. The rules of our profession prevent us from publishing the names of those we interviewed. We have kept their first name followed by the initial of the family name and their date and place of birth. The names of the persons cited in their memoirs have been changed except when they are famous personages.

ence with that of Doris Bensimon-Donath and Dominique Schnapper who were collecting oral archives at the time we conducted our interviews.

We also thank Aby Wieworka who translated and transcribed a long interview in Yiddish as well as Alexandre Derczansky who generously gave us the benefit of his erudition. Finally, we benefited from the material support of the Centre de Recherches Historiques at the École des Hautes Études en Sciences Sociales and from the Ministry of Culture, Direction du Patrimoine to which we are also grateful.

Cast of Characters[1]

CLAIRE A.,
born in 1916 in Constantine, Algeria, an attractive woman, she came to France much earlier than the rest of her family. Since 1948, she has been a worker and seems emancipated. Nevertheless, she feels a need to speak Arabic every day: "I think it's the most beautiful language. . . . Every day, three or four words of Arabic come to me, I say them, no matter where I am."

The interview took place in her home, amid the aroma of coffee. She showed a photograph of her father playing the mandolin (he was born in 1885 and had had a shop in Constantine). Claire A. is the first cousin of the next two narrators. We will find her on pp. 23, 235, 283.

ALICE B.,
born in 1913 in Aïn Beïda, Algeria. Remaining single, she lived with her mother in Algeria and in Paris. She fulfills the role of family chronicler and genealogist; another example of such a character will be found later on. Alice B. will be seen on pp. 24, 117, 279, 288.

MANOU B.,
born in 1926 in Aïn Beïda, Algeria, earned her living as a technician in Paris. See pp. 25, 59, 63, 113, 241, 278, 283, 285, 286. These three interviews were done by Raymonde Adda.

1. By order of appearance. Only the major characters are introduced here.

TITA,

born in Tunis in 1902, was questioned in her home, in the Belleville quarter of Paris, by her grandson, a young history teacher, who translated her long narrative from Arabic. The daughter of a shoemaker and a laundress, wife of a traveling peddler, a widow at 36, illiterate, she was employed successively as a servant, a chambermaid in a hotel, and a factory worker. Worn out by a life of trials, her narrative is nevertheless full of humor and love. See pp. 25, 54, 219.

CAMILLA N.,

born in Tripoli, Libya, before 1900. We interviewed her in her home. She has a lovely Italian accent and elegant manners. Serving tea, she is reminded of a Turkish prince in exile in Tripoli—he, too, reduced by circumstances, as she is now, to making his own tea. An image of fallen grandeur. Her childhood memories in fact present a series of vignettes illustrating a fairy tale. See pp. 30, 45, 59, 60, 151, 163, 224, 227.

LAURE A.,

born in Istanbul in about 1910, defines herself as a spoiled child. She receives us in her home, in a pink housecoat; she wears makeup, her hair is styled and dyed blond. She tells us that the only thing she has preserved of the Orient is her taste for sofas, on which she spends her days. So, stretched out on a sofa, she gives us an account of her gilded youth. She has preserved a thick accent, inserts English, German, or Italian expressions into her speech, thus demonstrating the good education she received (one of the central themes of her biography). Nothing in the apartment is reminiscent of Istanbul; there is not even a single one of those precious rugs her father dealt in. See pp. 32, 63, 149, 160, 216, 230.

GABRIEL D.,

born in Salonika in about 1910, came to France after being an inmate in Auschwitz Concentration Camp and nursed back to health in Sweden. In Paris, he worked as a peddler. During the interview, done by Monica Tiffenberg, he shows a photograph from his youth, "himself at 17, his sisters, his cousins, all the kids, each one on his bike," dressed in the style of the 1920s. Monica Tiffenberg comments: "How handsome you were!" And he replies: "Yes! We're Spaniards!" Iberian pride emerges in other memories of Sephardim from Istanbul and Salonika. See pp. 33, 63, 66, 111, 222, 263, 286.

IDA O.,
born in Salonika in 1906, in France since the 1920s. Widow of a textile merchant in the Sentier quarter of Paris, she has known a certain comfort. She receives us in her home, offers tea with Salonikan pastries she has made and bought for us: the only trace of the home country. There are some objects of European manufacture but brought from Salonika and an abundant collection of photographs on which she comments with great liveliness, in tones and expressions that are strongly Salonikan. See pp. 33, 65, 115, 221, 223, 229, 271.

GEORGES X.,
born in Tunis in 1908, studied medicine in Paris, practiced in Tunisia, emigrated at the beginning of the 1960s. He receives us in his home, surrounded by the furniture and the rich library he had in Tunisia. See pp. 35, 143, 148.

GIOIA A.,
born in Alexandria in 1909. The appropriately named Gioia receives us in her home, derides everything she tells us, and is amused by everything. Even the exodus that led her, her husband, and her young daughter to the south of France, Portugal, Africa, and finally Cairo is told in a joking manner. Of her life in Egypt, she kept only photographs, and she comments on them for us. But her memories are especially filled with the flavors of sweets, that reappear during the interview in the form of Egyptian pastries. See pp. 35, 143, 148.

EDMOND H.,
contemporary of Gioia, born in Cairo, a businessman. The reverses he suffered in Egypt feed a resentment that is still very

keen. Again, nothing in his apartment is reminiscent of his long stay in Egypt, except for the pastries he makes himself and serves at each of our meetings. See pp. 36, 152, 161, 273.

SUZANNE T.,

born in Sétif in 1910. Approached by H. Benzakki, then a student of history, Suzanne T. preferred to write the account of her life and give him the various chapters. During their meetings, she added commentaries and documents to the text she provided. He describes her as living alone in a suburban low-income housing project, speaking with a loud voice, a marked accent, and a great liveliness in spite of physical handicaps. From her kitchen comes "an odor of pimento and oriental spices," "the reception is warm, spontaneous, the bottle of anisette is quickly out on the table for the visitor."

Her text is first an epic of daily life, with the detailed account of family conflicts, the birth of her ten children, the death of two of them, the professional successes and reverses of the husband. It is also a testimony: Suzanne is deliberate in recounting the political climate and events, details of the material conditions of life (for example, the introduction of domestic electricity in Constantine in 1930), and everything else that seems to her to be typical in the life she has lived. But, underlying the chronicle and the testimony, the autobiography utters a protest: a protest against an unsatisfactory present that lacks dear and departed persons, that lacks the objects of love and hate that fill her memories, that lacks the repayment by her children for all the attention she gave them.

The writing of the account is almost bereft of punctuation, and its spelling translates the sounds of the spoken rather than the written language. Regretfully, we have had to correct the spelling and introduce punctuation to make this text intelligible to a reader. See pp. 38, 50, 106, 231, 236, 240, 276, 279, 281, 285.

GEORGETTE D.,

born in 1899 in Tunis, converses with her husband, born before her, a nephew born in 1906, and his wife, who hardly intervenes. The conversation is lively, constantly interrupted. I was taken to Georgette because she is considered the repository of the family memory. Indeed, on the basis of tenuous clues—a first name, an address—she immediately reconstructs the biography of an individual and his relatives. The names that populate her discourse ultimately go well beyond the limits of family relationships. The personage of the family chronicler is a widespread social type. Among North African Jews he (or she) keeps oral records of personal statistics with associations such as: "X had his bar mitzvah when Z got married and Y was living on such-and-such a street." And people turn to this data bank for every verification of identity.[2]

Georgette's husband comes from a Livornese family and is thus higher in the local hierarchy. That will be recalled at length in the course of the conversation but is not reproduced here. See pp. 41, 119.

LOUISE G.,
Aïn Beïda, 1921, is the first cousin of Claire A., Alice B., and Manou B. See pp. 43, 116, 278, 284, 285.

PAPOU N.,
born in Salonika in 1894, was interviewed by his granddaughter, who describes him as tall, erect, filling the space. With his abundant hair "thrown back with a crazy elegance," he laughs. And when he stops laughing, "you can see the blue of his eyes, very blue. Papou rolls his r's and talks with his hands, or rather, his hands also talk, in an ironic or earnest counterpoint, with those gestures which come from far away, which nobody else in that family still has. What remains on paper resembles Papou very little. The tone of his voice, his gestures, the expressions of his face, everything is lost except for the

2. This character is also found in Salonika: "The date of birth, already a big deal. Let Cousin Rachel and Aunt Binouta remember (that's all they had to do) the births of our twenty cousins, that was enough." Henriette Asseo, "Du miel aux cendres. . . . Où sont passés soixante-dix mille Juifs de Salonique?" [From Honey to Ashes . . . Where Did the Seventy Thousand Jews of Salonika Go?], *Les Temps modernes*, no. 400 (November 1979): 828–845.

meaning, a black skeleton on white paper."[3] We will see him on pp. 44, 164, 265.

HENRI Z.,

born in Cairo in 1913. Like Edmond H., Papou N., Laure A.'s father, and so many other characters who will appear in the course of this book, he is a dragoman par excellence: an intermediary between East and West, an importer-exporter and major entrepreneur by profession, and a master of several languages and cultures. See pp. 46, 66.

MATHILDE B.,

born in Bizerte in 1892, receives us at her home in a studio she occupies in Sarcelles. All that is left of her life in Tunis is the round table at which her family used to eat its meals, the children did their schoolwork, and friends played cards. Mathilde pours out countless photographs onto the table and comments on them. She sees her life as a love story she wants to leave to posterity. (Interview done by Lucette Valensi and Nine Moatti.) See pp. 60, 65, 103.

CHARLES H.,

born in 1906 in Nysko, a shtetl in Galicia. His father was first a bailiff in the court and then a bank employee. Charles studied in the State Polish high school and then immigrated to France (Nancy) in 1924 to study medicine. After marrying Hélène, he moved to a small city near Paris. During the Occupation, he hid with his family in a village of the Creuse. He speaks a very elegant French, modulated by a slight accent. See pp. 3, 70, 94, 133, 247, 295.

GEORGES F.,

born in 1915 in the Polish little town of Skarzysko-Kamiena (between Radom and Kielce). Childhood lived in poverty, a "happy poverty." Studied in *heder* and, at the age of 13, became

3. Since the publication of this book, Papou N. has become the subject of a book written by his son, Edgar Morin, *Vidal et les siens* (Paris: Le Seuil, 1989).

an apprentice tailor. He immigrated to France in 1936 (following his brother who left in 1933). Went to Lyon after the round-up of September 1941, followed by his wife after the roundup of the Vel' d'Hiv of July 1942. Returned to Paris after the Liberation. He has preserved a deep nostalgia for the places of his childhood and dreams of one day crossing the bridge of his village again. See pp. 6, 74, 82, 85, 89, 95, 99, 124, 129, 130, 133, 177, 245, 249, 252, 301, 339.

HÉLÈNE H.,

born in 1906 in Bialystok, descendant of a line of famous rabbis. During World War I, she fled with her mother to the Ukraine (to Ekaterinoslav). Immigrated to France (Nancy) in 1924 to study medicine. Married Charles H. A perfect mastery of French, which she speaks without any accent. See pp. 75, 174, 295.

LAZARE M.,

born in Kalisz in 1910, studied in heder, then the Jewish (Hebrew) high school. A poor student in Warsaw, in a seminary of the C.Y.S.H.O. (to become a teacher). Active in the leftist Po'alei Zion movement.[4] Came to France in 1937, where he continued his activism. Volunteered for the army in 1939, was assigned to a Polish regiment that crossed the Swiss border in June 1940; was imprisoned in various camps and then was able to resume his studies in education in Switzerland. Returned to France after the war and worked as a teacher in the institutions that took in the children of deportees. See pp. 76, 80, 126, 135, 249.

MATHILDE R.,

born in 1928 in the suburbs of Paris, her father was from Lodz, her mother from Brest-Litovsk. Her assimilationist parents first raised her in ignorance of her Jewish origin and sent

---

4. C.Y.S.H.O.: Central Organization of Yiddish School. *Po'alei Zion:* a movement that combined Zionism and Socialism, it began in Russia in the 1890s and then spread to other European countries. The leftist branch joined the Third International.

her to a Catholic school. She discovered her Jewish identity during a trip to Poland in 1938 with her mother. Hid during the Occupation, first in Toulouse and then in a village of the Cantal, she returned to Paris after the Liberation and later became a psychoanalyst. She received us in an apartment in the chic neighborhood of Faubourg Saint-Germain and spoke with elegance, intensely reliving the emotions of the past, accompanying her account with a running analytical commentary. See pp. 81, 197, 253, 258, 292, 303, 317, 320.

LOUISE M.,
born at the turn of the century in a little town in Silesia, she then lived in Berlin, where she got married. Daughter and granddaughter of an educated middle-class family, she was one of those "assimilated" German Jews who were taken by surprise by the onslaught of Nazism. Immigrated to Morocco via Holland in 1936. See pp. 88, 178, 251, 257.

ANNA D.,
born in Lodz in about 1918. A poor dressmaker, she spent the war in Poland; was deported to the camp in Skarzysko. Immigrated to France in 1946. This interview was conducted by Claudine Guittonneau. See pp. 34, 327.

YACOB-JACQUES L.,
born at the end of the last century in a shtetl in the area of Lublin, Yacob is the son of a watchmaker, and he studied in the heder; his reading (particularly *Around the World in Eighty Days,* translated into Yiddish) led him to question religious beliefs. He became a watchmaker too and moved first to Warsaw and then to Moscow (where he experienced troubles during the Revolution of 1917). He immigrated to France in 1920 and worked as a watchmaker near Montbéliard, then in Besançon, and finally in Paris, where he becomes Jacques. Speaks French with a very thick accent. His speech is constantly interspersed with biblical allusions. His family having been exterminated during the war, he had always kept silent about that period. He

welcomes us gratefully, relieved to have a chance to tell his story at last. See pp. 94, 100, 128, 134, 172, 189, 324.

MAURICE N.,

born in 1920 in Okouniev, near Warsaw. His father, first a hasid, later became a Communist. Studied in heder, then in Polish school. The father immigrated to Paris in 1929, and was followed by his family in 1931. At the age of thirteen, after one year of schooling, Maurice went to work tanning leather. Member of the Yiddish Arbeiter Sportive Klub, then the Communist Youth and the Communist party, he joined the Resistance in Lyon (Décines). After the war, he went into the leatherworking business on his own. Left the Communist party in 1956 and states his sympathy for Israel. Interview done by Alex Kurc.[5] See pp. 98, 132, 188, 200, 210, 246, 309, 314.

ROBERT S.,

born in 1907 in Przemysl, in Galicia, to a family of modest means (his father, a traveling salesman in rather poor health). Studied in the Polish high school. Came to Nancy, France, in 1928. He led the life of a poor student (of dentistry), forced to work to support himself while also regularly sending help to his parents in Poland. Obtained French citizenship in 1935. Then he brought his brother and one sister to France. Drafted in 1939, he was taken prisoner and then freed. He lived in a town in the center of France during the Occupation and then hid in a village of Auvergne. He established his dental practice only after the Liberation, almost twenty years after his arrival in France. A longtime fellow traveler of the Communist party, he finally returned to his former Zionist sympathies. Speaks perfect French with a slight accent. See pp. 101, 171, 191, 207, 246, 250, 253, 298, 322.

5. This character also inspired the joint article of Martine Cohen, Michèle Feldmann, Colette Guigui, Claudine Guittonneau, Alex Kurc, Monica Tiffenberg, and Inna Weber, "L'histoire de Maurice: essai d'analyse d'un récit de vie" [The Story of Maurice: Analysis of a Life Account] *Yod. Revue des études hébraïques et juives modernes et contemporaines* 6:1 (first and second trimesters 1980): 78–86.

VIVIANE B.,

born in Constantine in 1929, in France since 1926; profession, secretary. She is the first cousin of Claire A., Alice B., Manou B., Louise G., and a few others. She is seen again on pp. 112, 278.

REINE A.,

a cousin of the previous characters, was born in Aïn Beïda in 1917. She was a seamstress and "sewed the trousseau" of several young Jewish girls of Constantine. She is loquacious and vociferous, her French mixed with Arab words. See pp. 114.

BERNARD P.,

born in 1922 in Kalisz. His father was a worker specializing in lace. Studied in the Jewish (Hebrew) high school. Immigrated to France (Roanne) with his family in 1938. He went to work immediately in the hosiery trade and was then a member of Hashomer HaZa'ir, the Zionist-Socialist youth movement. During the war, he joined the Resistance in the U.J.J. [Union de la Jeunesse Juive] in Roanne and later in Lyon (Décines). Left the Communist party in 1956 and declares his support of the State of Israel. Interview done by Alex Kurc. See pp. 127, 134, 197, 246, 252, 309, 317.

MARC B.,

born in 1900 in Warsaw (Praga), to a family of Hasidim. An apprentice leatherworker at thirteen, he was active in the Bundist movement at a very young age (he was especially involved in the organization of the large Bund library in Warsaw).[6] Came to France in 1925, where he worked as a leatherworker. Continued to be active in the Bund and was one of the founding members of the Medem Library. Arrested in May 1941, he was sent to the Beaune-la-Rolande camp, where he spent eleven months and then managed to escape. He hid successively in Toulouse, Lyon, and finally Grenoble. Interviewed by Claudine Guittonneau. See pp. 137, 199, 306.

6. Bund: Jewish Socialist party founded in Russia in 1897, very active in Poland between the two world wars.

JULIEN K.,

born about 1914 in a village in Galicia. His father was principal of a Yiddish school in Chelm, then editor of a Jewish journal in Cracow. Julien K. studied in the state Polish high school in Cracow and became a political activist at an early age. He followed a rather turbulent personal itinerary, moving from leftist Zionism to Communism and then to Trotskyism, later to Bundism and Socialism, all the while preserving his revolutionary faith intact. Condemned as a Trotskyite in Warsaw, he escaped before he was sentenced and, after much wandering about, arrived in France in May 1936. Participated in the Spanish Civil War with the troops of the P.O.U.M., the left-wing anti-Stalinist party. Arrested in Barcelona by the Stalinists, he was back in France in 1938. Managed to escape in 1941 to Switzerland, where he was interned in various camps. After the war, a journalist in the Yiddish press of Paris. The dramatic vicissitudes of his life are a surprise, coming from one with such a weak voice and such an apparently sickly constitution. An account that keeps us constantly charmed by its intelligence, its liveliness, and its quiet humor. See pp. 128, 138, 179, 200, 252.

MADAME K.,

an elegant and lively woman, who has known comfort ever since her childhood in Tunis. She meets us in a large café in the Opéra quarter of Paris. Love of music figures prominently in her memories, a sign of the high culture, good taste, and fine education with which she was raised. Her pleasure in those memories does not prevent her from offering critical remarks on the prejudices of her milieu. See pp. 156, 218.

GOLDA R.,

born about 1910 in Warsaw (Praga). Came to Paris for the first time at the age of thirteen but had to return to Poland. Immigrated to France ten years later (preceded by her parents). Worked first in a restaurant in Belleville, then as a salesgirl in a pastry shop, and finally as an operator in a textile workshop. Married a construction worker in 1937. Interview done in Yiddish. See pp. 172, 202, 319, 338.

LÉON W.,

born in 1905 in Kalisz (where he lived in the same building as Lazare M.). After studying in heder, he began to work as an apprentice tailor at the age of thirteen. Immigrated to France, to Metz, in 1923. Enlisted in the army in 1939. After the German invasion, he hid with his family in Clermont-Ferrand in 1940, then in Brioude in 1942. Continued to live in Auvergne after the war, practicing the trade of tailor. See pp. 177, 245, 249.

ANNETTE B.,

born in Mogador in the 1920s, did not go to school in Morocco. She simply learned leatherworking. She was not yet twenty when she married a young grain dealer. Starting out with nothing, he succeeded in amassing a comfortable fortune, symbolized particularly by the construction of a big house in Casablanca. Moving to France was accompanied by a social decline and a reversal of roles: at the time we speak to her, Annette B. is a dressmaker and supports the whole family, her husband being unable to find work. But the rise begun in Morocco is picked up again by the children. She encourages us to meet one of her daughters, who is married to an Ashkenazi intellectual in Paris. Exile was at the center of the mother's talk. It remains at the center of the daughter's, Sonia.

Annette B. received us in Strasbourg, at the end of Passover. All the tastes of spring in Morocco appeared on the table for the ritual of *Mimouna,* in which we were generously invited to participate. See pp. 280, 281, 287, 289.

PART ONE
The World of Yesterday

<table>
<tr><td>

I

From Salonika to Sefrou

</td><td>

SETTING: CONSTANTINE BETWEEN THE TWO WORLD WARS

"Everything happened together," "we were always in each other's houses," "the ghetto, after all, did us a favor": all the women who describe the city between the two world wars recall a closed space which stopped, significantly, at "Breach Street" and where you were with your own people. Far from complaining about being confined, they recall a rich world where social

</td></tr>
</table>

relations were intense and incessant. Far from denouncing the absence of privacy, they exalt the close acquaintance everyone had with everyone else, an entire population composed of only relatives, neighbors, and friends. Besides, those three categories were superimposed on one another: neighbors were like members of the family, friends were our cousins, our cousins became our spouses. In this homogeneous space, "private life" was unthinkable; on the contrary, today, deprived of these close relations, life loses its taste.

Claire A., Constantine 1916:

I was born in Constantine; I am the last of fourteen children. We were born in a kind of house, "Dar Mahmud Ali," which was very famous, a little like the mosque here: everybody knows where it is. There were thirty-three families there and no family had fewer than six children. And the houses, what was special about them is that they didn't close. The houses were open and you knew family X just as well as family Y. You were with family and everything happened together. You knew what your neighbor bought, you knew your neighbor's poverty as well as your neighbor's wealth. And anyway, they were all

Jews on Rue Ferrand. You see the high school, the synagogue, it was on this street, down by the hospital, the barracks. So imagine thirty-three families with those children who grew up, who had more children, everybody knew *everybody* else. There were two stories. We ourselves had two rooms and a kitchen. Once a week, Mama washed us, my father dried us, and then my oldest brother dressed us. And we had a table, a round one, my father cut the bread, he threw pieces of bread like that, and we stuffed it in the plate to augment the soup.

Those are memories that stay with you for your whole life. Of course, there was hardship as well. We lost my father, he was a shoemaker, he did everything, poor man. He sold cloth, he gave so much credit that they didn't pay him, he sold shoes, he went bankrupt. Then he did shoemaking. . . . Poor Mama, she had a tough time. There were a lot of things we didn't have, but not love.

Alice B., Aïn Beïda, 1913:

The family, we were always in each other's houses. First, it wasn't far, not the kind of distances you have here. You went out of one house, you went back to another one because everything was close by; you went to somebody's house, there were my aunts, my cousins, my cousin Yvonne who lived on Rue Thiers—she's in Marseille now—and you went out, you went to the movies, you went to the casino, on Saturday. In fact, they called us the pillars of the casino, we went there so much.

You visited the family almost every afternoon, visiting back and forth. First you had your mother Yvonne and your aunt Nono, every day, every day they came to our house, then it was Vivi, then it was. . . . When there was some event, no matter what event, everybody ran to see them.

Some came to our house, we went to their house. First, Mama, if you remember, she went down to your mother every morning to have coffee and your mother, she came in the afternoon. . . . They were very close down there, very. Daniel, Jacky, they don't have any pals anymore. Down there, every one had five, six pals. Roland he had Sylvain, Guy, Vivi.

"Were they not cousins?"

Yes but, even so, cousins but also pals. . . . There was Guy A., the hairdresser, Jacques's brother, Adelin, I tell you: at least seven or eight. There was Prosper, my cousin. See, we loved the family so much that we didn't have any friends except for our cousins.

Manou B., Aïn Beïda, 1926:

The ghetto, after all, did us a favor.
"How?"
Because you did what you wanted, you stayed in your own element. There weren't any strangers coming in, no mixed marriages, not all this stuff we see today. I, for example, I know that for Kippur, it was marvelous because we had a lot of synagogues right there in the ghetto. Across from the boys' high school, you see the Rue de France? There's Rue Thiers, Rue Damrémont, that whole corner there, right up to the Place de la Brèche, there were only Jews living there.

A man, born in Constantine in 1916. (Says in an objective tone of voice, without measuring the effect of unwitting humor):

The Jewish quarter has a particularity, it is typically Jewish. You can't say it's a ghetto, but a little Jerusalem in Algeria.

A woman, born in Aïn Beïda in 1907:

It was a little Jerusalem, Aïn Beïda, I swear. There were a lot of families who were very religious, very pious, you were hand in hand in that village, eh, you loved each other a lot and you knew each other well.[1]

TUNIS, AT THE BEGINNING OF THE CENTURY

A miserable childhood, right in the middle of the Jewish quarter, the Hara: *Tita, born in 1902, recalls the house where she grew up*

---

1. With about thirteen thousand Jews, Constantine was one of the most populous centers of Jewish life in Algeria between the two world wars, after Oran (twenty to twenty-five thousand Jews in the 1930s and 1940s) and Algiers (twenty-three to twenty-six thousand). Aïn Beïda numbered one thousand in 1931, and fewer than five hundred ten years later.

with her parents and two brothers. We have several descriptions of what she calls the "Arab house." Whether this house was in Algeria or Tunisia, it always evokes the same images, associated with the same impressions: the shortage of water and the drudgery that imposed; the lavatory which had to be shared with the neighbors, and the consequent immodesty and discomfort; the smallness and, at the same time, the neatness of the room occupied by the entire family; the courtyard as a place for meetings and as a female bastion; the life that circulated among the cells of that organism and through the courtyard.

When the same persons indicate their subsequent move into Western-style apartments, they feel no need to describe them, since they continue to live in a similar environment, whereas the Arab house belongs to the past and is no longer familiar. Rather than life in an apartment, people then recall, as in Constantine just now, life among *the apartments, life that circulated from one house to another.*

"What was your house like?"

My house? One room.

"Only one?"

One room. There were toilets: not in our house, for everybody. There was the courtyard; there, everybody had his own corner.

"A single room . . . and a kitchen?"

No! A single room! There was one corner inside and that's where you cooked. When it rained, you did the laundry; you did everything in that corner.

There was a mat, a piece of sheepskin. In winter, we sat on it, my mother and me, next to each other. We used the *canoun* [*a clay brazier*] to warm up and my father sat on a chair next to the table to pray and read, and read, and read. . . . When my father finished the meal—he ate a little salad, a little bread, and was content—he said the prayer and stayed like that until he finished digesting. Then he told us a story. Mama made coffee. He drank and finished his story. About 10 or 10:30, he got into bed and said *Shema Israel Adonai*" [*the profession of faith*].

"How did he read? Was there enough light?"

How! We had kerosene! No electricity, no; kerosene. You

put it in the room, on the cabinet. Sometimes, when you didn't have enough, you used candles.

As for me, ever since I can remember, there was water in the house. We were in the house of Caïd Nessim, a big house. We had a well but that water was salty. You cleaned the house with it, did the dishes and the laundry. But fresh water, the water seller brought us that. He had a water skin on his shoulder. "Hey water seller, bring water!" You took a little, you washed the laundry and soaped it. Then you rinsed it in the well. Sometimes, there was spring water. Fresh water.

"Where did people wash?"

In the basin, at home. Always.

"And the Turkish baths?"

Ah yes! The Turkish bath, there was one. But every day at the Turkish bath? No! We didn't have the money! The Turkish bath, you paid for it. Women went there once a year, twice . . . three times. For married women, it was an obligation! But it was expensive. Two hundred fifty, that was something! Who could go there?

Tita doesn't cross the threshold of the house except sometimes on Saturday to go to the port or the public gardens. She spends her day playing in the courtyard with her little neighbors.

When I was little, I didn't go to school because we were poor. My mother couldn't outfit me or buy me a blouse or shoes or school things.

World War I breaks out. Tita is thirteen or fourteen years old. Only an event of such magnitude can send her rushing out on an adventure: to leave the Hara to see the troops sail. She will never reach the port, barely a mile away.

I was with my girlfriend and I said to her: "Come on, we're going to the port to the parade of Jewish workers who are leaving." She said to me: "Shut up. Us, go to the port?" I insist, she says: "Fine, what else have we got to do anyway?" We went and we came to the church, the one of the Gate of France. When we get to the Residence House [*the Résidence Générale, symbol* and seat of the protectorate in the center of the European town], I said to her: "That's enough. I want to go back home. I'm scared." Going to the port, we could have been followed by some bad boys. What did we know? They could beat us up or . . . anyhow, we went home.

Married to an old clothes dealer at seventeen, Tita moves into the sort of house she has lived in since childhood: "From one dump to another, that's life." In the double room she occupies, she will have seven children and two miscarriages; she will not leave the ghetto until 1952, when she immigrates to Paris. Her jealous husband keeps her shut in and under close watch. This seclusion left ambivalent memories on Tita: on the one hand, a strong resentment against her husband; on the other, the memory of the modest joys obtained by the intense complicity between the women who shared the same courtyard.

With Aouïda, everything was fine, except that he was jealous. He would start up with me. I said to him: "But you really have nothing to complain about! The house is clean, dinner is ready, and I keep quiet." "Yes, but you want to go out!" "I don't want to go out! I don't!" In spite of everything, I wasn't sad like here. Because it was an Arab house: here's one neighbor, here another, there, yet another. . . . Here Shmina, here. . . . They would stand at the window talking. As for me, I'd be at the window too, looking at them. That would amuse me a little! It wasn't as if there was no one to talk to, like now.

He was too jealous. Sometimes he'd come home early; work hadn't gone well. I didn't know when he was going to come back so early. He'd find me standing around, and chatting with the neighbors: "Why are you there? Get into the house!" What a bother! I'd go back to the room. "They're all outside and I'm the only one to come in? Am I a rat or a snake for you to lock up?" "Look out the window!" Do you realize how tough it was?

When Aouïda died, I went everywhere: to Kalaline, to Bahri. Whatever he didn't let me do when he was alive, I did afterward.

One day, the neighbors enticed her into violating her husband's prohibition and attending an Arab wedding. Fifty years later, the escapade is told with relish.[2]

Once, there was an Arab wedding. . . . That old woman I told you about worked for them. She made *mhamos* [*a kind of semolina*] and other things for them. . . . They said to her: "You're coming to the wedding?" As for me, I was pregnant with the little one, in my seventh month. She says to me: "So, you're coming with us?" I said to that old woman, Meinou: "Yes, I really want to go!" I had made a *bsal ou loubia* [*a stew of beans and onions*] on the canoun, under the table: everything was neat. Aouïda was sleeping. Softly . . . I took my shoes, I put them on, and I went out! She asked me: "You're ready?" "I'm ready!" "Come out to the courtyard so Aouïda doesn't see you!" At three o'clock, we left. In the meantime, the cat spills the meal, the stewpot on the floor! Aouïda wakes up, gets up, and sees that meal. . . . He comes out and shouts: "Hey, Tita! Tita, Tita!" And where is Tita? At the wedding! You know what time I came back? Maybe, no kidding, it was in summer, nine, ten o'clock! But there, not all alone, with the neighbors! Ah, that night! Poor me! What he couldn't do! "By God, you won't come back, slut! [*Laughs*] You won't come back into the room tonight! You sleep outside!" There I was right in the middle of the house. The woman who was with me: "I beg you, do a favor, for me!" He had locked himself in: "She could die for all I care, she'll sleep nowhere except in the street to-night! Or in the toilets." One of my daughters, Hnina, was crying. She went to get Deïdou. It was far away, his house. She was crying and calling from downstairs: "Uncle! Uncle!" "What's the matter with you?" "Come down! Come down! Father has locked Mama out!" He came running. He begged, over and over again. Deïdou was respected: "Hey, Aouïda,

2. The same sort of woman is found in the memories of Albert Memmi, *La Terre Intérieure* [The Internal Land] (Paris: Gallimard, 1976), p. 21, who recalls his mother: "Even now I am amazed at the character of my mother, an almost mysterious blend of trickery and resignation, of suffering accepted and revolt intact to the end, of submission to the extraordinary harshness of her fate and the liveliness and tenacity of a weed, the confidence of a wild animal, born, raised and having spent almost all her life in the Hara, until that fabulous departure for that world that was unreal and crazy to her, Paris."
The same character appears in Georges Memmi, *Qui se souvient du Café Rubens?* [Who Remembers Café Rubens?] (Paris: J.-Cl. Lattes, 1984).

open up! Aouïda!" At first, softly, nicely, then, finally: "Shit, Aouïda! Open up!" He knocks on the door and finally Aouïda came down: "Wait till your brother goes and you'll see what I'm going to do to you!" I said to him: "What can you do to me? Beat me? Go ahead, beat me! You want to slit my throat with a knife?" Finally, Deïdou stayed a while and said to him: "Come on, eat some dinner!" The other one answered: "What dinner? There it is! The cat ate it!" Then he asked me: "And you?" "I ate!" Then we stayed like that, on two benches, one opposite the other: Then he started to talk and talk. . . . And he became coarse. . . . I let him talk until he'd had his say. Then, we stayed like that. I slept standing up. What could I do with him? He was born that way. Finally, he slept and I slept too. . . . We didn't sleep together, though, in the same bed. Never. Ever since I had Habiba, he slept on the bench and I slept inside on the bed with my children.

"Why?"

He didn't want to. He was disgusted. Ever since I had Habiba . . .

TRIPOLI BETWEEN 1908 AND 1920
A MAGNIFICENT HOLE

Camilla N.'s memory of Tripoli at the beginning of the century is the memory of a world of plenty. Unlike the previous witnesses, Camilla grew up in a rich family, open to the outside world, mixed with non-Jews. But the memories of grandeur arise mostly from the big house in which all of life's dramas were played out, from the patio teeming with noise and activity: abundance prevailed, men and animals abounded, including an entire population of white and black servants, clients, craftsmen, and artisans who worked for the family; visitors and relatives bustled about. Beyond, the town was nothing but a "hole," but it is recalled as a place rich in human and natural resources and so important politically that the great powers sent only personages of the highest quality.

Tripoli was the capital. It wasn't called Tripoli, Libya; it was called Tripoli of Barbary. When we were in school, it was

Tripoli of Barbary and I remember that there were only sixty thousand inhabitants in that whole capital: I had studied it in the *scuola elementare* [*laughs*], that's why it stayed in my mind. It was very small, insubstantial, nothing much to speak of. Only, it was like *le Isole Lipari*, if you like, where Sultan Abdulhamid (I don't know if you're familiar with the story of Abdulhamid, but you must know that he was a most terrible tyrant) sent those who supported freedom. That meant you were in contact with high-class people in that hole. In that hole which wasn't a hole, because on one side was an oasis with very tall palm trees that were very imposing and on the other side was the sea, the open sea. Without a port, without anything at all. There was no port, there wasn't anything, in fact. What was it then? It was a beach, where a few families had settled. And the rest, a small town: there was the ghetto, the Arabs, the Europeans.

What made it special was that Tripoli had been Turkish, but it couldn't remain Turkish because everybody was out colonizing. The Germans had colonies, the French had colonies, the English had colonized Egypt, they had Syria and all that. Anyhow, they had taken a lot of things. And Italy, which was just born, wanted her share. Only there was a lot of competition because the Germans wanted to occupy Tripoli. That meant it was extremely important politically and that's why there had to be politicians. There was even a consulate; there was almost nothing, but the men they sent there, from the political point of view, were very able men.

Camilla's father occupies a central place in her childhood memories: "I can't remember anything about him that wasn't extraordinary." Generosity, grandeur, ingenuity ("He was ahead of his time"), tolerance—all the qualities she recognizes in him are illustrated in the life of the house and the caravanserai attached to it.

There was a house that looked out onto a caravanserai. In the middle of that caravanserai, there was a small garden. And, all around, there were all sorts of animals. . . . In the morning, he [my father] woke me up to give me a cup of warm milk which had just been drawn. [*Later, she will give details: "In the dining*

31

room, there were all kinds of fruits, all the earth's seasonal bounty."]
Then we would go out onto a little terrace, overlooking the
caravanserai, and we saw the horses being washed and combed
and groomed. We would watch.

For example, at that time, there weren't any pipes, there
wasn't any water. We had cisterns, yes, we had cisterns in the
courtyard. There was rainwater. Okay, but to take a bath, you
had to have Negroes to bring the water up. There were a lot
of servants because down there it was easier. But him [my
father], what did he come up with? He had made a bridge like
this [gestures] and he put a big contraption on the terrace. And
when he came home at noon and at night, he used to take a
shower.

The Fezzanis, they gave us a lot of gazelles, parrots, mar-
mosets, small leopards. The leopards, my father gave to the
governor, they put them in a zoo. As for all the others, the
caravanserai was full of them: peacocks, talking parrots, there
were four or five of them in the house, canaries, dogs, everything. It was impressive, so impressive.

ISTANBUL, BETWEEN 1910 AND 1930

*Like Camilla N. between Tripoli, Tunis, and Paris, Laure A. has
always lived in comfort, often luxury. Neither of them suffered a loss
of status in moving to France. But Laure A. also recalls the splendor
of her childhood home and the sense of being superior to others comes
through in all the details of her story.*

I was born in Péra. Being the youngest, I was the only one
in the family to have had that privilege. The others were born
in little villages, not very elegant. All the rich Jews were in Has-
keuy but me, I was the smallest, the most advanced, I was born
in Péra. It was a chic place. When I say I was born in Péra,
people take me for a snob. But it's because I was the youngest.
Mama wanted to move. She thought it was common down
there, so we came to Péra.

Then we came to Kheidar Pasha. That was another suburb,
like Enghien, for example, where there was fresh air. It was very
bourgeois, you know, we were the aristocrats of the place.

Everyone lived in his own house. They were two-story houses. So you had a lot of servants, there would be ten of us at the table, and we had ten servants in the house. Papa and Mama, that makes two, and six children, that makes eight, the governess, who ate with us, that makes nine, and grandmother brings it to ten. Downstairs in the kitchen, there were as many servants: there was the cook, there was another governess, a maid who was almost a governess; there was a chambermaid; there was a girl who helped the chambermaid; there was the girl who ironed, there was the laundress. Anyway, there were a lot of people, I don't know. Oh, there was the servant with white gloves who waited on us at the table.

It was a different life in Turkey, we were free. We went to Moda: like Enghien, you might say, only nicer. There was the sea, there were big hotels; in summer, we vacationed there, we'd take the small boats and just go. And there was dancing; we used to dance with Turks.

SALONIKA BETWEEN THE TWO WARS

Gabriel D. begins his tale with his date of birth, "1911, the official date; the informal date is 1909," then he links up with "Salonika at that period." He does not describe the city but, as with Constantine and Tunis, the warmth of human relations.

Well, people lived, people visited each other, everybody, because in Salonika, it's not like in Europe. The family was very close. We got together all the time, we saw each other all the time, we would never miss being together on a religious holiday, we went to see each other and wish each other happy holiday.

Ida O., born in 1906 into a rich milieu, has memories of a more differentiated society but also talks of lost happiness. Of that country of which she knew only Salonika and its surroundings, and Athens barely, she repeats: "Greece, it's marvelous!"

There were three categories of people in Salonika. There were the poor poor, the middle class, and the upper class. We lived on one side, like Neuilly here; it was on the sea, and there were boats that came to get us. In the daytime, people didn't go out because it was so hot. From one o'clock to four o'clock, everything was closed. And at night we went to the sea. The house I knew with my parents was on the sea. And even if you only had a hut, you still had the sea for yourself.

These are the descriptions of the places where all these Jews grew up: illuminations of circumscribed spaces, reduced to a house, a street, a quarter, while the rest of the city remained in a kind of shadow and the rest of the country seemed almost not to exist. At a time when cars were rare and the means of communication barely developed, many people did not really travel through their own native land. At most, the name of a summer resort, a beach, a spa comes up in the memories of adolescence. It is not the image of a picture postcard that we are given—not a landscape, not a view of ruins, not monuments, but the evocation of a social fabric. Nor do people talk about the climate and fragrances of the Mediterranean. Yet the family environment and the savor of food that people prepared together and shared recur in all the memories. Images of wholeness come up repeatedly—Reader, have you counted how often the words "everybody" and "each other" are used? Whether one knew poverty or affluence, human relations had a powerful intensity.

A SOCIETY OF MUTUAL CREDIT

To be among your own, to live together, to visit one another, to marry with your own: among the Jews of North Africa, more than among others, this is both memory and ideal. This is happiness. However, tensions were not lacking and people do not hesitate to recall them. Crises were also the spice of life. The friendliest words could be a prelude to tragedy and seem to provoke it; demonstrations of generosity were also demonstrations of power; mutual exchanges were not without social competition. Each anecdote reveals the rivalries, the threats, and, hence, the constant wariness they imposed. An ostensibly innocent social game, the visits and receptions: they illustrate the conviviality that prevailed in Tunis, Alexandria, or Cairo between the two world wars as well as the atmosphere of prying: everyone did it and everyone was the victim of it.

*Georges X., born in Tunis in 1908, recalls his paternal grand-
mother, "talking all the time, a kind of easy, pleasant, witty speech"*:

She didn't visit the other families, not out of any disdain for
them, but because she was so attached to her own family that
that was enough for her. So, they came to see her on Saturday
morning, you know? My grandmother used to sit on a bench,
so either her old women cousins or even cousins from my
grandfather's side would come by. And they always came with
a handkerchief and a key. A handkerchief because they had to
have a handkerchief in their hand; and the key, the key to their
house. And all the women did this [*gestures*] and there was a
constant jiggling of keys around my grandmother. That really
made an impression on us kids, that. . . . And then came the
men, my grandfather's brothers. Not all, some of them. And
that went on until noon, with conversations you can just imagine: this one and that one, what she did, what she said. In short,
a lot of small talk. Then at noon, everybody left. And the light
was incredible! You can only find that light in Italy. You know
that Saturday light. . . . In Rome, you find that light. . . . But
here, never, never, never do you find that light.

Gioia A., Alexandria, 1909. Told with wit.

You want me to tell you about the receptions? They were
magnificent, those receptions! My mother had tons of lady
friends who received, one the first Monday of the month,
another the third Wednesday, one the fourth Thursday. . . . So
the ladies came. And, as far as I remember, my mother was very
liberal, she had Italian and Egyptian friends; that is, she didn't
make any distinction. And they served; on a silver tray there
were engraved silver jam dishes and around, there was a place
to put the spoons. The jam dish itself had a crystal bowl inside
where you put the jam. My mother spent her life making jam
from dates. It was so good!

So the date jam, they were big yellow dates. You cleaned
them, you pitted them, you replaced the pit with an almond
and you cooked them with cloves. Now, there were at least two
jams, quince jam and another one.

"And they let you come to these receptions?"

Yes. We came home from school. The maid who came to open the door for us told us: "Go to your room today, it's the '*bul*.'" *Bul,* there's the same word in Hebrew and Arabic, it means reception. So I'd put a big bow in my hair and put on a dress and I go to say hello to all those ladies, very hypocritically. And they said: "How pretty she is, how she has grown!" I was short and fat with fat thighs. [*Laughs*]

With Edmond H., born in Cairo in 1909, the memory of the receptions becomes frankly critical. Imitating the commentaries that would have followed the parties:

"Why, what a reception, what a reception! What didn't they have! Just imagine, my dear, that she ordered such and such a thing from Groppi's. She ordered such and such a thing from Hildis. [*And if they were kosher*], she ordered from so-and-so. . . . But you know, three days she worked. . . . And grandmother and the cook! And Madame So-and-So made the *kubebat,* the other one the *pastelles* and the *zambuzek,* and the cakes and all that. . . . You know, my dear, she was wearing a coat! Her husband, when he was in Europe last year, brought her a fur coat. And then, when her little girl was born, you saw the diamond he gave her?"

And that's how it was. Unfortunately, it's gossip. Okay, but it didn't stop there. Madame So-and-So was to give a reception in two weeks. While she was there [*at another reception*], she told the others: "Come." But she said to herself: the first one to entertain did thus and so but I have to do better. This was the kind of sick mentality that you found in Jewish families. That's my opinion and I'm sure it was the opinion of many others, especially many husbands. They said to their wives: "Just because Madame So-and-So invited forty people, you have to invite sixty? Where are you going to put them?" "Why, that's not important, there will always be room for everybody." "But how are you going to manage the serving?" "Why my sister's going to send me her servant, and the neighbor's servant will come help me." "And the dishes?" "Why I borrowed some dishes from the neighbor." And so on. That's how it happened.

Behind these courteous exchanges of visits, words, delicacies, there was calculation and judgment of the deeds, merits, and talents of every woman, one-upmanship, all the subtle strategies of social classification. Rich pastries, gestures, outfits were all pieces of information everyone could use in the game of social climbing. Was it a minefield? That is not how people remember it, for, if you knew the rules of the game, you were sure to find partners, friends, future mates among the same actors. In fact, people remember the community where they grew up as an enterprise of mutual aid where it was not necessary to be related to lend a hand. The social cohesion that people emphasize with such pleasure was the sum of all these credits and debits that bound individuals together. Moreover, if you were not from the same family, you could become a part of it, and not only by marriage.

One woman, Suzette, born in Tunis in 1911, reports the facts from before World War I. (Later, her husband joins her.) They begin by talking about first cousins.

She: I have to tell you that my cousins, if they were adopted, there was a reason. It was because my aunt lost the boys, so she sold them. She sold Albert to Ba-Lalu. Ba-Lalu was a clerk for her husband. But that, that's not adopted, that's symbolic. Khalu Bank [*i.e., the "uncle of the bank"*] also, he sold his boys: Georges, wasn't he with the son of the shoemaker Mesh'ud? So! Yes, but not adopted, sold.

Nani, he was with Ummi Nejeïma, he slept in her house, he stayed with her. Loulou, he was almost adopted by Corinna N. Frida [*another cousin*], she was adopted, and Esther, and Lucie my sister, poor girl.

Lucie, she was adopted by Maïssa. They were my parents' neighbors. When Lucie was born, she was real pretty, she had very beautiful eyes, all that. Maïssa said: "No, the real beauty is Gilberte, but Lucie has the eyes" [*Lucie was later to lose her sight*]. And since they didn't have any children, Lucie went, she slept in their house. She wasn't adopted, not really.

So, it's because they didn't have any children that they adopted her. And the X.'s too, they were friends and neighbors of the S.'s, they took Frida. They took her completely. But without a formal contract or papers or a civil status or nothing.

He: And Judith, she was taken away, it's terrible. She took the names of her adoptive parents, she didn't want to go to her mother anymore, she didn't want her father to greet her in the street.

"What word do you use for adoption?"

He: *Mshtebnia, Shtebnet.* It must be from the Torah [*from Hebrew*], in Arabic, they don't say *shtebnet*.[3]

Sétif at the end of the last century. Suzanne T., born in 1910, begins the tale of her life by recalling the material hardships her father knew in his childhood. In passing, she gives a first example of how one member of the family took care of others who had less. In the course of her autobiography, which takes us to Constantine, Batna, and Algiers, this practice recurs several times: family responsibility is one of the connecting threads that weaves through the whole of her memories.

My grandfather was in the war of '70. He was from the Elbez family, my grandmother was from the Guedj family. My father came from Sétif. He was the seventh in a family of twelve children, seven boys and five girls, two of them twins. His father was a mattress maker, he changed the cloth on old mattresses and made new ones too. Life was very hard in those days. My grandmother would cook for weddings, communions, baptisms. It was not easy for her to work and also take care of her family. One year, there was a very bad flu that took my grandfather.

Later on, my grandmother also died. She had children at an early age. In those days, girls were married off very young. The oldest girl was barely sixteen. She was already married when her parents died. She couldn't leave her brothers and sisters alone. In Sétif, the houses had big courtyards, upper floors, and balconies that went around the courtyard. My aunt had rented out all the rooms. Around the courtyard, on one side, she had set up bedrooms, and, on the other, she had set up a big kitchen

3. It is indeed an Arabic word in its local Jewish pronunciation. *Istabna*: tenth verbal form, "to make someone one's son."

and a big common room. She herself had her own children. She worked for people as a servant. Her husband was a house-painter—in whitewash, of course; oil was for doors and windows—and he was also a glazier. He had a hard time earning a living. When her brothers and sisters started growing up, she sent the boys to learn a trade. As for the girls, there were no options. The girls were sent out as servants.

Then the aunt marries off two of her sisters and one brother and begins to breathe a bit more easily. Time passes.

In 1928, Suzanne, who is eighteen, marries her cousin Leon, a carpenter. They are in Constantine, in a house with a central courtyard that is home to forty families. The young couple occupies "a large, long room" on the first floor of the house.

We were barely married a month and a half and we didn't have anything, we still had to buy everything. . . . One night, we saw my father-in-law and mother-in-law coming. We were surprised to see them. My father-in-law had lost his young sister in childbirth. She had two boys. And a few months later, her husband followed her. He was very rich, he had warehouses for hides and a shop where he sold leather to the shoemakers. Nobody wanted the children. They had tried to take them for a little while, but it didn't work. The young one was very nice. But the older one, Joël, was a daredevil. He was ten years old, and his brother was eight. After the funeral and the week of mourning, my father-in-law and the whole family gathered to see the estate left by the brother-in-law and sister. When they opened the warehouses, they were empty and the leather shop was also empty. There was nothing left. So they found their sister's father-in-law; he was in the same trade as his son. They asked him why he had taken what didn't belong to him. It belonged to the children. He answered them that all his son's wealth came back to him, that he didn't recognize the children, didn't want to hear about them. They were alone and disinherited. Nobody wanted them. So he put them in the public orphanage, while he figured out what they were going to do. The night my father-in-law came to see us he wanted his son to take in the older one to teach him his trade. The younger one, the

Z. family adopted him; they didn't have any children, and he took their name.

My father-in-law got a letter that if he didn't take the child out in a week, he would be adopted by the child welfare people; that they would change his name, that he shouldn't try to see the boy anymore. The boy would be lost. Of course, I didn't want to take him in and my husband didn't either. Our house was just big enough for us. I needed time to have my own children. They left and we just didn't know what to do. The next day at two o'clock, we had to be at the office of the child welfare people. My husband signed and so did I.

And that was the start of my woes. . . . And since then, nobody ever came to see what became of him. They washed their hands of him. I wasn't comfortable with him around. He stayed until he was twenty-five. He left the night before his marriage.

In 1930, the couple, who have a child and are responsible for young Joël, leave for Batna, where the husband becomes an independent entrepreneur. They move into a little apartment.

In Batna, you couldn't find workers; you had to send for workers from Constantine, guarantee them a bed and food, and pay them; they didn't want a hotel or a restaurant. Since he [*the husband*] needed them, we took them into our house. We arranged two rooms in our house, they ate with us, I washed their clothes. Four workers, Joël, and my husband: six men. My daughter was a few months old. I had to take care of everything all by myself. And I was pregnant.

In 1938, the family is now in Algiers and numbers four children plus Joël. Now, Suzanne's youngest sister, whose husband abandoned her to join the Foreign Legion, gives birth to a daughter. The event takes place in Suzanne's house.

On January 25, a Sunday morning, my husband went out to buy his paper. At that time, there was no paper seller, no grocery, no bakery in the neighborhood. He had to go to town for that. I myself was up in the laundry room doing my wash. My daughter came running up: "Mama, come fast, Auntie N. is sick." I went down and she said to me: "I'm having the baby."

I was alone with the children. I sent my daughter to call the neighbor, an old Arab woman. Seeing me in a panic, she said to me: "Don't worry, it'll be fine." A half hour later, she gave birth to a little girl, Josiane. But she wasn't any bigger than a baby cat. [*Three months pass.*] With every passing day, she became a normal baby. We didn't know where the father was. One day, we got a letter and, from the numbers and letters on the envelope, my husband guessed where he was: in the Foreign Legion, in Sidi Bel Abbès. My husband went to see him, to see if he could do something. He spoke with his commander but he had signed up for five years. My sister went back to Sétif with my mother a month after the baby was born, leaving me with the baby. She didn't see her again until she was eighteen years old.

The family tribulations continue. Suzanne will have nine children altogether, the births spread from 1930 to 1947. One of the photos that accompanies her autobiography shows eleven young people, lined up in a row, all of whom she raised to adulthood. In the 1950s, when the oldest daughter got married, the marriage soon fell apart—and it is again Suzanne who took her in with her son.

Such memories of an intense, hectic life, devoted to taking care of one another, feeding children you didn't bring into the world: many other women share them as well.

Here is the tale of another transfer of children in a family from Tunis, between 1906 and the end of World War I. First, the maternal grandfather "adopted" his first grandson at the time of his birth: blessed with six daughters, he had no son to say Kaddish[4] on his deathbed. Then, the father of that child died and the grandfather took in the whole family—three other children and their mother. Between the two events, his daughters were married off, but the house wasn't left empty since other members of the family lived under the same roof.[5]

Dialogue between Georgette, born in 1899, and her nephew André, born in 1906:

Georgette: It's André, the oldest. He had his bed in our house.

4. Prayer for the dead.
5. A similar memory opens the autobiographical narrative of Jules Tartour, *Carthage* (Paris: Promotion et édition, 1969).

André [*interrupting*]: They put me in my grandfather's house a week after I was born.

I: But why did the grandfather want a son so much?

Georgette: Because there were six daughters and that's all. He took the oldest boy.

I: But was that a legal adoption?

Georgette: No, he lived in our house. It was next door.

I: In the end, who did live together?

Georgette: In our apartment . . . let's see, there was Mama, Papa, us [*six daughters*] and André, that's all. Ah! There was my aunt, my mother's sister, Geija. She was in our house because she was older than Mama, but she never got married. She was a midget.

André: Hunchback, hunchback.

Georgette: Small, and she had a hump, there. She stayed. Mama didn't want to leave her. She's the one who raised us. And she stayed in our house permanently, that's all.

André: She lived in the *maqsura* [*a closet in the apartment*].[6]

[*Nine years later, four sisters are married off.*]

Georgette: Afterward, his father died and then we lived together on Avenue de France. There was Marie and her four children, Papa, Mama, Olga, and me. . . . The aunt was dead by then. . . . Oh, no, they had also taken in Mama's brother, who was divorced. He came to sleep in our house.

André: He was divorced, Kiki? Oh, I thought he never got married.

---

6. This character of the poor relative, who is so much a part of the furniture that a closet serves her as a bedroom, recurs often in memories. Further on, we shall encounter "*tsia Bergana*," p. 61. The character can also be found in the features of Rachel, "an old ageless Jewess," in the autobiographical novel of Nine Moatti, *Mon enfant, ma mère* [My Child, My Mother] (Paris: Stock, 1974).

Finally, here is a formal adoption. It takes some effort, but this time the boys take the name of the aunt who takes them in.

Louise G., Aïn Beida, 1921:

When my parents died, I was eighteen years old and it was my grandfather M., my father's father, who took us in, my three brothers and me. We stayed with them till I got married when I was twenty-one, and I left my poor brothers all alone.

"Alone with the grandfather?"

Sure, but even so. . . . There were two of them who went to war. The war of '39–'40, that one. Then, once the war was over, they came back to Aïn Beïda and were adopted there. It's my aunt and uncle, my father's sister. She didn't have any children and, seeing that my brothers were alone, they took my poor brother F. and, after the war, she took G. They took the name of the M.

[*As for the third brother*], he got married to a cousin, Simone, a first cousin. My father and her mother are brother and sister. . . . And since the father of Simone, my cousin, was in banking, he also chose to take a job with his father-in-law.[7]

GOOD AND BAD DEALS

This subject of professional relations that intensify family relations comes up in many memories, from Salonika to Morocco. If, in the women's tales of their past life, we see solidarity or selfishness exhibited especially in the domestic space, for men, those values also intrude themselves into the economic area.

Family networks generally provided a springboard for professional activity. You got your training, you got a job, you formed a partnership with a relative; sometimes you broke with them. When that family network was missing, the narratives insist on ingenuity, hard work, and initiative to explain economic success. The image of the self-made man

7. Emile Durkheim, *Le Suicide* [The Suicide] (Paris, 1897), p. 159, defines the Jews as "a small compact and coherent society having a very strong sense of itself and its unity." Other sociologists after him have characterized that society by endogamy, a less marked distance than in other groups between different social strata and between intellectual and economic factions, observations that are all substantiated here.

is often proposed and highly esteemed. We will see that success is not universal. There are those who suffer from extreme poverty until their dying day.

Papou N., Salonika, 1894:

[*Going back to the middle of the nineteenth century, he recalls the activities of his grandfather.*] He worked as a partner in the flour mills of Salonika, the Alatanik [?] mills they were called. It is fair to say that he knew his business; he was familiar with grains. When my grandfather died, my father's oldest brother took his place, still in grains. Okay.

So my father was raised in his family. When he was about twenty, he took over some of his father's trade, especially in grains—his specialty was durum wheat. The durum wheat of Macedonia was famous all over Europe and was sold in France. In this way he started his work, that is, his relations, with France. He signed a contract with the French consul in Salonika who, along with being consul, did a little bit of business on the side. So, my father exported wheat to France. He was attached to the consulate and he became his dragoman, as they call it, because the consuls in Turkey needed somebody from the country who spoke the language and to take them to the prefectures, the city halls. . . . That went on for almost five or six years; in the meantime, he met the Belgian consul in Salonika, who made the proposal that he represent Belgian metallurgical factories in Turkey. Since you're so good in exports, he said, you can certainly take care of imports. And, in fact, my father started to do just that. In the meantime, since my oldest brother finished school, he gave him the import branch; that is, he gave the representation of Belgian metallurgical factories, still in his [*the father's*] name, David N., to my oldest brother. And he's still at it today.

Meanwhile, he also met a producer of Russian oil. Because all the oil in Europe came from Russia, from Batoum; that's the port on the Black Sea where all the deposits were. He got an oil warehouse from the Mentachok Company, as it's called, for all of European Turkey, and he was director of the warehouse. So, on the one hand, he takes care of that, and, on the other, my oldest brother takes care of the metallurgical branch. And he's still attached to the Belgian consulate as a dragoman and very proud of the fact. . . . My third brother finished school in the meantime and went into banking in Salonika and, well, he pursued his career.

Then comes the Balkan war of 1912–13. Crash, everything collapses, including Turkey. As for the oil, the Russians don't want to send any more to Salonika since Salonika isn't Turkish anymore, it's Greek. There are different laws, different regulations, customs, etc. Poof! Everything falls apart, the metallurgical deal too because European Turkey is divided up. So there was all of European Turkey, with all its supplies in Salonika, and it's cut into four: one part for the Bulgarians, one part for the Serbs, one part, in short. . . . So what happens? My oldest brother went to Constantinople, where he still continued to represent the Belgian metallurgical factories. And my father in Salonika continued with the oil, but on a very, very, very modest scale.

Comes the world war of '14. Now, that's really the catastrophe.

During the war, the N. family will again find itself in Marseille. In the meantime, let us return to another family called N., one we have already seen in Tripoli. International ventures in big business are also presented as a series of risks to be exploited intelligently; the father doesn't "meet" any European consul but he "finds himself there," at the right moment.

Camilla N., Tripoli, before 1900:

The whole hinterland of Africa at that time, that is, the ostrich feathers, the finest skins they made into bags, it *all* came from Fezzan. And it was the Fezzanis—I don't know, of course, maybe you should know, among the Ar . . . [*She was going to say "Arabs" and catches herself*], among the blacks, Fezzanis were very advanced, they were the best; at that time, they had a matriarchy. So those people brought their goods to the closest beach. It took them three years to get there. Riding on camels. So they came there, and my parents were there.

There were enormous possibilities with those caravans from the interior, with extraordinary riches, you know. And they needed a certain cloth, a specific type, a color. So, naturally—it's really because of my father, he had that knowledge—they [*the father's brothers*] left to sell the ostrich feathers that were brought there in such great quantities. They left, one for Tunis, two for Manchester; one stayed in Tripoli, while his son was in London.

When the caravan came, it was something extraordinary, with all those Fezzanis. The camels stayed outside the walls. Because the camels that came from Fezzan were racing camels, for the trip, they couldn't come in. They brought gold, elephant tusks.

In England, one of my uncles—along with my father—they set up a small factory in Manchester. For white cloth, of good quality. Because they were buying right and left, they were able to find exactly what they wanted, a white cotton called *Asso di Pique,* that's the trademark. Then, they made them blue cloth and then cloth for when they died; then they brought them sugar and tea, and what else I can't even begin to know. Whatever they needed.

In Cairo in the 1930s. Henri Z. (born in 1913), venturing out from the paternal protection, went into business without either training or capital. He was tremendously successful, however. Our hero was close to the royal entourage, politicians, chiefs of police, the biggest businessmen. He tells a spirited tale, and even the epilogue—the ruin following the Anglo-French-Israeli action of 1956—is recounted with humor.

In '40, a friend proposed that I charter a ship called the *Zamzam,* an Egyptian ship blockaded in Japan. It had to do with delivering a letter of guarantee to the Misr Bank because the ship belonged to the Misr group. . . . I worked on my father little by little until he finally agreed.

Well, we made the *Zamzam* deal, which was enormous at the time. My father, scared as he was. . . . My idea was to fill the *Zamzam* with merchandise on our own instead of taking freight from this one and that. The other way around, I've got a ship, let's fill it up. When the documents come, well, the banks are there: merchandise that comes to the docks, especially in wartime, there's no problem. But my father didn't want to. He was perfectly happy with the profit from the freight. I had friends who bought tea. A case of tea originally sold for eighty piastres, that is eight francs [*a pound*]. When it got to the docks of Alexandria, they sold it for twelve pounds a case; from one pound to twelve! That story of the *Zamzam,* that was the memory of my life. In short, after that, I said: "No, I can't follow in my father's footsteps" and I started my own construction business.

"But did you know anything about building?"

Very little, very little, practically nothing. Obviously, I learned. Practice makes perfect. And we built a good part of Cairo, the new buildings, of course, in Zamalek and in all of Cairo.

Henri Z. then built the Shepheard's, the Hilton, and other symbols of modernization of that large metropolis, one of which was "a building twelve stories high with a surface of at least two thousand square meters, a luxury apartment building, one of the most beautiful buildings of Zamalek, no doubt about it, an absolutely divine location on the Nile." He explains how he got into big public works, won all the bids, and, especially, how he conceived of his most grandiose plan to bring running water to all the villages of Egypt—a project he figured at fifteen or twenty million pounds sterling—and how he submitted it to the ministry. Let us listen to that episode, for it indicates clearly the climate, the places, and the maneuvers that were necessary to bring off big deals.

That, it's the project of bringing water into all of Egypt. My idea, that was on July 22 or 23, 1954, the ministry would announce that it was giving water. Because July 22 was [*the commemoration of*] the abdication of Farouk. My idea was to avoid a public tender since I had created the project. And fearing— since we were a Jewish business. . . . They certainly weren't anti-Semites, but I did say to myself: "All the same, in the present situation, aside from Israel, there are incidents all the time." I said to myself: "Let's try to get an Arab involved in my deal." There was an Arab engineer who worked as an adviser for me because we had to have 90 percent pure Egyptians. So, I had this fellow, who was a businessman himself and my adviser. It was a day during Ramadan, his name was Ismail. I said to him: "Tonight, come have dinner at the Automobile Club so I can tell you about a project that's going to knock you off your feet." He came. Meanwhile I myself had already seen the head of the cabinet, who went nuts over the project and said to me: "Why, all that's very nice, but he won't understand, I have to explain it to him [*he was speaking of the minister*]." What I wanted was for him to give me the work and put the whole government, the bookkeepers, and the experts behind the enterprise . . . so they would control all the prices and give us a percentage of the total amount. I went to the Automobile Club that night and explained the project to Ismail, who, yellow as he was, turned red. That very night, I was summoned by the head of the cabinet, to whom I had already explained the whole project. In less than six weeks, all Egypt knew about the project of the pipeline! There was a factory that made the pipes of asbestos and cement, whose president–director general was M. M., and his engineer, B., a graduate of the Central school,[8] was director of the factory. The head of the cabinet called me in and said: "Here are the letters you're going to give to all the businesses so they'll submit bids to you." I went to M. and told him: "Here." M. looked at me and said: "That can't be right." "What do you mean, that's not so? I'm not telling you that I'm inviting bids, I'm telling you you're going to have an order of four million sterling on condition that you offer good prices." He tried to sabotage the thing because his factory couldn't produce so much. Four million sterling in two years! . . . As I saw it, I didn't need M. anyway. I could set up a factory in three weeks; I had all the contacts in Italy. It was Italian pipes that would have come set up the factory for me, and I didn't even have to pay for the factory. I explained all that to B.: "He doesn't want to! Let him go." And we set up a factory. . . . Then this guy N., who worked for some business in Egypt, left the country and went to work for Edmond de Rothschild.

8. One of the most prestigious French schools of engineering.

Right away he sent a representative to finance the operation. This representative came to me and I told him: "Nobody asked for financing." I was afraid they would cut me out of the deal, and, in fact, that's just what they did. The Lyonnaise des Eaux was interested in the deal. Twenty million sterling, that's not small potatoes! And they talked to Ismail, who was my partner. We should have made two offers, one in his name and one in ours, in exchange for sharing the operation. The Lyonnaise des Eaux insisted and went into partnership with Ismail. So, they were forced to make a public, even international, awarding of the contract. I knew in advance that Ismail and we would have at least a third of the contract. So, instead of dealing in 1954, we negotiated on December 22, 1955.

It required letters of guarantee from the bank because the government demanded a bank guarantee of 400,000 sterling. What bank was going to go along with us? I had some money in Switzerland, which I declared confidentially at the bank. . . . We get the letter of guarantee. In February 1956, someone from the ministry said to me: "Listen, you'd better resign from all your business interests right away." I had created a special company for the pipes, and then there was the regular company I worked in. "Appoint somebody, but resign, it's in your own interest, believe me." I did put in a straw man and I resigned from all my business dealings. So I left in February or March 1956; a few months later, it's the infamous war of '56. My father was interned; everything was confiscated. I was about to sign a contract with Pont-à-Mousson for four million sterling with at least 10 percent . . . in partnership with the Arab who had refused to sign the contract—because he was an Egyptian. I had set up the whole operation from A to Z, they finished all the work, and I didn't even get to see it begin . . . and I was out 400,000 dollars. I'm laughing today, but . . .

"And you already had bases here in France?"

Bases I had, but I had to bring the money back to get a contract in sterling. At that time I was building the Hilton Hotel, the city hall . . . I had five million in civil revenues . . . five million pounds! That's not peanuts! And a million sterling. . .

"I think you really have quite a sense of humor. . ."

What's past is past. You have to forget about it, and that's all.

Here is the account of the difficult social rise of Suzanne T. of Sétif. As far back as her family memories go—to about 1870—their material circumstances were hard: they worked and lived in poverty, and they died young. Her maternal grandfather was a tinsmith. Her paternal grandfather, we recall (p. 38), was a mattress maker, her paternal grandmother, a cook. Orphaned young, Suzanne T.'s father was raised by an aunt, servant to a pharmacist and wife of a house painter. He left them to do his military service and got married right away. But the war of 1914 broke out; he wound up at the front, was wounded and disabled.

He didn't have any toes left; he had shell fragments in his head; very often he didn't see anything out of his eye. He coughed all the time; his face was always swollen from coughing so much. He had spent seven years away from home and had gotten into the habit of drinking more than he should have. When he came back from the war, he wasn't the same man; of course, he was sick. He received a miserable little pension. He didn't know how to write; you had to be intelligent to fight and get a good pension. Every time he asked them to increase his pension, they refused. And the little bit he did get every three months had to go for something or other. He needed two packs of cigarettes every day and a liter of wine every day, not counting what he drank outside. He didn't do anything at home. My mother was forced to pay him for all the things I mentioned, and many times she gave him the money she earned painfully. He was never happy. My mother was miserable with him.

She worked from morning to night, nonstop. She did laundry. She had regular customers: rich people had their laundry done only twice a year; it took her at least two or three weeks to finish. She went to wash at the school of the nuns. I was little, so she took me with her.

Suzanne had to earn her living from a very young age: she was hired as a children's nursemaid and then as a maid.

At twelve, I got my certificate from school; the exam lasted three days. It was in July; in August I started working. I took care of a child, from morning to night. The parents were Spaniards; they had a sandal factory. There was a woman who took care of the household, and I took care of the child. I got fifteen pennies a day for two years. Afterward, I wanted to learn another trade, dressmaking, but to learn a trade, you had to pay. I went to work for a so-called dressmaker, to learn a trade. She had four children. I had to tend to the house, take care of the children, run errands. Afterward, if she had time, she would teach me to sew! With me she had a maid she didn't pay. For two months, I was patient, then I got fed up and I left. I went back to work for some people from France; he was an engineer of roads and bridges. I prepared the food, I took care of the house, the errands, washing, ironing, mending. I arrived at six in the morning and I left at 2:30, but three or four times a month, I stayed until nine o'clock, sometimes even until 10 o'clock. I got only two francs a month. I didn't quit my job until a month before my wedding.

Right after the wedding, the young couple tried their luck in Algiers but stayed there only a month ("I couldn't get used to the big city, I had never traveled") and then returned to Constantine, where we saw them taking in their young cousin Joël (p. 39). The husband worked as a carpenter in a workshop six days a week. September 1930 marks a turning point in their lives: he set up his own business, and the family moved to Batna. After one of his workers suffered an accident at work, the husband was the victim of a shady insurance agent and was blackmailed by the wounded worker.

The insurance agent was indicted, but we had everything else on our backs. K. [*the worker*] was lazy and found a source of income: he started blackmailing my husband. Every time he came back, he asked for bigger and bigger sums. He knew he couldn't be punished, and he took advantage of it. My husband couldn't pay his bills anymore, for wood, hardware, everything he needed to run the workshop. He wasn't making ends meet anymore. There were two bailiffs in Batna who shared an office. One was French, Mr. G., and the other a Jew, Mr. K. [*who was related to the worker involved in the litigation*]. When I would see him, he never wanted to help us, and when it was Mr. G., he did all he could. In the end, we just couldn't manage anymore. We sold everything for whatever we could get, and we paid all our debts. We had nothing left. One morning, my husband insisted that I do the errands; when I came back, I understood why. I returned from the market to find the house empty; there was nothing more than the clothes in the suitcases and the dishes in boxes. The children were dressed, ready to leave. The night before, he had made the arrangements. At noon, we took the train for Constantine, two children, me pregnant, and a sick husband [*he will be hospitalized and will recover slowly from a stomach ulcer*].

Return to the previous situation: in Constantine, the husband was employed as a foreman, one child died, another born. At the end of 1935, the family tried its luck once again in Algiers, where the husband was first employed as a simple apprentice. Once again, a Frenchman helps them out.

He had to find work. A carpenter had put a notice on his door that he was looking for an apprentice—he didn't want a worker. After both of us thought it over, he went back to work as an apprentice at seven francs a day. At least I could feed my children and pay the rent . . .

One day a candymaker named K. wanted to redo the front of his shop. He called my husband's boss. He took my husband with him, and he started working right away. It was urgent, he finished the front and the windows in the shop. He was very happy with my husband's work; he asked him to redo his apartment. [*A long narrative follows: the candymaker discovers that the "apprentice" is underpaid, summons the boss and concludes after a long discussion*]: "You dare to make me pay a hundred francs a day for the worker—you even told me he was greedy and cost you a lot—when you're not even paying him for a week half of what I pay you for a day! Now I understood and you're going to pay him everything I paid you for him and I never want to hear from you again." He said to him: "And the work?" He answered: "As for the work, he'll finish it, and he'll be paid at the normal price."

Not only did he [*the husband*] bring me a large sum of money that day but he finished the work for the candymaker. The other shops next door—when they saw the new shop front, they wanted to change their fronts too. There was an old tailor's shop, a glove maker, a shirtmaker. When all these shop fronts were finished, you couldn't recognize Rue d'Isly anymore. And ever since then, thank God, we never wanted for anything. He worked hard, of course, but he was happy.

1939: In Suzanne T.'s tale, the family chronicle once again encounters world history.

In June 1939, I gave birth to a daughter, Hermine. I named her Hermine because my husband had a Spanish worker who worked with him. He was called Henri and his wife was Hermine. We were very close to them, so if it had been a boy, we would have called him Henri. Since it was a girl, we called her Hermine. He was the caretaker of a big villa that belonged to a lawyer; the owners came once or twice a year, during the fruit season. On Saturday night, we went up to that house. We came back on Sunday night with vegetables, fruit, flowers. Every morning, he passed by our house on his way to work, so he'd bring me what his wife picked for herself and for us. So many flowers, I didn't know where to put them. And on September 1st my husband got a telephone call from the city hall of Bouzareah that he had to go to city hall with the leaders of the neighborhood. They all went by truck to the city hall, which was five miles away. The mayor and his deputies were waiting for them. The mayor announced the declaration of war. There were police there too. The chief of police gave each one of them a travel order and said they had to take the train at eight o'clock the next morning. The mayor gave them posters to put up in all the neighborhoods.

When they came back, I understood right away that something was wrong. My husband filled me in and everybody gathered in our house. Men and women were crying. We knew that everything was going to be terrible.

On September 2, it was a Friday morning, we had only 20

pennies in the house. He left me 10, and he took the rest. He didn't want me to go to the station with him. Later on, I wondered about how I was going to feed my children.

Suzanne goes to work in a clothing factory. At the end of the war, the family numbers eight children (a last son will be born in 1947), and the husband resumes his activities. Family happiness is at an all-time high: they build a big house, the bar mitzvah[9] of one of the sons is celebrated with a great show of wealth, the family is able to entertain young Jewish soldiers every Friday night, the husband becomes one of the leaders of the Jewish community. He is even paid a visit by a French admiral: the photograph depicting this event shows them in a salon whose wide bay windows are shaped like the Star of David. The house really is the house of the Good Lord.

As for Tita, whom we saw escaping the surveillance of her jealous husband in Tunis, she began her life in poverty and continued in poverty.

My father? A shoemaker. He had a little shop, in the Hara, in front of the Italian woman who made chairs for children. A little shop. But his heart was a little cold, he didn't like work. God rest his soul. Leila, she worked; my poor mother, she worked. She worked in a hundred ways. She washed the women, she took them to the Turkish bath. She worked washing the dead. She washed clothes. She worked with all colors. God rest her soul.

. . . When I was little, we ate chicken only twice a year. At Purim and . . . when else?[10] At Kippur. That's all. Here, you throw the chicken [*she swears*], over my father's head, you throw it!

. . . Before, my mother went to the butcher and said: "Give me a few pieces of tripe and a little something for Friday's couscous." She only went there on Friday. Other days she didn't go there or he just gave her some skin. At home, she broiled it, she took off the hair, made it white as a lily, and then

9. Religious ritual of a boy's coming of age.

10. The holiday of Purim celebrates the victory of the Jews, subjects of King Ahaseurus, over the minister Haman who plotted to destroy them. The Jews were saved by the intervention of Esther and her uncle Mordechai.

you would serve that skin with chickpeas and cumin or with beans and cumin.

"How much did she buy, two pounds?"

Are you kidding! Maybe a half a pound, he gave her, a pound. Listen: with that, she made the couscous broth, meat balls, *tfina* [*a dish slowly braised for Saturday*], and stew.

The father worked listlessly. The mother washed the living and the dead and did laundry. At this level of poverty, the daughter very soon had to contribute to the family resources: she took over the mother's domestic tasks and took in trimming work at home.

I worked at home. Arabic work, Arabic buttons, tassels. Something else: I did weaving. I worked on the floor, one ball of yarn on one side, one ball of yarn on the other side. And I worked in the house, I was responsible for the house. I washed the clothes, I cooked, I prepared Shabbat [*Saturday, the day of rest*] . . . I went to bring water with the neighbors, everybody took a turn. In short, I worked, I worked, so much [*sigh*].

The husband her mother made her marry because he was a hard worker was only a peddler of secondhand goods. In 1936 he rises to become an apartment agent but he dies before he can enjoy the fruits. Like her mother before her, Tita has to go to work for other people.

He worked hard. Every day. Could he stand not working? He would have died of it. Whenever he came home without earning any money, he was mad. Right away I understood. Oh boy, I was scared. He turned the whole house upside down if he didn't earn anything.

"What did he sell?"

Roba vecchia. [*Taking up the cry uttered by that type of merchant*]: *Roba vecchia! Scarbi vecchia!*[11] Bottle dealer. Then he stopped. He used to dress like an Arab, you know? He wore a chechia, a sweater, and a sarwal[12] that could hold four people [*laughs*]. Later on, he was partners with H. So H. told him: "Aouïda!" "What." "You know, we have to go to fancy houses, on Avenue

11. Italian words in the local Tunisian spelling: used things, used shoes.

12. Translator's note: *Chechia* is the red cap, and *sarwal* the wide trousers traditionally worn by natives in North Africa.

de Paris, in the arcade. You have to dress like an Italian. Because when you visit a house—houses for sale were written in newspaper ads—people are going to say: 'He's a Moslem.'" He answered: "Fine." That's how it happened. Right away, he went to the tailor, made a suit, one or two pairs of pants. And he changed over to a shirt and tie. I said to him: "Aouïda, look at you!" "What can I do? They laugh at me and I shouldn't change?" The poor man, that year, he died with it all. He left his things hanging in the wardrobe. New suit, underpants, shirts, ties, shoes, socks: Lalou his son took them for his bar mitsvah. That's God's will; what can I do?

[*After his death.*] Somebody gave me this, somebody else gave me that, my brothers-in-law helped. Then they all stopped. So I went to Mchi'ad. God rest his soul, Mchi'ad. He said: "Tita!" "Yes!" "You want me to take you to work?" "I'd like it very much, Mchi'ad, I'm in such bad shape." So, he took me to work for a particular lady. I didn't earn a cent without tears running down my face as much as the water I was washing with. I had a very hard time.

Whenever life in the Hara comes into people's memories, several themes recur obsessively: small houses, crowded courtyards; small incomes; the luxury represented by the purchase of meat or poultry. These images are colored with contrasting tones. Those who have always lived in the ghetto talk about the cleanliness of "well-ordered" rooms; they recall an orderly world. The courtyard illustrates a sociability marked at times by boisterous laughter. Meals are tribute to the ingenuity of the maternal cuisine. Those who escaped from the ghetto or who never lived there, however, denounce the poverty, the crowding, the unfair disparity between rich and poor. Among many other memories, that of André A., born in Tunis in 1926:

I was born right in the middle of the Hara. We lived there until we were communion age, twelve, in 1938.[13] Then we lived on Rue Pierre Curie, next to Avenue de Londres, down below. It's a more middle-class neighborhood: the bus went by, the streetcar, all that. There were cars . . .

13. The narrator borrows the word *communion* from the colonial Christian population to evoke his bar mitzvah.

My grandfather, he never went to school. For forty years, he worked as a hairdresser; when he died he had never left Tunis, except once. He traveled forty miles to Testour, on a pilgrimage to Rabbi Fraji. That's the only time he left. There's a man who lived seventy years in poverty, in whadycallit. He never left. Except for La Goulette [*a resort suburb of Tunis*]. And La Goulette, he went there maybe once a year, once every two years, because he didn't have any money. It was a big deal. That was the kind of life it was.

Meat, you ate it once a week, on Friday night. And *m'alaq*, not even *l-marjou'a*[14] because it's less expensive. And I was the one who went to buy it at the butcher, with all those flies around.

Yvette A., cousin and sister-in-law of André A.:

X. tells that his mother, in order to encourage him when he went to school, told him: "If you're the best, I'll make you a hard-boiled egg on Saturday in the tfina." Okay, the first month that worked, he was the best, she made him his hard-boiled egg. The second month too. Then she said to him: "This won't do." Even one hard-boiled egg a month strained the budget.

THE RELIGION OF OUR FATHERS,
THE COOKING OF OUR MOTHERS

Religious rituals stand out vividly in memory. Summoning up memories, everyone sees Shabbat, Purim, Passover, Yom Kippur, and other important dates. Everyone emphasizes the consistency of practices, their expected repetition. They describe not one celebration, dated and unique, but a holiday that is the sum total of all holidays, a Saturday that encompasses all Saturdays. Everyone also emphasizes the fullness of the celebrations: "everyone" participated in them, "all" the laws were observed, "everything" had to be done just right.[15]

14. *M'alaq*, top ribs, *marjou'a*, beef shank.
15. The sequences of biography also follow the cycle of religious holidays, and individual life takes its rhythm from ritual in Camille El Baz, *Sarah, ou moeurs et coutumes des Juifs de Constantine* [Sarah, or the Ways and Customs of

One man, recalling Sefrou before the emigration of the Jews from Morocco:

Oh! The holidays! You had to live there. There just aren't enough words to describe the holidays in Sefrou for you. You felt the holidays in the house, you felt the holidays on the street. Shabbat, let's begin with Shabbat! There wasn't a single Jewish shop, a single store that was open. All the Jews were gathered in the *mellah*[16] and were in the *shul*s.[17] There were seventeen plus three, twenty shuls in that town. So you can imagine! . . . . You won't find it there anymore. Those who didn't live there can't ever experience the holiday the way we did. And every holiday had its own color, its own traditions.

Passover,[18] that was the preparation of the wafers right after Purim because you didn't get the wafers ready-made in packages, like now. Every family, they had to buy their own wheat, select it, bring it to the mill—a mill that was koshered[19]—made sure everything was kosher. Oh! The feeling on those occasions was really something indescribable. So Passover came, all the houses were gleaming, shining, cleaned up, whitewashed, painted. Some houses were painted although each family had only one room. Most families were big, when I say big, there were ten children. They all lived in one room and it wasn't

the Jews of Constantine] (Nice, 1971); and in Edmond Zeïtoun, *Les Cadeaux de Pourim* [Purim Presents] (Paris: La Pensée universelle, 1975).

16. *Mellah* designates the Jewish neighborhood in Moroccan cities.

17. *Shul*: Synagogue. The word is borrowed from Yiddish, which indicates that, for the narrator, the Ashkenazi Jews represent a stricter Orthodoxy than the one he claims for his own community. It signals the hierarchies prevailing in France or at least the way they are perceived.

18. Passover, commemorating the Exodus from Egypt. The following holidays are then recalled:

1. Purim, see p. 54. The Book of Esther is called a *megillah,* which will be used later (p. 60);
2. Sukkot, the Feast of the Tabernacles, which takes place in autumn;
3. Hanukkah, which celebrates the reconsecration of the Temple by the Hasmoneans in the second century B.C.E. The *hanukia* (also see p. 59) is the candelabra used during the eight-day holiday, with one additional branch lit each night.

19. *Kashrut,* the combination of rules of dietary purity. *Kosher,* fit for consumption. *To kosher,* to make something fit for consumption.

always large. I ask myself . . . How did those people manage? And yet they lived, they were happy, that's how it was.

On Sukkoth you saw huts everywhere. There wasn't a street that didn't have huts; there wasn't a house, if it had a courtyard, that didn't have a hut.

Weeks before Hanukkah, they were already beginning to prepare olive oil to light the *hanukiya*. For each holiday, and I tell you that in practice they couldn't even imagine what assimilation was or how there could be a Jew who didn't keep the Shabbat. I don't mean all Jews were pious and observant. There were some in the Jewish population of Sefrou who weren't very pious, very observant. But what does it mean to say very observant? It means somebody who doesn't observe to the letter what he is told. But you couldn't imagine a Jew who didn't go to shul three times, for *shaharit, minhah,* and *maariv,*[20] that just didn't exist. Or an artisan, a hairdresser who opened his shop on Shabbat—that just didn't come into our heads. Or a businessman tempted by profit and opening his shop on Saturday—that just couldn't be.

Manou B., Aïn Beïda, 1926, speaking of Constantine in the 1930s:

For the holidays, it was marvelous, for our own holidays, because we felt them. Saturday, we felt it because we lived in the ghetto and Saturday, everybody made Saturday. For holidays, everybody was dressed for the holiday. That was the way it was. That's what we don't have here anymore.

Camilla N., Tripoli, about 1900:

My father was a real believer. He prayed every morning and on the holidays. When it was a holiday, for instance, it was a holiday, it was a religious thing, it was a holiday. For instance, on Friday night, I can't tell you how that table was: the flowers, the candlesticks, the prayers. . . . Not so much the prayers, it was everything. He said the prayer, the blessing over all the children, we kissed his hand, there, that's how it was.

20. The three daily prayers that must be said, respectively, at dawn, at sunset, and in the evening.

And the maids! In the morning, there was a bath for us up-stairs. Then, downstairs, on the ground floor, that was where they washed the clothes, a kind of laundry where the maids went when they had made the couscous and everything else. And all of them dressed up special with henna and everything. And then they put on silk, they were dressed, all of them. And then, until Saturday night, they didn't touch anything.

Each celebration had a corresponding act, gesture, a libretto in which everyone had a role to play. Children, for example: Purim in Bizerte at the end of the last century:

So, what did my brother Ernest do? We got the catalog from the Samaritan department store and there were women and men in the catalog. He unfolded them, put them on a cardboard and when my grandfather read the megillah to us, because he had to read it to us aloud, when the name of Haman was uttered, we sang and hit the pictures with little rattles they sold for the occasion. It was very picturesque! [*Mathilde B., Bizerte, 1892.*]

Tripoli at the beginning of the century. The destruction of the Temple was commemorated on the ninth of Ab. In the book of Ezekiel, the prophecies against the people of Israel and on the ruin of Jerusalem are followed by the "resurrection of the people of God" and the rebuilding of the City. Then there is the vision of the dry bones restored to life: "The hand of the Lord was upon me and carried me out in the spirit of the Lord and set me down in the midst of the valley which was full of bones. . . . Then He said unto me: Son of man, these bones are the whole house of Israel." Camilla never studied this book because girls only learnt practical things and not traditional texts. But she unwittingly acted out Ezekiel's vision. She recalls her childhood gestures, and something of their meaning has remained engraved in her memory: to collect the pearls was to reassemble the bodies of the Jews. She had acted out the rebuilding of the "house of Israel," prepared for God's return to His people. All that is left of the awesome biblical prophecy are these little pearls:

Many beliefs were attractive because they weren't fanatical. For example, one of the things that was very moving was when there was—what do they call it?—the destruction of the Temple. *Again,*[21] that's it. For *again,* for example, everybody fasted and for the children they bought us a lot of little pearls, you know, tiny little pearls. With those little pearls, I could make a little fish. It was to collect the bones of all the Jews who were killed and scattered. That was for that holiday.

The festival, the toilette, the clothing transform even the humblest persons. In Tripoli again, "the maids" put henna on their hair and dressed in silk gowns for Shabbat. Here is Aunt Bergana, a servant during the week, in the glory of Friday night.

On Friday night, we had an old aunt of my father's who was a sort of household drudge and who was always at home. All week long, she was in the kitchen, you know, like all Jewish women, like all women. She took care of this one and that one, and, naturally, everybody loved her a lot, but she was like a piece of furniture, an old piece of furniture. So what was special is that this aunt that you almost didn't see, who came to the table, who sat in a corner—on Friday night, she put kohl[22] on her eyes out to here, she put on her nicest *barracano,*[23] she made herself all beautiful. And when they said the prayer, she stood up for the prayer. And I always remember my cousins coming from England, Cairo, London; they were very rich and so very advanced in their ways, very snobbish and everything. There was one cousin who was there one Friday night, as they were saying the prayer. And he sees *tsia* Bergana. "*Tsia* Bergana, *tsia* Bergana, look, what happened to her? She's so tall!" He had always seen her sitting down. And here was a woman who was tall, with big black eyes, who was standing up.

For the end of Shabbat, which marks the return to secular life and produces a kind of pang of anxiety, "a bad mood," the father officiated. He recited the havdalah prayer,[24] *and with that the old aunt resumed her humble position:*

21. *Again*: the ninth of Ab—Ab is a month in the Jewish calendar that corresponds approximately to the month of August—is the annual commemoration of the destruction of the Temple.

22. Kohl, eye makeup.

23. *Barracano,* a woolen garment in which women wrapped themselves.

24. Havdalah: prayer of separation that ends the Sabbath repose and ushers in ordinary life again.

So, on Saturday night, it was funny, you know, on Saturday night, papa said the prayer and Saturday was over and so you saw that woman start laughing giddily, hee-hee-hee, hee-hee-hee, until the whole family caught that contagious laughter. Why? Because they said that if you start laughing on Saturday night and you're happy, the whole week is happy, so in families there's always a little bit of a bad mood, a little . . . something—it's like that in every family. And that woman, as soon as she saw there was a bad mood, she started her ridiculous laughing, like a clown. She knew she would set them all off . . .

Noises, sounds, voices also return to memory. Tripoli again, at the beginning of the century: Camilla N. recalls the holiday of Shavuot, which commemorates the giving of the Tablets of the Law to Moses on Mount Sinai. But this is not what her tale is about. What remains is rather a night of vigil and the whispering of the rabbis who "talmodize."

Then the *Tomotoura*[25] came to the house, and it was a real wonder, because all night long there was the rabbis and the children who came to pray and especially to argue, they argued the whole Talmud, they argued all night, they argued and they argued. But, by five o'clock in the morning, we went to bed, we were young and it was so nice, those kids' voices, you know. And so, all night long, there were maids serving coffee, bringing them cakes, bringing them things, coming and going. We stayed downstairs a little bit and then we got bored hearing them talmodizing,[26] arguing and everything. But at five o'clock in the morning, they had special songs and there, that's just the way it was. It was really a strict form of religion but it wasn't oppressive because it came in that way—there wasn't any fanaticism at all, not at all.

To speak of religion, then, is not to recall a faith, beliefs, or study but rather to evoke shared acts, forms of fellowship and of sociability.

25. *Tamotoura* [Talmud Torah]: children studying the Torah. The locution is condensed into one word and indicates children who *only* attended rabbinic school, i.e., the poor.
26. The narrator invents the word talmodize, shaped on psalmodize.

When faith disappeared, gestures remained. At its extreme, religion became practice without knowledge, an orthopraxis without orthodoxy.

Repeated, one seeming just like the next, the holidays are ultimately confused in memory because their meaning has been lost or never was really grasped in the first place.

Gabriel D. (Salonika, about 1910) is unsure of the order of the holidays and then resumes:

Once *Shavuot* is over, then came New Year's Day . . . New Year's Day before Kippur . . . First was Yom Kippur, then it was New Year's Day, I think. Or first it was New Year's Day and then Yom Kippur, I think so, yes.

Laure A. again, about her father:

In synagogue, for example, on Kippur and on the Day of Atonement, my grandmother said to him: "Jacques, everybody has already come out of church [*sic*]." "I'm waiting for them to go. Because they haven't eaten, their breath, I can't stand it." "So, come on, it's already late." He went, unwillingly. Then, on the Day of Atonement, he went.

"The Day of Atonement *is* Kippur, isn't it?"

"No, the Day of Atonement isn't Kippur! Kippur is the fast. The Day of Atonement comes a week later."

It takes a long discussion, interspersed with laughter and exclamations to finally establish the order of the holidays.

Women's participation in rituals was exercised primarily in the kitchen. The image of the ritual blends with that of the table, a masterpiece created by the mother and offered to her kin, a center around which the family circle was linked, and an altar of the family's religion.

Manou B., Aïn Beïda, 1926:

My husband was strict. On Friday, it was special, holidays were special, and I keep it up here. I can guarantee you that on Friday night in my house, there's a table, a beautiful Friday night table. Friday night in my house is very beautiful. You see here, it's all full. It's a beautiful Shabbat table.

The women recall less what they did than what they had to do: pre-
pare a meal. If you think about it, that's what they devoted themselves
to every single day. Why did the preparation of holiday meals leave
such a strong impression? No doubt because these occasions gathered
the "whole" family and demanded more effort, more dishes, more uten-
sils. Some celebrations were also accompanied by unusual acts laden
with significance: the preparation of the Passover dishes, the sacrifice
of the Passover lamb, the sacrifice of the chickens on Yom Kippur. But
those meals, more than the daily routine, had particularly to conform
to the norms. No initiative, no improvisation, no delay was permitted.
You had to bend to the rules, prove that you had internalized them.
Cooking was basically the female expression of orthodoxy since women
did not go to the synagogue—and when they did it was as spectators.
Hence, the preparation of food constituted the feminine part of each
holiday and the first act of the libretto that the whole family was going
to perform. Men came on stage only after the ovens were cold.

The paradox, then, is that Yom Kippur, a day of contrition, of
withdrawal, remains in memories as a moment of culinary fever.[27] Yom
Kippur is associated with tastes: of stuffed chicken, lemonade, and cook-
ies for the Jews of Tunis; of chicken with tomato sauce in Salonika.
The association of food and ritual is so close in memory that a woman
born in Algeria, wanting to talk about her estrangement from religion,
recalls her fears when she stopped eating on Yom Kippur for the first
time.

The first year I didn't eat on Kippur, I said to myself: "Is it
true that something bad is going to happen to me next year?"
In Algeria, the boys had to go to Hebrew religious school, while
we didn't have any. . . . You weren't good for anything but
making meatballs [*to go with the Shabbat couscous*] and knowing
what dish to make for what holiday. [*Paule S., Tlemcen, born
in 1940.*]

The thousand and one ways of making chicken for Yom Kippur
finally casts doubt on the religious practice: that is the experience of

27. A literary echo of this fever of preparation for the fast is in Katia
Rubinstein, *Mémoire illettrée d'une fillette d'Afrique du Nord à l'époque coloniale*
[Illiterate Memoir of a North African Girl During the Colonial Period] (Paris:
Stock, 1979).

Ida O., who sees in the diversity of Jewish food practices the proof that it is people who make the laws. Surely God would not have wasted His time inventing such prescriptions.

On the Day of Atonement, I don't eat. I do what I can but I don't want it to go any further because I think . . . I don't know . . . I'm going to explain these ideas of mine to you: I myself used to play a whole lot of poker, I visited a whole lot of people, and one of my friends was an Alsatian woman, from Alsace. She was born in China, but she was really French. Then I had a certain Madame C., a high-class Moroccan, if you please, surely no *pied-noir*.[28] We played a whole lot of poker, we were at the table, playing. Okay, next week was the Day of Atonement. So we asked what do you plan to do? Our custom—and this I still observe—was first that we fasted and all that. My father went to the synagogue. And at night, we started with a spoonful of jam with coffee, and some soup. My parents always made chicken, chicken cooked in tomato sauce. That was the custom of Salonika. You made broth, you left it in to make a soup with noodles. And the rest of the chicken you cooked in tomato sauce. That stayed with me, that habit. So my friends asked: "What are you making to eat for Kippur?" I say: "We make soup and then chicken." "How awful! We make couscous!" The other one who was Polish: "I do this." [*She:*] "Do you think that the Good Lord had time to tell you 'Do this' if you're Polish; 'you pied-noirs, you do this,' You believe that? It's people who make the laws in every country. The Good Lord didn't have time to do that. In every country, the Shkenazis have one way of doing things and we Sephardim have another way." And maybe that's why my father kept a certain distance, you know, while believing, while being a Jew.

Among women, the memory of the tension brought on by the holidays sometimes leaves a bitter taste and leads them to criticize religious prescriptions and taboos. In Istanbul, Laure A.'s mother fell ill at Passover. Mathilde (Bizerte, 1892), speaking of her brother-in-law, a "very religious" man, goes on:

28. *Pied-noir*: the European settlers in colonial Algeria and their descendants.

You see, he saw only one thing, his religion. So there was no way to talk to him, you couldn't get him to the theater. He prayed. On Saturday, he prayed all day long and it was pure agony. You know how it was, on Friday, you had to run to do the cooking because at four o'clock, the candles were lit and all the rest. It was murder! Moses, he was very pious, very . . .

"And you did that yourself?"

Me, no. My sister, yes. My sister suffered that agony. It's an agony, eh, because you've got to rush so. Fortunately, she had help; there were always servants who helped her with the heavy work, and she did the cooking.

And she took her bath every month. When she had her period, she slept in another bed. So, it meant fifteen days with the husband and fourteen days without coming close to him. It was her mother-in-law who kept count! Yes, she would say to her: "Tonight, I calculated, today, you go to the Turkish bath." And that day, she had to go to the Turkish bath in order to sleep with her husband. So, for the first fourteen days, she slept with her husband, then it stopped.

If religious practice is located between the kitchen and the holiday table for women, men more often recall the synagogue. The memories of Henri Z., born in Cairo in 1913, show clearly that this difference corresponds to a real division of tasks:

We did Passover, Kippur, of course . . . Passover and Kippur . . . Naturally, my mother had an open table. But that was every night. And on the holidays, there were naturally twenty, thirty, forty people. Especially during the war, the war of '40, every day at lunch or dinner, she had fifteen or twenty soldiers or officers.

"OK. That's the meal. But the ritual as such, who did that?"

That was my father, though my mother also knew them. My father read Hebrew. Badly, but he read it, maybe in his own way.

The mother shared her table; the father read Hebrew. For Gabriel D. (Salonika, about 1910), ritual meant going to the synagogue:

On Yom Kippur, everybody went to the synagogue because, in Salonika at that time, there were almost seventy or eighty thousand, so . . .[29]

There were a good many synagogues. I can't list them all for you. When I was little and my father took me to synagogue, that synagogue was in the central marketplace of Salonika. I went there . . . and then to another one they built later, in some street. What was the name of that synagogue? And then there was the big synagogue of Beth Shaul, I don't know if you've heard of it. That synagogue of Beth Shaul existed during the time of Jesus Christ! I was married in that synagogue in 1937.

Religion is also a questioning, sometimes a doubt. M. M. (Sousse, 1900) was bar mitzvah, he learned to read Hebrew, but he doesn't understand it. Speaking of Jews (after indicating his family origins), he goes on:

That race which has lasted for five thousand years, there must be a reason for it. . . . If I were to tell you my views, you wouldn't believe me [*laughs*].

"Tell me anyway."

29. Salonika numbered 120,000 inhabitants at the turn of the century. With about 50,000 individuals in 1901, 90,000 in 1908, the Jewish community was the most important in the city, which also included communities of Moslems, Greeks, Bulgarians, and a few thousand people of other nationalities. See Paul Dumont, "La structure sociale de la communauté juive de Salonique à la fin du XIXe siècle" [The Social Structure of the Jewish Community of Salonika at the End of the Nineteenth Century] *Revue historique* 263:2 (1980): 351–393.

Only the Jews of Salonika recall the numerical—hence social—importance of their community as a claim to glory. Note that the Jewish population of Turkey was estimated at about 300,000 inhabitants at the turn of the century, before the dismemberment of the Ottoman Empire and the begining of Jewish emigration. M. Franco, *Essai sur l'histoire des Israélites de l'Empire ottoman depuis les origines jusqu'à nos jours* [Essay on the History of the Israelites of the Ottoman Empire from the Origins to Our Own Day] (Paris, 1897).

In Egypt, there were about 65,000 Jews in 1950 of a total population of 20 million; in Tunisia, more than 100,000 at the end of the Protectorate, most of them living in Tunis. In Morocco, the Jewish community numbered about 250,000 individuals at the end of the Protectorate, that is, 2.3 percent of the total population. Their proportion was less in Algeria (about 110,000 Jews in the 1940s and 1950s). See D. Bensimon-Donath, *Évolution du judaïsme marocain sous le protectorat français, 1912–1956* [Evolution of Moroccan Judaism Under the French Protectorate, 1912–1956] (Paris: La Haye, Mouton, 1968).

Maybe Jesus really *was* the prophet sent by God. It's to punish us for burning him, for killing him, that we are . . . [*he doesn't finish his sentence but he wants to evoke the misfortune of the Jews*]. Because, because, you surely read: the Dead Sea Scrolls, the Essenes, my boy, they were Christians. We refused to admit it, but you know, we've paid dearly for it! [*Then, after a digression*]: You know, aside from a few fanatics, there aren't many [*Jews*] anymore. The religion of our milieu's is extremely simplified. There isn't that fanaticism anymore, that pride in saying: "I'm a Jew."

"Were you observant in Tunisia?"

When I was young, yes, because I came from a very religious family. Now, on Kippur, Passover, more out of tradition than anything else. Now, I question. As soon as you question, you're not a believer anymore.

Sometimes the testimony goes off into a criticism of religious taboos, sometimes it expresses a doubt about the divine presence, sometimes it questions the meaning and validity of tradition. Finally, some people, objecting to fanaticism, indiscriminately reject the whole constellation of practices. Contrary to what might have been expected, it is not by virtue of adherence to the letter of religion that all these individuals assume their Jewish identity but much more through the sense of belonging to a local community and to a local tradition and through the experience of a combination of social practices that are recalled as having been shared only with Jews.

2
Between the Oder and the Dniepr

YIDDISHLAND, *of so many lost worlds, is different from all the others. It was not the inexorable course of time that carried it off—it was murdered, victim of a genocide unparalleled in history. Thus, a world lost several times over for Jews of eastern Europe: first, when they emigrated, for the most part, with no idea of going back; then, when it disappeared totally, millions of human beings gone up in smoke. This is why the nostalgia for childhood in the voices of the witnesses we are going to hear is not the nostalgia for any childhood: restrospectively, their memories bear the imprint of that tragic end. They feel not only a regret for a bygone past that formed their identities, but their memories are also mixed with complex, sometimes contradictory, feelings and reactions: tenderness, of course, at a return to their most private selves but also lucidity, even a critical spirit, as well as a sense of moral obligation. For if they know that they have lived an experience that cannot practically be transmitted, they also feel, as survivors, a manifest duty to make their testimony known.*

Speaking of themselves, they also speak for the others, for those who cannot speak anymore. Memories intersect, echo, correct one another. What we hear are shared, multiple memories and memories of memories: people tell what was told by parents and grandparents, everyone they knew and loved, those who made them what they are. Long digressions and parentheses within parentheses follow the sometimes strange windings of recall: one must remember such and such a character, an episode, a scene, a dialogue, simply for themselves, for the simple reason that they existed. The expansion of memory responds to a concern for exhaustiveness, an effort to achieve a total reconstruction of the past, analogous to the collective enterprise of the Yisker-biher *(the "books of memory"), whose many pages bear rows of quotes, lists, inventories, so as not to lose anything of what once was. A duty of piety and loyalty, an obsessive concern not to forget anything: individual memories, like the "books of memory," are so many tombstones for the world of yesterday. In speaking of himself or herself, the individual erects a living memorial to those who are gone.*

THE SHTETL

The shtetl, the Jewish or predominantly Jewish village, was the space where people lived, among their own and felt at home. More important, in literature and folklore the shtetl meant a way of life, a combination of values that gave "its mark to Ashkenazi Jewry."[1] The reality of the shtetl, however, was more complex, less idyllic than is projected by the somewhat sublimated image. Its representations in memories are not without nuances: the warmth of human relations, the outstanding moral qualities, combined with religious or political contradictions and extreme poverty.

Charles H., born in 1906 in Nysko, in western Galicia, comes from families that illustrate the diversity of the shtetlach*: on his father's side, the rationalist tradition of the Haskalah,[2] along with an opening onto the wide spaces (with the rafts of wood that went floating down the San and the Vistula to the Danube); on his mother's side, a life of peasants of Hasidic stock who nevertheless harbored a certain fascination with the prestige of the Polish nobility.*

My paternal grandfather died young, about forty, before I was born. He had a very special trade: he was a *Danziger soyher*,[3] that is, he cut down forests (there were immense forests in the region). They took the wood to the river, the San, and made wooden rafts, just as they do everywhere in that flat country. Having made his raft, he went down the San, then the Vistula,

1. Rachel Ertel, *Le Shtetl. La bourgade juive de Pologne* [The Shtetl. The Jewish Village of Poland] (Paris: Payot, 1982), 16–17.
2. Enlightenment movement, an opening up to the modern world, which emerged in Germany in the second half of the eighteenth century and spread to eastern Europe during the nineteenth century.
3. *Soyher*—merchant (from the Hebrew *sokher*).

to Danzig. He built a cabin on that raft and it served as a house for him to live in. In Danzig, the wood was sold for use in the mines of England (they were pine forests). The expedition took place in March or April, as soon as the snow melted and the water was rising. It was important to calculate the date carefully, it went very fast. It all had to be done before the river overflowed. Either he returned rich after an expedition like that (he returned by train), or he returned poor, if the wooden raft ran aground on the banks. From time to time, he had to ask the Jewish community in which he found himself to help him get back, and he returned destitute, absolutely destitute.

[. . .] I knew my maternal grandfather very well. He was another type. My mother came from a little village, a real village, where there were a half dozen Jews, a classic village. So, my grandfather was a peasant, a rarity among Galician Jews. I still remember my grandfather behind the plow. He was the owner of a little farm, maybe fifteen *morgen,* which corresponds roughly to three-fourths of a hectare. It was rather strange because my mother's village belonged to a count. It was still very feudal: I saw my grandfather go to *Hrabia*[4] Horodjinski to kiss his hand. Everything belonged to him. The peasants and my grandfather had little patches of ground. My grandfather's farm wasn't his own property either; it belong to Horodjinski. He cultivated five or six hectares that he rented from the count (aside from his patch of land). But the horses, the cows, etc., were his.

There was a large building, a hunting lodge, which my grandfather rented and managed; he had prepared some rooms and he also made a restaurant and tavern. I think the count could sell alcohol. They accused the Jews of causing drunkenness—they ran the taverns after all—but the actual owners were the count or the priest. My grandfather wasn't rich, he worked as a manager. Even today, I still see grandfather wearing a long frock coat and that frock coat floating in the wind and him behind the horse that pulled the plow.

But he was influenced by the count, by the life of the nobility.

4. Count.

So my grandfather played his Horodjinski. He had a beard in the style of Franz Josef. Tall, strong, with broad shoulders, a good appetite. For several months, in about 1910, an artisan had come to live in my grandfather's house to make him his pretty little carriage, his *bryczka* (with two wheels). I still remember my grandfather driving us in autumn before the holidays of Rosh Hashanah and Yom Kippur, to a branch of the San. He rented that branch of the river for fishing. We went by boat from the other side and held long lines. We went out fishing at four in the morning. We would fill cases, barrels full of fish, put them in the bryczka, and then go to sell them in town, in Rozwadow, some six miles away. On the eve of the Jewish holidays, we always did a good business.

We also brought fish back home for grandmother to fry on the stove. She breaded them with flour and then salted them, and we filled barrels with them. They used them in the inn and we ate them in the winter; it was good to crunch them.

So, grandfather played a bit of the count; he imitated him. In his building, at home, he had set up one room like a kind of synagogue. That is, he bought a Torah[5]—that was expensive— with a little closet. There were a few Jews in the area, peasants like him, in the little villages around the castle. And on Saturday, since there was no synagogue in the little villages and since you need ten men to say prayers, they came from all the villages to pray in grandfather's house. He was the host. After prayers, he offered everyone a glass of vodka.

There's the character. Religiously speaking, he wasn't very well versed in Talmud. But for the holidays, he also played the Hasid, he had his *tsaddik,* a somewhat miraculous rabbi. A big court with a lot of people. And, since he played the count, he brought a lot of money. When he came, they greeted him: "Rebbe Herschel!" and they sat him on the right of the tsaddik, he had the privilege of receiving the first piece of meat when the tsaddik distributed it, and he was very proud of that. He probably went there for the holiday of Sukkot because, for

5. This expression already appears very secularized, for the traditional formula was: "had a Torah inscribed."

Rosh Hashanah and Yom Kippur, I think he stayed home. But I know that it must have been expensive. Since he had a lot of daughters, when there was a girl to marry off, grandmother came to ask my father (her son-in-law), who had influence over him, to find a way to keep him from going to the tsaddik that year because they had to have enough for their daughter's dowry!

My grandfather had a lot of respect for my father because my father was a learned man; he gave him a gift of an edition of the Babylonian Talmud in at least twenty volumes, bound in leather.

Here is another vision of the shtetl, fleeting but dazzling. Isaac P. was born in Kiev at the end of the last century. He spent his early childhood in the big city, which he left in 1904, at the age of seven, after the pogrom of Kishinev, to hide with his mother in the village where his grandparents lived.

At the time of the pogrom, my father got the idea of sending us to his shtetl. He sent my mother, the children, all we could carry; we made the trip by boat on the Dniepr, to B. [. . .] The village was divided into two completely distinct parts, separated by a little river. On one side were the Jews and on the other, the goys; on one side the synagogue all black, on the other a church all white. To go from one part to the other, there was a footbridge. But nobody (at least not the children) ever crossed the footbridge.

In the shtetl, it was Jewish life par excellence. In Kiev, even in the Jewish schools, you learned Russian. In the shtetl, you spoke only Yiddish and everything was Jewish: language, clothes, customs, way of life. You recognized a Jew a hundred feet away, with his black hat, his long frock coat, usually black, all buttoned up. In the shtetl, it was a total Jewish life, with Shabbat and the holidays, a Jewish life as it was conceived at that time, in that place, but total. You couldn't be anything else. It wasn't thinkable. When there was a holiday, there was a holiday all over. A fast, everybody fasted. It was the Kingdom of God, in its way.

The shtetlach lasted for centuries and centuries by preserving a spirit. In a different form, I find that spirit inside me, attenuated, but very deep. Those shtetlach were separate little kingdoms, which had established a spiritual permanence in the midst of precariousness. They were so many little Jerusalems. Every one of those shtetlach was a little Jerusalem.

On the contrary, the tale of Georges F. (born in 1915) lingers on the desolation, the archaic aspects, and the poverty of the Jewish town. The town is Skarzysko, between Radom and Kielce:

It's a village that was truly primitive. At the age of six or seven, I saw that they walked like it was still two hundred years ago. Now, with hindsight, I see that it really was a primitive state. They walked barefoot. There weren't any sidewalks, nor a paved road in the middle. Naturally, there wasn't much traffic [*laughs*]. You were almost mixed up with the animals. It wasn't organized, that's how it was, savage. I always went barefoot in summer. During the war of '14, when the Russians chased the Germans, they put tree trunks across the paths to be able to move their vehicles. That's what allowed us to cross from one house to another avoiding the mud. Afterward, it improved. They became aware that life isn't exactly like that, and they started to put in sidewalks, roads.

When I was little, there was real poverty. The Jews were the tradesmen. You lived on nothing. This one sold apples he bought from the peasants; that one sold potatoes. My mother sold poultry. She used to get two or three chickens to sell to people who were a little better off. That's how she was able to feed her children. We lived in a house built of logs. There weren't any roof tiles, nothing at all; the roof was also made of wooden boards. We didn't have electricity either. It did exist in the village a little farther away, but we didn't get it until I was sixteen or eighteen years old. Until then, I didn't see a light; we always used kerosene lamps, like in the old days. It was still archaic, a little primitive. There were wells. We went to get water with buckets.

The shtetl wasn't the only place where the Jews of eastern Europe felt at home among themselves. Statistically speaking, in Poland between the wars the Jewish minority represented 10 percent of the population (3.2 million out of 32 million inhabitants, according to the statistics of 1931). However, its distribution was geographically imbalanced. A third of the population in cities like Warsaw (352,000 out of 1,171,000), Lodz (202,000 out of 604,000), Lvov (99,000 out of 312,000), or Lublin (38,000 out of 112,000) was Jewish.[6] In those areas of heavy concentration, the Jewish community, despite its extreme diversity, imposed its structure and rhythm on daily life. While the city did not include a ghetto in the narrow juridical sense of the term, the Jews generally lived in neighborhoods where, as in the shtetl, they were among themselves. Following a suggestive formula of one of our informers: "There was no wall; the wall was only spiritual." One could spend years, even a whole lifetime, without venturing into non-Jewish neighborhoods, without mixing with "the others" (except through the concierge or, in the rarer case of well-off families, through servants). Thus, the number of Jews, the relative homogeneity, and the web of relations result, in the memory of the city as in the shtetl, in the same image of completeness, of a world that was totally Jewish.

Hélène H., born in 1906 in Bialystok, descendant of a line of famous rabbis, emphasizes the contrast between the two parts of the city. At the beginning of the century, the city numbered 42,000 inhabitants, 28,000 of them Jews (i.e., 66 percent):[7] the Polish quarter stretched over vast spaces, residential and empty, where one never dared to go; whereas commercial activities, movement, and bustle were concentrated in the central Jewish streets, teeming with life.

6. Pawel Korzec, *Juifs en Pologne: La question juive pendent l'entre-deux-guerres* [Jews in Poland: The Jewish Question Between the Wars] (Paris: Presses de la Fondation Nationale des Sciences Politiques, 1980), 164; *La Situation des Juifs dans le monde* [The Situation of the Jews in the World], published by the World Jewish Congress, Vol. I, Part 1 (Paris, 1938), 208–217.

7. *The Bialystoker Memorial Book,* ed. the Bialystoker Center (New York: 1982), 4. The figures mentioned by Hélène H. represent those of the 1930s.

I was born in Bialystok, one of the biggest cities of Poland. The Jews were two-thirds of the population; seventy thousand Jews out of a hundred thousand inhabitants.

There was a main street, Linden Street, which went from the station to the spacious quarter down below, where there was a public park. Almost in the middle, the street widened, you know, like in Cracow. There was a kind of square with a little clock. On every side you had perpendicular streets and we lived there, a street that wasn't very wide (hardly wider than Rue de Tolbiac), but very commercial. All the trade was concentrated in the main part, and it was all Jewish trade. You could go in and speak Yiddish in all the shops; that was completely normal. I don't remember seeing any Polish shops there (except later on, when I returned for vacation in the '20s and '30s). Then, a little farther on, the main street was cut by a street that was a little wider, more residential and less commercial. There were bigger, maybe richer houses. My grandfather (the rabbi) lived on that more spacious street. There, that was the Jewish city, all that.

Beyond, in the extension of Linden Street, if you like, you came to a more spacious neighborhood, where there was the public park, the administration buildings, the state high school, and maybe the theater. That was the Christian part. And we practically never went there. We lived in the main part of the city, the Jewish part. I tell you, the Christian part, that wasn't our city.

[. . .] That wasn't exactly Poland, it was the part of Poland that was Russian-Lithuanian. I really didn't know anything about the Polish except that we had a maid named Zoche, who was Polish. That's all. For me, the Poles were the maid. Nobody in our house spoke Polish until the '20s.

"But in the Polish part of the city?"

I don't know what was there. We never went there!

Here is the description of a house in Kalisz, a city of about sixty thousand inhabitants, almost half of whom were Jews.[8] *Lazare M.'s*

8. *The Kalish Book,* ed. I. M. Lask (Tel Aviv: The Societies of Former Residents of Kalish and the Vicinity in Israel and the U.S.A., 1968), 10.

memories revive from inside (from attic to cellar) the neighborly, friendly, and family relations among those who lived there.

The Jewish quarter wasn't a compulsory ghetto. There was no wall; the wall was only spiritual. Everybody spoke Yiddish, even the concierges. In the Jewish streets, in the Jewish neighborhoods, it was rare to find a non-Jewish resident or tenant, except for the concierges. You needed a non-Jewish concierge for Saturdays, to light the lamp or, in winter, for the fire. He would come on Sundays, and you gave him ten *groschen* and a piece of *challah*.[9] It was part of his salary. Because the concierge was even poorer than the poorest ones in the building. I remember, I can tell you, everybody who lived in our house.

It was like this. There was a wooden gate and then a courtyard and the house. With most of the houses in the poor neighborhoods, you entered, and there was the courtyard and then the house. There were also houses that fronted onto the street, with another house in back. In the big cities, in Warsaw, there were three or four courtyards, and then you came out into another street.

Our house had three stories, and with the cellar and the ground floor, that makes five floors of dwellings. There were three apartments per floor on four stories. One apartment of two rooms and kitchen and two apartments of one room and kitchen, the kitchen without a window, without light, and the room being the extension of the kitchen, twenty-five square meters in all.

Underground, let's say the cellar, because the windows were above, at ground level, that's how it was. On the left, in the apartment with two rooms and kitchen, lived a shoemaker. I still see him, with his one son and six daughters. The son was the oldest. On the right, in the apartment with one room and kitchen, it was your grandmother, Madame W., with five or six children, I don't remember. Your grandfather wasn't there anymore. The children were still little, three boys and two girls, I think. The oldest sons didn't live there anymore and your

9. Braided egg bread eaten on the Sabbath and holidays.

grandmother worked making shirts. All that in a room fifteen by fifteen feet large, as in our house. Next to the W.'s was someone who practiced a trade that doesn't exist anymore, with pans: a tinsmith.

So, that was on the bottom. On the ground floor, that is, on the mezzanine, there was somebody who had a shop, a little shop. A haberdasher, a worker who made hats, with two daughters. He worked at home for a boss. And another one was a peddler. A peddler, that doesn't mean like here; there, they spread it out on the ground, on a piece of cloth, or they brought two or three chairs and put the merchandise on a chair. He did business in the little towns around Kalisz. He used to leave at midnight with a cart and horse to make his rounds.

On the first floor, my uncle was the one who lived in the two rooms and kitchen. He was a *melamed,* you know, a teacher; one room in his apartment was for his heder.[10] We lived next door, in one room, my father, my mother, and three children, that is, my brother, my sister, and me. My father was a lace worker; it's the local industry of Kalisz. Most of the manufacturers and workers in lace were Jews. They sold it everywhere, in all of Russia, even in Siberia. Next door to us, in the other room and kitchen, lived the Diaments. One of the children was my friend. His older brother was a great hero in the Warsaw Ghetto: Abraham Diament. He had been a noncommissioned officer in the Polish army in 1920, a sergeant or, rather, a corporal because they called him "the corporal." And since he knew how to handle weapons, he had a rifle in the ghetto. Who had weapons in the ghetto? You know it wasn't everybody who had them. And he fell with a rifle in his hand, he fell from a roof of a burning house. I wrote an article about him, it's called *Gestalten,* "Faces of the Ghetto"; it hasn't been published yet. He lived right next door to me. His father worked in the city mill, at night, a night watchman; that's not a Jewish trade. And his mother was a teacher. She taught girls to read and write, Yiddish and Polish—because the girls didn't go to heder. She taught two or three girls, every day another class, all that in

10. Traditional Jewish elementary school.

the one room. The room was smaller than this one and not so light. There was no bathroom either, just a garbage can and the kitchen without a window.

On the second floor, oh! On the second floor, the two apartments of one room and kitchen were joined into one. It wasn't actually an apartment. I'll tell you in Hebrew: it is called *haknasat orhim;*[11] it was to take in the poor to sleep. A night's shelter. I know it well because I went there often. At one time, it was my father who took care of it. It was an association, maybe the Jewish community, that paid my father a little something to open it at night. You had to register in a book because the police checked. The poor came there to sleep. It was dirty, because who was it who came? Beggars, Jewish beggars, *schnorrers!* But not the beggars of Kalisz. Because begging is a trade, not just a trade, a caste. The ones who came were the beggars who made the rounds from one city to another, from one village to another. Let's say, one night, somebody comes that night and afterward he does twenty or thirty villages before he comes back to Kalisz. That was in '20, '22. I was ten, twelve years old. I was already somewhat aware of these things. I remember saying: "Papa, you'll see, next week, so-and-so will come." And, in the city everybody had his own domain—it was like the sidewalk here in Paris. One person didn't have the right to trespass on somebody else's sidewalk. Everybody had his own hundred yards, two hundred yards. Like the whores here. You see beggars here too. But the tramps of Paris are rich compared to them! Because really, what did you give them? And the schnorrers, there were a lot of them in Poland. They didn't all go from city to city. Some had their own place—in front of the synagogue, say, like in front of a church. Those places were the best ones. They'd sit in front of the synagogue, not on Saturday, not on holidays, but all week long: "*Git a groshen, git a groshen,*" give a penny!

But let's go back to the house. We were on the second floor, and the shelter was the two apartments. Next door lived somebody who was already old, already retired. He had a daughter,

11. "Welcoming guests," shelter.

and when she got married, she lived there with the son-in-law, in the two rooms and kitchen. The son-in-law was a roofer, a trade that was quite common among the Jews.

Now the third floor. There was only one apartment. On the other side was the attic for drying clothes. The tenants of the house followed a schedule; sometimes they argued. And on the other side lived somebody called Franzuz. He had a tiny little grocery. The grocery was a quarter of his room. He would sell a herring or a liter of oil, a few apples, a few eggs, that's all.

Oh! I remember something that will interest you. If somebody died in the house, when there was a death, you had to empty all the buckets, all the water. You know why? Because the *Malhemuves*,[12] the Angel of Death, when he comes, he kills a man with his sword. And afterward, he cleans it, he rinses it in the water of the whole house. So you have to throw out the water. My mother did that. Those are superstitions. You threw the water in the sink outside, in the staircase. It went down to the courtyard.

POVERTY

Childhood memories are set against a background of poverty, as in the description of the house we have just heard. It is one of the subjects that recurs most frequently, whether in the shtetl *or in the city: hunger, the cramped dwellings, bare feet in the snow—it all provokes a retrospective pity that does not preclude lucid reflection.*

The episode of the hidden bread, told by Lazare M., is a sort of memory once removed since the narrator himself was not present at the scene. He reconstructs it, sixty years later, assuming his brother's subsequent confession. This is an example of a concatenation of memory: the individual here acts as a relay for his family, the spokesman for the group, while integrating the memories of others into his own experience. Individual memories, thus intersecting and reassumed, blend to constitute a collective memory:

The first time I saw my brother again after I left Poland was in 1955, in Israel. Because he had been in a concentration camp

12. "*Malhemuves*"—Hebrew *Malakh ha-mavet*—the Angel of Death.

and afterward, he went to Israel. I saw him again for the first time in Ramat Gan, in Israel. And he told me this story, he said: "You remember when you went to the Diament's house to listen to the megillah of Esther? I had stayed home alone. There was a loaf of bread; it wasn't whole; it was already sliced. Without Mama knowing, without anybody knowing, I cut a piece of bread and ate it. And until now, you're the only one I've ever told the story to."

That gives you an idea of how well-off we were. In 1917, I was six and a half years old. My brother was born in '06; he was ten. How you ate, like that, a piece of dry bread. And the bread, in '17, that was black bread. There was more bran than bread in it and more potato, you know, potato starch. It wasn't a baguette like today.

And I'm telling you this story today for the first time—to you, for the first time since my brother told it to me. From '17 to '55, that's thirty-eight years. After thirty-eight years, he told it to me, thirty-eight years later. And I'm telling it in '80. From '17, that's sixty-three years. I was six years old.

I wanted to tell that story so much.

There are also memories of memories in Mathilde R.'s account (born in France in 1928). Before getting to her own story, she goes far back, to a time she knew only from the family tradition her parents passed on to her:

My paternal grandparents lived in a shtetl near Lodz, in a little village called Glownow [. . .] Often the children didn't have enough to eat, but my grandmother could work wonders. For example, one thing really struck me when they told me about it. She went to a street where there was a guy with a little cart of potatoes. She bought potatoes from him and said: "I'm going to take the cart home; I'll get money and bring the cart back to you with the money." Then she went to the next street and sold the potatoes for a little more than what she had paid for them. She brought the cart back, gave him the money, and kept the difference. And for that she could buy a few kilos of potatoes for her children.

Georges F.:

There was a very pretty field, like a park, on the banks of the river that went through the city. Every Saturday, when the weather was nice, from May on, we put up little huts of branches and we slept there. That would free our parents of four or five children. We spent the night and the next morning went back home to eat. That was poverty. We came to sleep, to clear out the room we lived in. Our room was maybe twelve or thirteen meters; we were seven children and our parents.

We built a house there out of logs, with trees, and that's how we lived, on the flattened ground. I remember that the house had two windows. There were three beds, a cabinet, a table, and chairs. That's what made us go outside in the morning, as soon as it was light. Every now and then, to clean up, the practice was for my sisters to get white sand and put it on the ground. That makes the room cleaner. That's how we lived.

Pieces of bread were rationed; children couldn't just eat whatever they wanted. The peasants we knew before (before the arrival of the weapons factory) helped us. I remember I had to go get milk in a jug, in winter, with a brother who was two years older than me. Then we sold the milk to Jews who wanted to buy it. We'd bring it to their house. Once I happened to slip in the snow and spill the jug of milk; so my brother said: "We'll add water; nobody will notice." They did notice, but we said that the cow wasn't as good as before for giving pure milk. We did really primitive things, even after civilization came. We carried milk and, every now and then, somebody gave us a piece of bread as payment and once a week they gave my mother a few pennies to pay for the milk.

There were also water carriers, men who carried water, in exchange for food, with a device on both shoulders, like you see in the histories of old cities, I don't know if that still exists in France. We too, we children, we also carried water; that's how we managed to get the basic necessities.

And in our house, in front of the room, they built a little hut for a Jewish merchant. He payed us by the month, a small rent. He put in a grocery. A grocery, it wasn't like today. When you bought a pickled herring, it was by the piece. Cigarettes you bought one by one. When you had a piece of bread on one side, you went to get a piece of herring. It wasn't a whole herring you bought, they cut it up into maybe twenty pieces. That's how you ate. You managed to get through the day. And most of the time, you lived outside.

You went barefoot, even in winter. You wrapped your feet in potato sacks, that's how you walked. Once, the Americans arranged a social welfare setup, a kitchen for the poor, for the children. Sometimes I would carry my brother on my back because I had sacks on my feet while he was barefoot. I carried him all the way down there to get food. I was maybe seven years old. That's how we helped each other in the middle of winter. There were people whose feet froze; that was really poverty.

It was Georges F.'s mother who supplied the needs of the family with an indefatigable ingenuity because the father—a classical cultural feature, recalled here with some bitterness—spent his time praying. As for the children, still very young, they were forced to find ways of helping the mother.

My father could have worked, but he didn't want to because he was a religious fanatic. We weren't allowed to touch anything at all on Saturday. He went to pray every day, to study the Bible. It wasn't so much for the prayers, because you say prayers three times a day, in the morning, at noon, and at night. But he stayed in the house of prayer all day long. I don't know if it was to avoid eating or to study religion. There were a lot of men who did that. The synagogue was almost full.

It didn't start out as a synagogue. It was built by the villagers. Little by little, it developed, and that house eventually became a real synagogue. The poor even came to spend the night and sleep there. Those who wandered around on the roads had their meeting place in that house; they came to tell each other stories about their day, and they slept on the wooden benches.

I loved my mother very much—she was a really terrific woman. To be able to take care of seven children, go out in the morning, at four o'clock in the morning, winter and summer alike, to get things. She went to get poultry. She had to go all over the countryside to find a peasant who wanted to sell a chicken or a goose. She brought it back and had it killed by the *shoihet*;[13] then she'd sell the goose in pieces, by quarters.

When she left in the morning, at four, five o'clock, she'd come back by one, two o'clock in the afternoon. And we fasted while waiting for her to come. She had to walk: five miles for a woman, going and coming, naturally that took almost the whole day. She went on foot, since she didn't have money to take the train. She left us children to manage on our own. My father, he almost wasn't interested at all; he expected, just like us, that she'd be the one to bring home the bread. It's really a terrible memory that won't go away even now. Poverty, it's the same everywhere, but in Poland it was very common.

From seven to twenty-one, I remember the jobs I did. I wonder how I could have done all that in fourteen years. I don't even know how I learned to read and write. All I did, you can't imagine. There was lots of willingness, to see, to do . . .

Among other things, Georges F. helped porters unload merchandise.

Those porters, with their wagons, came from our town, from Skarzysko, to Kielce or Schidlovsk, because that was the railroad center, carrying sacks of flour, sugar, beans, food. I went with them, it took the whole day, to go and come back. The porter was well paid, and me, what did I earn? Almost nothing.

There were three of them, those porters in the village, who went from one village to another with their wagon. Once, the merchant came to see one of those horse owners and said to him:

"Listen, on Tuesday, there's a market in Vorotzk, you have to come. We'll go to the market, we'll spend the day, and then we'll come back. I'll pay you."

"I really want to, but you have to give me the money in advance to feed my horses and get them ready."

Horses were usually fed hay, but when you wanted them to do an especially big job, you had to give them oats, straw. That

13. Ritual slaughterer.

meant paying in advance. And the next morning, there was a terrible storm, they couldn't leave. The merchant comes to see the porter:

"Give me back the money, since I gave you a deposit."

"Here, I'm going to show you what I did with your money."

And he takes him where the horses were; it wasn't even a stable:

"Pick up the droppings, you see, that's your money there!"

"Are you crazy?"

"What do you want from me? I got my horses ready—they ate. If it rains, it's not my fault! How would you like me to give back the money!"

So he gave him the biggest horse droppings. And that's the way it happened.

That horse dropping, proposed as payment for a debt, seems to stir up a repertoire of jokes (from a folklore perhaps more peasant than Jewish). But it is remarkable that Georges F. insists on the authenticity of the anecdote, and that he piles up a wealth of details which make the episode unique and real. Here the individual—with unquestioned sincerity—takes the collective memory for his own and inscribes it in his personal memory.

APPRENTICESHIP

After these early activities, recalled in a joking tone (these were mere child's play), one soon went on to serious things: in these large, poor families, children started working very young, from the age of twelve or thirteen. For Georges F., memories of apprenticeship blend with those of his passage to adulthood: as he learned his trade as a tailor, he also learned the harshness of exploitative relationships.

A day of my apprenticeship in the shop: it meant coming in at five, six o'clock in the morning in winter. Then making the fire. That was the first thing.

Making the fire, bringing coal, it wasn't all that easy to carry the coal. It meant bringing forty-four pounds on my back from the coalman. We used coal for the fire. We used a cookstove, like they used to have here at one time. Then you had to heat the pressing iron. That was the first thing. The irons weren't the same ones I have here either. The iron was made of iron. You put it in the fire, on hard coal. Not charcoal. Charcoal came later, that was already an advance. We heated up the iron on the coal; you poked inside with a *shareizen*.[14] The iron weighed about ten or twelve pounds. When the workers came and started setting up, I had to take the irons out of the fire to put them by the big table. They weren't anything like the irons we used after the war.

Later, the iron was a wood iron, heated by charcoal. The work was even harder when they invented that business. You had to go outside and swing it with your hand like that [*gesture*] so the coal would move to the front of the iron.

There were three men and two women who worked in the shop. As for the girls—one of them passed away in Paris; the other one was deported. They used to talk about all sorts of things, gossip. This one told how he went out with a girl; that one told about his worries—things I didn't know, coarse things. It shocked me terribly.

Then, afterward, at noon, we didn't make a hot lunch. Everybody went out to buy bread and sausage, and then we went back to work. It was very hard on an apprentice. Just learning to do the work, to learn to hold the needle on the thimble, that took at least three months. Yes, because that finger had to be bent like that [*gesture*]. Because men, they sew with a thimble that doesn't have a bottom, they don't prick like that, but here. So, to have that finger bent right, you tied it down and you slept that way so the finger stayed bent the right way and you could hold the needle to go through there. Bending the fingers that way was hard.

And when I took the irons out of the fire for the guys who were going to iron, that was a very important thing. It was a big deal to iron a piece; it took all day. When the piece was ironed, the worker showed it to the boss and he said: "See, that garment is alive; I put my soul in it."

The worker who had a piece to iron, you better not talk

14. A poker.

to him! So much so that I once got smacked because the iron wasn't hot enough when I took it out of the oven. It was a real scandal. The guy who smacked me, he lives in Paris now. We see each other every now and then. He's a little older than me, maybe ten years older. And when the iron was too hot, it burned.

He showed the piece to the boss. The boss would say: "It's not worked enough." And he would explain how it should be done: "You have to put your vest on the iron!" *Your vest* meant put your chest on the iron, lean on the iron, to make it even heavier than the ten pounds. A worker could work on the same few inches for an hour pushing the iron like that.

And the day went on like that till night. Sometimes you slept in the shop, especially the men. If there was a garment that had to be finished for the next day, you had no choice. That's how it was: you slept on the big table a few hours, and then you went back to work.

Almost all the work was done by hand. There was a machine, but, for a garment that took thirty-six hours, it was used maybe three hours, not even that, to make the big seams. All the rest was done by hand; that's why it took so long. But a garment, it wasn't like now: when you made one, it lasted from marriage to grandchildren. There was even a time when you turned it inside out; we also did that in the Liberation.[15] When you turned it inside out, it's the apprentice who had to undo it and take out all that dust that had piled up: you came out of that with your hands black as a coal miner.

And that all happened in one room. The boss had a room, and the boss's wife had a room on the side. Because, in general, at that time the boss's wife wasn't in the business. You would see her when she brought her husband something to eat. But she wasn't really involved with the business.

When you took on a thing, you did it from beginning to end. Nobody specialized, except for one finisher who did the detail work. The worker was paid by the piece; when he took on a piece, he had to finish it. That's how the work went. During

15. In France after World War II.

the week, you made . . . Of course, you can't compare with now. Here, my wife and I, together, how many did we make? Three times six, eighteen to twenty pieces a week. But back when I was an apprentice, a worker, a good worker, if he did two pieces a week, he was already somebody, a fine worker.

Now it's not the same at all. At the time we used the iron with the charcoal, that poisoned the shop because, in winter, the doors and windows were closed, and it gave off a toxic gas. One time, while preparing the irons for the others, I became sick, poisoned, and I passed out. The boss and his wife came. They were scared; I had passed out on the floor. It was winter and they took me out on the snow. It was the only way to make me come to, to lay me down in the snow. That wasn't the first such accident. You knew that when somebody was poisoned by charcoal, you had to get him out to the snow. I came to, returned to the shop, and went back to work.

[. . .] When I left, when I left home, my mother cried like a child. I was the only one who provided some relief to her poverty. The other children also worked, but they didn't earn as much as I did. Maybe I was more responsible than the others: everything I earned I gave to the family.

JEWISH INGENUITY

The social conditions of the Jews of central and eastern Europe were actually more diverse than the preceding images or scenes would suggest. If most of them did indeed belong to the lower and poorer classes, some came from an educated or economic elite. Were they privileged people? Not always. They proudly recall that some ancestor or some relative owed his success only to his intelligence, his inventiveness, and his hard work. Memories of poverty find their counterpoint in praise of Jewish ingenuity.

Louise M. (born at the turn of this century):

My grandfather was from another region of Silesia. He had the idea, the almost absurd idea, of starting up a factory there. There wasn't anything—no coal, no water—there was very little water. There was only one thing in that region, rape, a lot of rape, that yellow plant with a captivating smell. He had this idea because they were already exporting it; that is, merchants from other regions were buying it to extract the oil from it. Then they sold the oil because it was the only means of lighting. So, he said to himself: Why not extract the oil on the spot?

He was very young; he didn't have any money. He looked and looked and it was very hard because you needed a steam engine, a big machine. Naturally, there was no such thing, but he, with all his ideas, said to himself: Certainly, in other parts of Germany, you still find machines for scrap that aren't very modern and that don't work very well, but that do the job all the same. And he found exactly that in a former monastery, and there he set up that factory, with that old machine. I even have a photo of that machine—it's quite something—with my father and my grandfather next to it.

HAPPINESS, NOSTALGIA

"In spite of poverty, we were happy." Is this just retrospective illusion? It is certainly a sense of happiness, however, that dwells in the heart of memory. The fullness experienced during childhood has at least three dimensions: familiarity with nature, solidarity with members (near and far) of the Jewish community, and especially the warmth of the family nucleus. This environment, composed of concentric circles, formed a totality in which individuals, as they remember it, were harmoniously integrated.

This is how Georges F., the apprentice tailor who described himself as a kind of "street urchin" of the shtetl, sees the joys of his childhood, as rural scenes unfold before his eyes.

That's my youth. I don't know if children now are happier than we were then. We were happy all the same. It really was something. In winter, we were cold, but we had fun. What were our toys? We could have fun with anything: on the snow with wooden boards, that was one of the pleasures. Especially the things we made ourselves. We made shoes out of potato sacks, but we were happy. And sleds, skates: a piece of iron wire and you made a skate and you learned. That's how we had fun. It was really . . . I think we were happier.

I don't want to judge; maybe it's because I didn't know anything else. It was nice; it was nature. There was the river. In the summer, you learned how to swim. We lived like savages, outside, and it was good. We ate what we could. Our parents gave us pieces of bread and butter to go to the beach, and we shared—there wasn't any selfishness. We protected the other children, watched over them. We banded together; that's how we managed to survive, to feed ourselves. That's how we lived, spending whole days in the fields, on the moors (the *lonke*).

This solidarity between groups of children extends to all members of the Jewish community and is accompanied by the simple happiness of being together. People take pleasure, for example, in recalling the gatherings of men, women, and children who assembled in the house of prayer to listen to the storytellers who went from village to village. The pleasure of the tales and the conviviality it sustained are certainly not specifically Jewish, but, in his narrative, Georges F. emphasizes the role of oral transmission and his concern for preserving a living memory:

Oral transmission is really something terrific. I was talking with some friends the other day: "How can you remember all that?" In my opinion, what is transmitted by speech is as solid as by writing. You saw the transmission from parents and grandparents to children. All you have to do is press a certain spot, a button, and people start talking to you. I could spend twenty-four hours telling you stories that have remained engraved on my memory and that come back. Of course, in a book, when you're reading, you can go back. Oral transmission will disappear with my generation. My children, of course, learned by reading, not by listening to stories.

We were in contact with the person who told the stories, we sat there, we listened to him. When the guy came, they called him *a bal'-darshan*.[16] It was something terrific. He stayed for

16. Teller of biblical stories.

twenty-four hours talking to us. We got together in the *shil*.[17] He'd come on Friday about noon and stay for Saturday. He talked to hand down certain things, Bible stories, Rachel, Joseph; he told stories from his own life too. Everybody was there to listen to him. On Friday night, they'd invite him for dinner. The richest family or somebody who wanted to hear him some more would take him home. He'd invite him without telling his wife, and she'd be so surprised she wouldn't want to give him anything to eat. She'd cut a little piece of bread for him with a little bit of soup. He'd be hungry when he came back to sleep on the bench of the house of prayer.

The next day, he'd start telling again, after noon, because, until noon there were prayers. When it was a famous storyteller, the shil was full. There wasn't any room to come near. Everybody came: children, adults, men and women separately. Some people came to learn and followed his stories in the holy books, like somebody who knows a piece of opera and who follows the score. It was all the joy and life that returned. It was a satisfaction like we have now when we see a play we like a lot. For half a day you listen and forget all of life's woes.

That lasted from Friday noon to Saturday night. Then he left again. He'd make a tour of the villages. All week long, he'd walk. It was only on Saturday that he could gather such a crowd. He fed himself however he could; sometimes they barely gave him enough to survive. But he didn't get discouraged. He went on all the same, to transmit what he had to say. All week long he was on the road, and on Saturday he started again . . .

At the center of all childhood happiness is that which one has lived with one's parents. Even more than in the shtetl or in the Jewish quarter, it was within the family that one felt at home, sheltered from surrounding hostility. The family circle generally meant father, mother, brothers and sisters, sometimes an aunt or an uncle. Memory here rarely goes beyond grandparents. It is this early refuge of peace and affection that appears in memory as the ideal of all joy. The rest of life will preserve a longing for it. Later on, in the course of returns, encounters,

17. Shul, synagogue.

or dreams, the trace of paradise lost looms, stirring up the most intense emotion: one has a sense of finding oneself again.

Georges F.:

But to tell the truth, going back fifty years, it wasn't as bad as all that. You see, I still have nostalgia for my village, it was good.

[. . .] That village, my memories come back to me now. I miss it somehow, even though I live in France. It's an amazing thing. I can't explain how a human being, after fifty years, can feel such nostalgia: to see that village again, in spite of all the hardship he had gone through there.

I tell you, I miss it—even though I've been in France for so long already—I miss that courtyard, that life. What cooking do you love best? Your mother's. In spite of the poverty, we managed to live. I ate dry bread all week. I was solid as a Turk. Of the seven children, no one had a sickness. No vaccinations against smallpox, diphtheria, nothing. We lived like animals, but we were sturdy. I see my grandson, at eleven; you push him with a breeze and he falls over. Me, at seven, I was dragging bulls and cows that could have carried me off like a fly, but I broke them. I was very sturdy.

Martha F.: All in all, in spite of the poverty, you have better memories than me, childhood memories.

Georges F.: Because you, you didn't grow up in that environment. What was your experience?

Martha F.: I was in Paris.

Georges F.: In Paris! That was something else altogether. You didn't know . . .

Martha F.: I had a different form of poverty. You had a happy poverty!

Georges F.: A happy poverty! Me, I just had poverty! [*Laughs, then explains*] I had a happy poverty because we lived together. But you had a lonely poverty, without any family. We, in our poverty, were surrounded by everybody—cousins, aunts, powerful things. I had an aunt. At the time she was, I don't know, she was born before the twentieth century. She was a midwife; she delivered all the children in the Jewish village. She never knew what it was to read and write. And she used to tell us stories; we'd gather in that courtyard. We forgot poverty, we had other joys. And the cousin who took a tour of Europe—he also came to tell stories. It took your mind off eating. And others came to tell us. There was really a family life in that courtyard that just doesn't exist anymore. The family cell is broken. It's over. That story is over.

Martha F.: You don't have any photos of your mother . . .

Georges F.: I had a whole suitcase of photos, and the Germans took them away, on Rue du Chemin-Vert. The only photo I had on me, of my father, that remained. Otherwise, they took everything from me. They emptied the apartment. Yes, there was a whole suitcase of photos! What would you see on those photos? You'd see old people, like in that book.[18] They all look alike, like two drops of water. It was only the *soul* that changed, the way they gave themselves to the children, the way they took care of the house. Otherwise, the people didn't change. You can look at your grandmother and a person who's in there—it's almost the same.

TRADITIONS

In the city, as in the shtetl, to live with your own meant to respect those norms theoretically accepted by all the members of the Jewish community. There were certainly dissonant voices (as we shall see in the next chapter), but they could not escape the constraints of the ever-present tradition. This tradition was composed of various elements (language, dietary rules, cooking, religious practices and beliefs) that coalesced in Jewish memory as a specific and coherent whole. It is there where collective identity sank its roots. Even among those whose families were hardly devout and who called themselves atheists, nos-

18. *The Old Country: The Lost World of European Jews,* ed. Abraham Shulman, preface by Isaac Bashevis Singer (New York: Charles Scribner's Sons, 1974).

talgia for the lost world included a religious dimension. Either they evoke Shabbat (often blended with the image of happiness within the family circle) or celebrations of major holidays, which were inscribed in the larger Jewish environment.

Anna D. (of Lodz, born around 1918):

On Shabbes, nobody worked. All the shops were closed. On Thursday morning, you bought what you needed to prepare by Friday afternoon. Then you lit the candles. You ate a good meal, on Saturday too. So as not to cook on Saturday, to keep for a long time, you made *cholent*.[19] It had meat with grated potatoes and you left it with the baker until Saturday noon when people would go to pick it up. You can't imagine how good that was. There was also stuffed fish. That was very good, believe me, it was better than here.

Now, after the war, all that's over. The meat was better than here, like all the food. You can't imagine the bread! There weren't baguettes; bread came by the kilo. Cholent, gefilte fish,[20] stews, strudels. . . . Here they don't know anything at all. It was very good, everybody was happy—until the war, that is.

Yacob-Jacques, L. (born at the end of the nineteenth century in a shtetl in the area of Lublin):

On Shabbes even the poor did something special. They didn't have money to buy big fish so they bought little fish. They ate a bit of a small chicken, soup with noodles, with beans. Have you ever eaten it? On Friday night people went all out. They'd sweep the house, put a clean cloth on the table—and the rolls, the challah, with little cloths. My mother made the challah herself. And she lit candles before my father went to shil.

Charles H.:

I remember the atmosphere that prevailed in a synagogue on Yom Kippur. It was something extraordinary, that atmosphere.

19. A stew of meat or poultry, potatoes or dried beans, cooked on a slow fire from Friday afternoon on and served as the main meal on Saturday.
20. Stuffed carp.

I don't know, I've never gone to a synagogue for the holidays in France—I should do it before I die—but I did go in the United States. I went with my brother-in-law to a synagogue, in Bridgeport, where there's a big Jewish community. Well, personally, I was pretty shocked because the atmosphere just wasn't there.

First the smell, the smell of a hundred candles lit since the night before (afterward, you mustn't light them). They are candles like in church, big candles that last a long time, more than twenty-four hours. Every family brings at least one, or even several, that they light because it's also in part in memory of the dead. Then, that smell all evening, all night. More than that, to get through the fast, they breathed smelling salts so as not to be sick.

At home, we had a real *tallit* of linen, with black stripes. And, on Yom Kippur, the adults, the heads of families, all wore a *kittel* over their clothes, a kind of white cloth tunic, as a sign of mourning, penitence. That's the clothing of the dead; they're buried nude in that shroud. Back then, in that little town, the Jews were buried nude in a shroud. That's the shroud they wore on Yom Kippur. So, imagine that white color, with the tallit spread over their head. The prayers were chanted by a *hazan*[21] and repeated aloud by everyone, all day long in that fashion.

Georges F.:

At Pesah, the father was the king and the mother was the queen. To prepare that holiday, once a year, they cleaned the house by taking everything out to the courtyard: the cabinets, the beds, the chairs. Everything was taken out and cleaned so there wouldn't be even a trace of the food from the year. It was all renewed. We waited for that holiday like for the Messiah. The children waited for that holiday like for the Messiah because they took out everything, they cleaned, they swept. They even took out the mattress to change the straw. Bread was forbidden, so whatever bread they collected they burned in the courtyard. All the neighbors together lit a fire and burned it.

21. Cantor.

Then everyone set up for Passover. Believe me, it was a fantastic holiday. People bought food for eight days—unleavened bread, potatoes, eggs. There were two sets of dishes. You know, that bread, the unleavened bread, could only be made by Jews. They made it in a special oven, eight days in advance, and prepared it by hand, nothing but water and flour, no salt, nothing. Now they manufacture it in factories and it comes in squares. Before, back home, they made it round. Then there was a moment of prayer with a glass of wine. That wine was made with dry grapes a year in advance—every year—and it was used for the next year. It wasn't only the eight days: all year you worked for that holiday. They made goose fat in advance too, in the winter, and since Passover comes in spring, they prepared those things for the holiday six months in advance.

Martha F.: Where did your mother get money for all that?

Georges F.:

There was a fund. We all had to buy food for eight days though not everybody could manage. So they made a fund. The rich helped the poor, especially for unleavened bread. It was distributed almost free. On that holiday everybody was equal; people were on the same level. The richest and the poorest were on the same level. The rich man couldn't eat anything different from the poor man. Maybe he ate more meat, more unleavened bread. But it was the same, he didn't eat anything different.

And then, on the night of the Seder, at home, that prayer, it was terrific. There were five of us left at home, father, mother, the five children around the table. The table was set with unleavened bread, the pieces of unleavened bread were put on top of one another, separated by a clean napkin so they wouldn't touch each other. There was horseradish, hard-boiled eggs. The Seder began at about eight o'clock at night and lasted until one in the morning. Father said the prayer, he told the whole history of the exodus from Egypt, and the youngest child asked nine questions: why do we eat unleavened bread, why do we eat nine kinds of raw vegetables, bitter herbs. You had to taste nine kinds of food that night, nine, always that uneven number: why, I don't know.

At one particular moment in the prayer, father picked up a piece of unleavened bread. He gave it to the children and mother to taste, he took some himself, and they ate around the table. The piece in the middle stayed all year, until the next year. Then, there was a moment of prayer for which the glass of wine was prepared. It was reserved for the Messiah. I don't know if it was the Messiah. They called it *Ele Nuve*.[22] *Ele Nuve*, it's not really the Messiah, it's a chosen soul, I don't know exactly, a chosen soul from the family, who came to taste the wine at the table. So that was the most solemn moment, the most awesome moment of the night. Father would get up. Everybody stood up, and they opened the door and began the prayer to make that soul enter, that holy soul that came down from heaven to taste wine with us. It was really the most awesome moment, we trembled with fear. Then, I don't know how it's done, we looked at the wine and the wine moved. It's unbelievable. My father remarked: "You see that somebody came to drink!"

That's how it happened. It's an unforgettable memory. I've been to Seders in Paris, but they were imitations. What happened in my youth, I was six, seven years old, it wasn't that at all.

In recalling the episode of the wine that moved, Georges F. has almost relived in the present the emotion he felt on those Seder nights. But at the same time, he distances it by injecting it with humor, which modifies the tone of the tale. The scene he goes on to describe is found in the memories of others and seems to belong (like the history of the horse droppings above) to a certain folkloric and rather irreverent tradition! Here, too, individual memory works as a relay of the collective memory.

One day—it was when I was grown up—I remember that somebody played a trick on the neighbors. As soon as they

22. *Eliyahu Hanavi,* the Prophet Elijah. According to Jewish tradition, the coming of the Messiah is announced by the return of the Prophet Elijah; this is why one awaits the latter on Passover.

opened the door to let that holy soul come in, somebody pushed a goat into the house. They were terribly scared. It was quite a scandal.

From irreverent humor, one gradually slips into the critical spirit. Until he was eleven, Maurice N. lived in a small town near Warsaw. His father went from being a fervent Hasid to a "total atheist": his adherence to Communism even contributed to convincing him to emigrate. Maurice N. received a traditional education in Poland, but the memories he has preserved of it are inevitably inflected by his father's subsequent development and by his own convictions. Nevertheless, he levels his criticism with a bit of a smile; his anecdote sounds like a kind of parable.

Prohibitions—there were a lot of them. That's all there was. You didn't have the right to eat this, you didn't have the right to go here, you didn't have the right. . . . There were a lot of things. . . . You mustn't do that because a Jewish boy doesn't do that. For example, running, you mustn't run; skating, you mustn't skate. You mustn't do sport. You have to go to heder. You mustn't do the same thing as the goys. Prohibitions, from all sides.

I remember, when I was little, one day, I was maybe five, six years old. I was at my uncle's house. It was cherry season and I went outside with a handful of cherries. There was a little girl who wanted my cherries and I didn't want to give them to her. So she jumped up to catch the cherries. And this little girl was a goy. I threw away every cherry she touched, because it wasn't kosher anymore. That's how she ate up all my cherries.

APPARITIONS, MIRACLES

The world of ghosts, dybbuks,[23] devils, of visions, apparitions, miracles—that world magnified in Isaac Bashevis Singer by the magic of writing—does exist in memory. Earlier, in the description of the house, we noted the theme of the Angel of Death, who passes through and washes his sword in the water kept in the containers belonging to the

23. Dybbuk: an evil spirit that enters into a living person.

house. That supernatural universe appears in snatches, in certain de-
tours of the tale, surprising the narrator himself, who then breaks off
his recollection with a smile. Sometimes he talks spontaneously of
"superstitions" and proposes his own, thoroughly rational interpreta-
tion. Dybbuks, ghosts? Yes, those are the stories he was told. He even
witnessed them, but he certainly doesn't believe in them. And yet, he
recalls with a mixture of unease and affection that his parents and his
grandparents did believe in them: a received memory that he both
repeats and from which he distances himself.

We are not surprised to find a certain folkloric vein injected into
Georges F.'s personal story.

In the shop, we worked at night, as I told you. Once, you
know, the fellows were joking, and somebody said: "Hey, I'm
going to go to the cemetery and, to prove it to you, I'll plant
a stick there!" The Jewish cemetery was outside the town and
we were scared. . . : crossing the cemetery at night was something unimaginable. When I came to Paris, I lived right next
door to Père-Lachaise, on Rue Pierre-Bayle, but I wouldn't have
dreamt of going to the window and looking at the tombs of
the dead. . .

So he says to us: "I'm going to go to the cemetery at midnight, you'll see!" It was an idiotic bet, but he went just the
same. They gave him a stick, and he said: "I'm going to put it
on such and such a grave, and tomorrow you can go see if it's
true." So he went. And since we wore long clothes—you know
the long coats the Jews wear, he had a long coat like that, which
got stuck with that stick; it went across it. And when he wanted
to leave he felt something holding him back. The next day, he
was found dead.

It's terrible, but that's what happened. They went to see the
next day because they were worried, but they didn't dare go
there at one o'clock in the morning. And they found him dead.
He died of fear. . . [. . .]

I remember the rabbi who came, the most illustrious rabbi
who used to come to us, for a stay. Because they also went from
one village to another, to supervise what was going on, how
Judaism was developing. He came and the Jews came to tell

him. You had to bring him presents, food. For example, when he spent a Saturday in a village, all the rich Jews brought him food. They came to tell him, they'd come to say: "I have three daughters, I want to marry them off, give us advice." So he'd say to those people: "Go back home, you're going to see, you're going to marry off such and such a daughter this year, there will be a miracle," and all that. Sometimes it did happen. But pious Jews believed.

Yacob-Jacques L.:

So here's the miracle. My father met his father, who was walking down the road. They met at the crossing. The night before, my grandfather had been called to sell some rings or something. So, when he found my father on the way, he said to him:
"Michael, where are you going?"
"Down to the village, to N., to fix watches."
"That's just where I'm going; it's not worth it for you to go."
"Of course, if you're going there, I won't go."
My father returned home. My grandfather was away; he didn't return. That went on for eight days, ten days, he wasn't there. And all of a sudden, they bring him back—dead, killed. He was killed on the road. And my mother says to me:
"You see what that means. God didn't want your father to die."
But I thought otherwise. They wouldn't have killed my father because he didn't have anything on him. They killed my grandfather because he was carrying a lot of jewels, very valuable ones. But if my father had gone there, they wouldn't have killed him. I didn't dare tell my mother that. She believed, fine.
Listen, there was another miracle. They were preparing for the funeral and sent people to the cemetery to dig a grave. It was winter, and the ground was so frozen that they couldn't dig. They worked for two hours, three hours, they just couldn't do it. It was already noon on Friday. What were they going to do? You see the problem? What were they going to do? Everybody was crying.

Then, all of a sudden, they saw a soldier right next to them, and this soldier asks:

"What are you doing there?"

My father and his brother explained what was happening.

"Give me the thing for digging."

He took the shovel and, in five minutes, the grave was done. Then they buried my grandfather. Afterward, my father said to me:

"I wanted to thank the soldier or to pay him. When I looked, I didn't find him; he wasn't there anymore."

For them, what was that? A miracle. But I'm going to tell you what it was. It was a soldier on leave passing by who saw people crying. I don't know what—he was a peasant who knew how to dig a grave. I didn't tell my mother that, but that's how I understood it, see? Them, they always lived with miracles. Always miracles, they believed in them.

YIDDISHKEIT

Yiddishland *has disappeared;* Yiddishkeit *remains. The term cannot be reduced simply to linguistic or religious elements: it includes much broader connotations, indicating an entire way of life based on a mix of rules, customs, behaviors, tastes, and bonds of solidarity. It encompasses as well a totality in which individuals find not only a place but also meaning, to the extent that they preserve its indelible imprint in the most private part of their being. Even in those who admit their indifference to religion and proclaim their hostility to rabbinic teaching, there survives an attachment, sometimes unconscious, to values they themselves define as "Jewish." The religious tradition is transposed onto the secular world and henceforth seen magnified as moral law. These ever-present values inform thought, sensibility, all of life.*

A longtime "fellow traveler" of the Communist party, Robert S. (born in 1907), contrasts the education he received at home, within the family, with the lavish instruction in school, in this case, a Polish school. After immigrating to France in the late 1920s, he mastered the French language, thanks to strenuous efforts, and achieved a certain social success, of which he is proud. But fifty years later, he still resorts to Yiddish to express his deepest feelings.

This Jewish culture was given to me by my father. He handed down to me what he had received from the tradition. When I compare what I learned at home and what I learned in the Polish school (about either Polish or German or Scandinavian or some other literature), I'm all confused. Why? Nowhere do I find anything that corresponds to what I learned at home, to what the Jewish tradition taught me. A primarily Jewish education is the sense of solidarity and that love of living in a family-type community.

Yiddishkeit—I know I was there, my whole life—all the everyday things were made of it. The other culture I received, Polish culture, was in addition; French culture too. What makes me a Jew is what exists inside me. I feel it. I feel it every time I have to make a decision. When I came to France, in 1928, I spoke Polish and I sought the words I needed to express myself in French; I translated into French. Now, after more than fifty years, I still live in France and it's the other way around: I think in French and I translate into another language if I have to. Basically, when I want to say something closest to what I feel, the only word I can find that fits is the Yiddish word.

3
Happy
Holidays,
Family
Feuds

WHILE THE JEWS of Europe regularly recall religious rituals even when they are not believers, they do not willingly report those major
rites of passage that may have marked their own
lives or those of their close friends and relatives.
Was this perhaps modest silence? Or rather a
sign of the erosion of rituals, the secularization
of habits that has turned marriage or birth into
ordinary events? Among the Jews of the Medi-
terranean basin, more anchored in a traditional society where values
and gestures were handed down from generation to generation, those
moments have preserved a strong glow in memory. The arrival of
the first son, the bar mitzvah, marriage all occupy a large place in
memories.

"A VERY NICE LOVE STORY"

Marriage, as reported by women, is the drama most especially rich
in emotions, fears, and expectations. Sometimes they tell about it with
laughter, like Georgette A., who, in spite of her calculations, found
that she had her period on the day of the ceremony and so could not
consummate her marriage. Sometimes it is with heavy heart because
one has submitted to a forced marriage, had hoped for a better offer, or
at least a nice wedding. Happy or not, marriage always merits a story.
Sometimes it is a love story, the idyll—in the literary sense—of an
encounter, of trials one must face, of happiness that comes in fulfillment
of the hopes one had nurtured. Mathilde B., born in Bizerte in 1892,
sees her whole life as "a very nice love story."

I must write my memoirs because I have a very nice love story. It shows how many disappointments people bear, how much patience they have when they love each other. It's very beautiful and that's my life. It all rests on that.

He was a marvelous man. How good that man was! And handsome—what beauty! He was very handsome, blond. And he really must have had perseverance, because I met him when I was fifteen and I couldn't get married until I was twenty-seven! Our parents didn't want to let us, they didn't want to. Because when I came into the world. . . . First, let me tell you: our mothers are sisters, we're first cousins. Eugénie is my mother's sister. My mother's name was Clara, and my aunt was called Eugénie. So, when the oldest son was born, they intended him for the future daughter the other sister would have. The future daughter was me. They intended us for one another, the way they used to do. As for us, we were children. We didn't understand anything. He lived in Béjà, and I lived in Bizerte. We didn't know each other at all. And once, they sent the oldest one to us there, the one they intended for me, Sansonnet. And he was happy: "That's my wife, that's my wife, that's my wife." As for me, I didn't like that at all. I didn't realize the significance of the thing. Then he left; we didn't meet anymore. And Gaston, who became my husband, I had not yet met him. Because you didn't travel like nowadays. It was a big deal to come from Béjà to Bizerte, a big excursion. Even more so since my mother-in-law had had a lot of children and didn't move around easily. So one fine day, around Passover, they decided to take me to their house in Béjà. And who was to accompany me? Gaston, who was studying in Tunis. He was at the Lycée Carnot in Tunis and he's the one who was to take me to Béjà. By the way, Aunt Irène told him: "Gaston, pay attention, you're going to take Mathilde, you know that she's pretty. Careful not to fall in love with her!" She sensed it all, eh! I myself didn't know anything about it. He came; I didn't know him. "Oh," I say, "my God, how handsome you are!" [*Laughter*] "How handsome you are, what a pretty blond!" Gray suit, elegant, magnificent. Since I was very direct, I said everything I thought, you know. And I went on: "You are a handsome guy!" We had a good time

in a cousinly fashion. It just happened. We made the trip together. And when we got down there and they started saying
"This is Sansonnet's wife, this is Sansonnet's wife," Gaston,
poor boy, he thought I was his fiancée. He had fallen in love
with me and started crying and carrying on. Since he was still
very young, he had become surly. The two of them fought over
me. I myself didn't understand anything at all. And one fine
day, the family was behaving in an odd manner. What's going
on? My God, my God, I felt like a stranger in that world because
I had never been to their house. And what was it all about? It
was because Gaston, on leaving Béjà to go back to school, had
sent me a postcard on which he had written: "From the one who
knew how to love you."

But he sent it to his father's house, and they didn't tell me.
The father was beside himself and the mother too: "What, he
took his brother's betrothed. That can't be." Poor me, I hadn't
known. Later on they told me. And naturally I was very hurt
by the whole thing.

"Because you already loved him?"

Certainly. . . . It was love at first sight. Gaston, I loved
him. . . . That's normal when you see a man who kisses your
hands, who weeps to kiss your hand and to take a burning
kiss from you in secret . . . especially when you're fifteen. . . .
Oh, really, it's a nice story to tell, even though I did suffer
from it. We were both fifteen; he was two months younger
than me.

In short, I went back home, and I was roundly scolded.
"What have you done! You did something bad!" So my father-
in-law, who was so wrought up, said: "Well, too bad for her,
she won't take either one of them. She'll remain an old maid
like her sister." (Yes, my sister wasn't yet married.) So my parents had their pride wounded. They insisted that I make a rich
marriage. Aunt Henriette was there with Mama, Grandmother
Taita, and all of them. There was a rich young man, and they
wanted to stick me with him. But that wouldn't do at all. I refused. I was lucky enough to be able to refuse, because, there,
in those days, you didn't marry the younger daughter before
the older one.

The war broke out and affairs of the heart were somehow sorted out.

Sansonnet came on leave. And he told his parents that he wasn't interested in me. He was very nice about it. He said to them: "Since Gaston is so much in love with her, fine, let Gaston have her." And that's how, at the end of the war of '14, we were engaged. [*The wedding was finally celebrated.*] Now, that, I have to tell you. There we were, my wedding night, it was terrible. There wasn't any way of having personal satisfaction. It hurt me very much, and the blood, and the pain was excruciating. O.K., I put that down to . . . anyway. But the next day, when we went to Sousse [*for a honeymoon*] and, like everybody else, I wanted to have relations, it hurt me so much and I was bleeding so much that he had to go get a doctor. When we came back from the honeymoon, no relations, nothing at all. I still had pains in my lower stomach, it's scary. We didn't tell anybody because it was shameful. You think I'd tell that to my mother and my mother-in-law? My God! For a year, we stayed like that.

Does Mathilde think of the story of Jacob and Rachel when she tells her own tale, of Jacob's love for his younger cousin and the waiting twice imposed before he could take her as his wife? No, she hasn't read the Bible and doesn't refer to it. Nor does she refer to Bathsheba when, recalling the dangers of World War II, she tells how she had a scarf brought to her daughter, an adolescent in the full flower of her beauty, to cover her hair, the sight of which might have stirred the passion of the German soldiers.

Suzanne T. still has a painful memory of her marriage. "The blush of shame" crosses her face when she tells of it, for her husband's parents had fostered other ambitions for their son and had mounted a vain but cruel resistance to that union. Here is the story, now come to life and rich in details, of the course of the wedding. We are in Sétif, in 1928.

My mother's sister, the older one, lived in Constantine. She had nine children, six girls and three boys. Her husband was a secondhand dealer. In 1927, her oldest child, Léon, came to do a year of military service in Sétif. Naturally, he came to our house every night. One night a few months later, my father came home and said to my mother: "Tomorrow, my uncle and aunt are coming to ask for our daughter in marriage to their son." We were eating supper, and my cousin got up and said to my mother: "Aunt, I want to marry Suzanne." My father answered: "You know very well that your mother will never want this marriage. You heard her last week when she was here. What did she say? That she had found a girl from a good family who will bring you furniture to fill an apartment, a trousseau, jewels, and fifty thousand." In those days, fifty thousand was a fortune. "So how do you expect her to accept my daughter, who doesn't have either jewels or a trousseau or an apartment or money? Don't plan on my daughter because your parents will never agree." The man who was to become my husband answered my mother and father: "I'm the one who's getting married—I don't need furniture or a trousseau." On Friday, he asked for a twenty-four-hour leave to go to his parents. He informed them. So his father and mother said to him: "You'll never marry her." He told them he would get married in spite of them, that he was old enough to decide his own fate.

Two weeks before the wedding, the dressmaker came to the house to sew the gowns and the housecoats. In those days, you didn't go to the dressmaker; you had her come to your house. She made the wedding gown of satin and lace; and a satin gown for the henna night,[1] a dress of pink-beige georgette crepe for the day after the wedding, a blue dress of Moroccan crepe, a white dressing gown, a pink one, a yellow one, and a blue one. It was already a celebration, two weeks in advance.

A week before the wedding, in spite of everything, my mother went to Constantine to see her sister and brother-in-law. Mama told them to come, that that wasn't done. People would talk if they didn't come. Her husband answered: "Yes, we'll come." But she didn't want to hear of it. My mother went in the morning, and she came back at night. Of course, we waited for her at the station. We had understood that they wouldn't come.

1. *Henna* night: a sequence of the wedding ritual in which the bride's hands are smeared with the reddish–orange dye of the leaves of the plant henna (*Lawsonia inermis*).

Since she couldn't manage both the cooking and the wedding, she [*the mother*] had arranged for a cook. My cousins and my aunts were there to make the meals for the henna night and for the night of the wedding. And the whole family was there to serve the people at the tables and take care of everything. The dressmaker had finished sewing. She herself was my maid of honor.

The week of the wedding, that is, on Monday, they accompanied me to the bath all by myself. On Tuesday, it was the day of the girls who accompanied me. We were all dressed in blue. On Wednesday, the night of the henna and the *mikvah* [*ritual bath*], the married women accompanied me, but none of the girls. It was my oldest aunt who made me enter the mikvah and who said the regular prayer. She made me put my head in the water seven times, and then she helped me out. They were dressed in pink, like me. There were *youyous* [*ululating*] everywhere. During the day, my mother had made the bread and meat that were served to everybody. Then came the cakes, the jams, and the sugared almonds. (I forgot to say that on Monday and Tuesday there were also jams and sugared almonds.) In those days, that was the custom.

After the food, my aunt—the same one—put a pink veil over my head so no man would see me and so I wouldn't look at them. I was all in pink; even my slippers were pink. A woman on each side held my arms. Behind, there were musicians. The tables were set up in the courtyard, all around the house, with carpets in front of the entrance door. They sat us down, my fiancé and me, next to the musicians. They put a lot of mattresses on the ground, a rug, a low table; two candelabras with big pink candles, a large yellow copper plate in the middle of the table, a candelabra on each side, flowers. The middle of the courtyard was empty.

We got to the house. It was 7:30. The musicians were at their table and started playing. Arabic-style, of course. There were already a lot of people. All around the balcony, the neighbors and everybody were celebrating. The men started serving drinks at the tables. We had everything. Later, they cleared it away and started serving supper. That went on until after eleven o'clock. There were a lot of them to make sure the people had everything they wanted. They served them drinks, the women brought food, the men and the women ran around to see to it that everyone was satisfied. There were more than two hundred people and the next day, even more.

They left the middle of the courtyard free so there would be room for people to dance. The musicians started singing the bride's song. The older woman came to put henna on the palms of my hands with a gold coin and on the soles of my feet, which were tied with a red ribbon. My husband didn't want them to put it on him. Later on, it was the turn of the girls, the young men, and the married women. Then they brought fruit, cakes, jam, and liqueurs. The women danced, and the men gave them money to put on the musicians' plate. One man was standing up and shouting: "Twenty francs for the bride, fifteen francs for the groom," and everybody was singing and everybody was dancing. As for the musicians, if they got a lot of money, they were happy, and that was fine; if not, you gave them more money. But they collected beyond their wildest dreams. They answered yes when we asked them if they were satisfied. At two o'clock in the morning, the musicians left and so did the people. Then, we had to sweep the courtyard, pick up the dirty linen and wash the dishes, and prepare to make the bread for the wedding night. The owner of the house had lent my mother a big room and a big kitchen in the courtyard. So it was much easier.

After that night, we were very tired. Before going to bed, my mother asked my future husband to stay awhile. He answered: "Tomorrow she'll be my wife, I'll have time." My father shouted: "She's still my daughter and I'm still in charge," and he threw him out. I have to say that you came of age at twenty-one and I was barely eighteen.

Thursday morning, a dramatic turn of events: the fiancé's family finally agreed to join the celebration. In the afternoon, the civil marriage was celebrated at city hall, and then the religious wedding in the synagogue. Both buildings were on the same street, but a cortege of several cars was nonetheless organized. From the synagogue, they went to the photographer. In the evening, they went back to the house, where another night of celebration took place.

My father-in-law was very happy, he was laughing. You could tell he was happy. But his wife made a long face. When we came back to the house, the musicians and everybody else came to us singing the song of the newlyweds, in Arabic, of course. They escorted us to our table. Then the people sat down around us. The night started out fine, with everybody happy. They started serving drinks, and there were more people than the night before. My father-in-law started drinking and that's normal, it was his son's wedding. My father-in-law was the nicest man, but when he drank, you had better not get in his way. And that's just what his wife did, she started getting on his nerves in front of everybody. She pulled his wallet out of his hands so he wouldn't put any money in the musicians' plate. He wanted to make up for the night before, he adored Arabic music. But you shouldn't get on his nerves, and his wife knew that very well. He kept on drinking, which didn't help things.

During this time, they started serving supper. When my father saw what was happening, he sat down on a chair. He didn't budge. My father-in-law kept on drinking, and she kept on insulting him in front of everybody. Then he started breaking everything he found. He started hitting people. Everybody was shouting and was scared. Some newlyweds took us to our room on the first floor while the brawl continued downstairs. One musician got a sprained wrist; another one sprained his ankle; a third got a black eye. It was five o'clock in the morning, you know. At that moment, my mother had had enough. She didn't want to interfere, thinking it was going to calm down. But when she saw that all the guests had been beaten up, she threw them out at six o'clock in the morning. They took the train to Constantine. It was Friday. He had the nerve to come up and knock on our door; he wasn't ashamed at all. People wanted to kill him. It was Friday. Nobody could sleep, we were all so sick with shame. We didn't dare look people in the eye. The whole family was there, and we had to prepare for Shabbat.

The next day, Saturday, my husband, accompanied by my cousins and my uncles, went to the synagogue. After prayers, the people in the synagogue and the rabbi came for the Shabbat prayer. I had put on the white gown again. The musicians, outside, called out to know if he [*the father-in-law*] was still there. Everybody had some bruises. Of course, you'll tell me they were men, that they could have subdued him. But they didn't want to raise a hand against my husband's father, and everyone agreed on that.

We paid all the costs of the wedding before we left, except for the drinks. My two cousins had a café, and they bought the drinks wholesale, altogether nine hundred francs in those days. We wanted to pay, but my cousins said: "Keep your money. When you start working, you'll send it to us." That's what we did.

Even now, when I think of my wedding, I blush with shame.

SHREWD BARGAINING

Aside from romance, these narratives demonstrate that marriage was a complex intrigue with multiple stakes that could produce an intense crisis. This crisis built and developed before the betrothal, culminated and was resolved during the final ceremonies. The bride and groom were not the only characters in the action. Parents intervened and so did other members of the family, relatives, matchmakers—a whole cast among whom the various roles were distributed. And the whole thing took place under the attentive, even prying, eye of the milieu to which the couple belonged.

Thus, to talk about one's marriage is to pull a myriad of strings that were knotted together when it was concluded. It is to talk of love and happiness but even more of the subtle transactions that were undertaken between the families.

Gabriel D., Salonika:

My father and mother got married through a family connection. How did they meet? It was through a matrimonial agency, they called it a go-between. . . . I'm looking for the other word. . . . Here's the word in Spanish: *izviterdige*.[2] The go-between had acquaintances among businessmen, workers—everybody. He'd go to see a family: "Here, I've got an offer for your daughter." The go-between might be a full-time matchmaker, but there were others, who were rental agents who didn't have a rich clientele, and sought extra business. They got a percentage, according to the family they approached. Then came the matter of the dowry. If the boy had a good job, the dowry was higher because, since the wife wouldn't work anymore and maybe wasn't even working then, the boy's parents demanded a dowry a little bit higher than they would have demanded for a clerk or somebody poorer. Then there was the matter of the trousseau. That, I would say, was essential. The trousseau was essential. The girl brought a trousseau according to the economic status of her family, a big trousseau or a little trousseau. Eight days before the wedding, the two families made a party. Family and friends were invited to this party because the girl had to exhibit the trousseau. A girl started making her trousseau before she grew up; once she was married, she started making the layette for the baby who was to come.

Tales of brokers and their clientele, of the commissions they earned from the deals they handled, of fierce negotiations over dowries and trousseaus (whose value varied with the "status" of the groom) clearly show that matrimonial transactions assumed an economic dimension. The subject of the investment represented by the dowry and the trousseau—the nightmare parents lived through when they had several daughters to marry off—recurs as a leitmotiv in many narratives.

Viviane B., Constantine, 1929:

It's my mother-in-law who came to ask for me in marriage. She knew that we were of modest means, since there was no father. My mother worked; so did I. She wasn't demanding. But in those days, at the time I got married, certain families demanded dowries. For me, there was no dowry. But my mother had already been making a trousseau for me since I was twelve years old. So when I did get married, I already had a

2. A word we cannot identify.

pretty complete trousseau, and, to this day, I've bought almost no linens, sheets. All the linen in the house, the silverware, the dishes—everything was embellished with my initials. It was superb. But she did it with great difficulty. Ever since I was twelve, she had been collecting all that.

Manou B. (Aïn Beïda, 1926) suggests an interpretation of those practices and emphasizes the change in progress at the time she herself was married: in Constantine, in the 1940s, the salary of the young working wife replaced the dowry.

My mother, it was never the woman who had problems because she had daughters. While at that time, it was a catastrophe for a woman who had daughters, because you had to have a dowry. Why? Because quite simply the boys didn't all have means down there. Not much work, lots of unemployment. First of all, what could we do down there, us Jews? A Jew couldn't get a job in the administration as easily as he can today. A Jew was either a tailor or a barber or a shoemaker. And since they were big families, a shoemaker who needed an apprentice or a worker took his nephew or his son. So there just wasn't very much work. My brothers had to become barbers. But where could you work? There wasn't always work. That's why for a boy getting married, the only chance of getting ahead was to have a dowry and, with that dowry, to open a little shop.

For those women who had daughters, poor souls, it was a catastrophe because they had to come up with a trousseau and a dowry. That wasn't so in my case. Because my husband wanted me—not the trousseau and not the dowry. He was doing well. He was a grain dealer . . . and I was earning a good living. I was making eight thousand francs a month, in '45, that's seven or eight hundred thousand francs today [*about one thousand dollars in 1985*].

The economic stakes were not the only ones. There were social concerns as well. In fact, the successive stages of a marriage presented each of the two sides with a chance to evaluate its material and symbolic resources, to display them in public to one's friends and kinsfolk: for the amount of the dowry was known, the trousseau was displayed, and the scope of the wedding celebration gave a measure of one's discretionary income. The quality of the bride's education and her upbringing would be read in her gestures, her words, her dress, the embroidery with which she herself perhaps had trimmed her trousseau. This gave friends and relatives the opportunity to assess the capital thus displayed, but they were also expected to participate in the event: to contribute their services during the preparation and the course of the celebration, to be an active presence at the various moments of the ritual, to offer payments to the musicians and gifts to the newlyweds, etc. Marriage thus engendered an exhibition and mobilization of the family's economic and symbolic capital. Suzanne T. could pride herself on having set "more than two hundred persons" in motion when she got married, despite the resistance of her in-laws, who, she emphasizes, did not contribute to the expenses. Everyone aimed at maintaining or improving a status, confirming or accelerating a social climb, and reinforcing a network of relations. Marriage was thus an expression of these social strategies, and, at the same time, it allowed their efficacy to be gauged.

One of the components of the symbolic capital was family "honor," which also had to be preserved. Remaining single for a long time brought more discredit to girls than to boys but it also affected the whole family; being single was considered a sign of imperfection, a taint perhaps, physical or otherwise. So the family had to arrange for its children while they were quite young. Once an alliance between two families was concluded—indeed, until the wedding—family honor could still be jeopardized by acts of impropriety on the part of the young people.

OK, we met each other, but hey, we weren't allowed to talk to each other. He made that clear, Alfred, my uncle! That I'm not ready to forget—the lickings he gave me. He could never— he wouldn't let us talk to young men. So we would have to sneak around; we went to the Petite Vitesse—that's a neighborhood—to talk to each other a little bit. And you'd think it was planned, somebody from the family would always catch me. It was something! At night, it never failed, I got a licking.

You know who saw me? It was Rica, my aunt. Oh, she'd go gallivanting around all the time with Alice. [*Reine A.*, 1917,

Aïn Beïda. She thus had to wait eight years to get married, her fiancé's oldest sister not having found a husband.]

FAMILY ORDER

Marriage aimed at reproducing the social order and, first of all, the family cell. Each union was to guarantee the continuation of the generations by the transmission, not only of the family name but also of first names and, with them, the renown attached to the line, or more precisely, to two lines, since each union sealed an alliance between two families. This is why in the chronicles of marriages it is the parents who speak first rather than the future spouses: parents "ask for" or "give" a daughter in marriage; they "want" and "take" a girl for their son. Parents have the first word, if not the last, in matrimonial negotiations. The desires and feelings of the future couple are asserted only if they suit the arrangements made by the parents. And what of the personal inclinations of the couple? That was to follow from "being from a good family."

Beyond the two family lines, a matrimonial transaction also concerned the community, a community with fluid outlines but for which every wedding guaranteed the continuity of Jewish life. Hence, that insistence on the endogamy of family or place that recurs in so many memories. Mathilde B. (Bizerte, 1892) and Suzanne T. (Sétif, 1910)[3] both married first cousins. M. Z., born in Istanbul at the turn of the century, had lived in Paris since his early youth; but it is a first cousin from Istanbul whom he married in 1926. His contemporary, M., who came from Salonika to Paris in 1922, married his cousin, whom he brought from Salonika a few years later. Ida O., born in the same city in 1906, married a Salonikan Jew there; her older sister came to Paris before her but she married

a Salonikan, yes. That is, a Salonikan but one who lived in France, here. He had come very young. He had lost his parents,

---

3. The case of Suzanne T. shows that endogamy may not be a sufficient condition for parents: although she was her husband's first cousin, the latter risked losing or at least not gaining anything in social and symbolic status if he married a partner of modest means. Hence, the parents' obstinacy in fighting against that marriage. See p. 106 ff.

but his uncles were very rich. They had him brought here and raised him. They put him in a school run by monks. His name was Menahem. She married him. The other sister married a Sullam, from Salonika. The other one, the one who was deported, she married a Nefusi, also from Salonika.

Louise G., Aïn Beïda, 1921:

I had a young man from Tébessa. He was a relative of one of my aunts, from Aïn Beïda also. He was an orphan too. He lived in Tébessa. They sent him to Aïn Beïda to be introduced. And it's the truth, in that case it worked out well. I saw he was an orphan; I was an orphan myself. He was from Tébessa; I was from Aïn Beïda. We were distantly related, not very very much with him—on my aunt's side, the wife of my uncle, my father's brother. So it was almost done.

I was at my Aunt Cécile's. She was sick, in bed, and I was at her house. I got along with my Aunt Cécile. I had prepared for Saturday, Shabbat, and all of a sudden, we heard a knock at the door. I went to open it, and there was Uncle A., M.'s mother, Mother Y., and, if I'm not mistaken, Auntie A. Supposedly they came to see their sister. As far as I was concerned, it was perfectly normal since she was sick. Meanwhile, he showed up, that young man. He came on Saturday and on Sunday. Auntie Cécile said to me: "This afternoon, don't bother going out, you're going to stay here. Your uncle needs you."

[*The girl insists on going out. In vain.*] My Uncle A. took me by the hand like a little baby and walked me around Aïn Beïda, explaining to me: "That's why we came, for your marriage. We don't want you to marry a stranger. You're the only daughter of our sister Baya. We don't want you to go away. You have to stay with us, among us. There's my sister's son. He's very good, he's this, he's that." In short, all that nonsense.

Listen, it's not worth it to try to understand. The A. family found out I was going to marry that guy from Tébessa, and they didn't want it. I said: "Uncle, it's not nice what you're doing now. I've got that young man. He was waiting the guardian—since he's an orphan—to come ask for me in marriage. The young man, he's there." And uncle says, "Don't bother trying to understand. Here we are. We don't want you to go to Tébessa. We don't know what might happen."

"Was it far away, Tébessa?"

Maybe two and a half, three hours, that's all, by car. And it's nice, it's not like the buses from here to Paris.

They worked on me so much that I thought to myself: after all, they came for me, it's true—and I said yes. We were very modest. Here in Paris I don't think they would have done the same thing, it's not the same thing at all.

Alice B., Aïn Beïda, 1913, remained single:

My mother wanted to keep me with her. But I had offers from everywhere, even from Canada. A Canadian and an American. I'd be an aunt from America now or a Canadian aunt. Jews. When there were English, Americans, everywhere, in '42–'43, there were those two. One, who was called Daniel, the American, came every Saturday.

Just think! She didn't give me in Bône or Algiers and we're talking about her sending me to Canada or even America!

In a world and at a time when these Jewish communities were on the verge of rupturing and disappearing, their frontiers were still sharply defended.

RELIGION AND TRADITION

When Gabriel D. spontaneously approached the subject of his parents' marriage (p. 111), he immediately brought in the character of the go-between. Thus he moved imperceptibly from the narrative of a unique adventure to the recounting of the customs of his community. In the same way, the women of Aïn Beïda, Constantine, and Tunis take care to describe the rules of the game with a wealth of details, even when they didn't follow them. So, "I" illustrates what is done by "We," the community back home.

This insistence on the norm no doubt stems from the importance of the event in their own lives. Raised from childhood in the expectation of its realization and the terror that it might not happen, marriage for them was the major rite de passage, *perhaps the only one. For men, by contrast, birth was marked by circumcision and entry into adulthood by bar mitzvah.*[4] *Besides, they could show their stuff outside the family milieu, in work, study, or even, from what we hear, in sport, the arts, and—why not?—adventure. No such opportunities existed for women. So their tales of the wedding and their marriage is like the proof that they have passed the test: that's what had to be done, that's what I did. At that crucial moment when they had to conform to tradition and thereby demonstrate their adherence to the community consensus, they fulfilled their role.*

If women take so much pleasure in describing the wedding, it is also because it lends itself to a long, dramatic presentation, with costumes, music, and sets corresponding to each one of the acts of the drama. But as they recall the beauty of that show, these women indicate a distance with regard to practices fallen into disuse and now alien. When the lights of the party are extinguished and the noises disappear, the impression of excess remains—in the preparation of the trousseau, the requirement of the dowry, and the cost of the copper objects necessary for the ritual bath but useless once the marriage is celebrated. Yes, the memory of the excessive constraints imposed by the environment remains. Precisely because "that isn't done anymore" and "that might not be done anymore" are people so given to protracted descriptions.

What had to be done constituted the tradition. In the collected narratives, it was blended with religion. One's efforts to conform to the norms indicated one's respect for religious prescriptions. People don't seem to realize that the tradition was in fact a tradition, a version of local custom, which had no doubt changed over time and was devoid of meaning once it crossed the boundaries of the community. Quite to the contrary, local customs are presented as having an authentic and universal Jewish, and hence prescriptive, value. The descriptions of the whole wedding, lavish in their detailing of the social aspects of the celebration, ultimately say almost nothing about those elements in fact required by Jewish orthodoxy. The ketubbah[5] *is barely indicated, if at all; the kiddushin*[6] *is completely absent. Only the ritual bath and the blessing*

4. In the collected memories, we do not find any mention of celebrations for the birth of a daughter. There were no birthdays, no ceremonies for piercing ears, and none marking puberty.

5. Marriage contract.

6. Delivery by the future husband of a pledge accompanied by a formula which binds the girl.

of the rabbi are inscribed here and there in the series of scenes we are shown. In most cases, people don't seem to realize either that the practices they describe bear strong resemblances to those of Muslim families. This assimilation of the Jewish religion to the most narrowly localized practice, already expressed in cooking or rituals, is found here with regard to other social practices.

Among other memories, that of Georgette D. (Tunis, 1899), which begins with a particular episode, slips into a general and prescriptive discourse and soon turns to a questioning of customs that have become exotic.

[*Speaking of persons in her family*]: Her mother and father were neighbors. I was six years old when her parents got married. It happened just like weddings in those days, eh. There was what they call the *hammam ushekh,* where the bride was dressed in the local costume, wtih the *teguia* [*headdress*], the bolero, everything. And all the girls were dressed like that. Then there was an oriental concert and a big party. Then there was the henna.

For hammam ushekh, you didn't go to the Turkish bath. Then, afterward, there was a Turkish bath for the girls: the night before the wedding, the bride went into the pool there, and they gave her the *tbila* [*ritual bath*]. They put sugared almonds in her mouth and *tbarkallah.*[7] They used to give those sugared almonds to girls so they'd get married fast. Did you know that?

Here the order of the events is confused; the string of memories is broken. She insists only on what seems anachronistic to her.

The bride's last shirt, they gave it to the girl they wanted to marry off next—the last shirt before getting dressed to get married, on the wedding day.

There was a showing of the trousseau on the last Saturday. Somebody, a child that is, from the groom's family went "to take" the hen from the bride's family's house. Then, they gave

7. "God bless!" used here ironically. The fact that her description is addressed to someone who was not familiar with these practices contributes to distancing her from the tradition.

back half the hen. And the girls had the right to the wing, to both wings, yes. You wonder why it was a young child, who was always accompanied by an adult.

Yes, but there's something else that we didn't do for anybody except Henriette, because Madame S. [*the groom's mother*] was a little . . . old-fashioned. Before beginning all the marriage celebrations, they sent a woman to the mother-in-law to tell her: "There, we decided to make the wedding. And the hammam ushekh will be on such and such a date, the henna on such and such a date, etc." So it was that woman herself who prepared the *shebgha* [*dye and makeup*] for the henna. They said in Arabic: "We can open the wedding." You see, the translation is "to open the wedding." As if they weren't in agreement! [*Laughter*]

The husband then takes up the tale, emphasizing again the strangeness of the practices.

Oh, you know what there was that was special, that made me laugh, it was taking the hairs off the face, the down. They did that, *termertina*. It's a wax—I don't know—it's sticky. It burns sometimes. And the person who did it smeared her fingers with the stuff and put it on the face and then she pulled it off. And you'd see the bride grimacing. It was done at home, before she went to the Turkish bath.

Speech breaks off; memory is disconnected. While giving a description of customs they thought immemorial and immutable, inscribed in the slow move of tradition, they tell—and become aware—of a break. Tradition has lost its meaning.

PART TWO
Passengers in Transit

<table>
<tr><td>

4
Internal
Migrations

</td><td>

*MIGRATION FOR MOST was first internal,
that is, cultural, and preceded the physical de-
parture. On the whole, the Jewish communities
of Poland and Russia were beyond the reach of
the Emancipation, which, from the second half
of the eighteenth century, determined profound
transformations in western Europe (including
Germany). Nevertheless, even they were not
immune to the changes that affected the sur-*

</td></tr>
</table>

*rounding societies. From the mid-nineteenth century on, demographic
growth, the development of industrial activity, and urbanization mod-
ified the socioeconomic structures of the Jewish world. Until then composed essentially of artisans and small tradesmen, the Jewish population
contributed broadly to the constitution of new classes, including the
working class, the liberal professions, and the industrialists. Moreover,
if the Haskalah movement, a product of Enlightenment philosophy,
spread belatedly into Poland and Russia, it assumed specific forms there.
Its adherents (*maskilim*) were aware that the diffusion of their ideas
in Hebrew or Russian remained confined within narrow limits. The
use of the vernacular Yiddish and the criticism of the conservatism of
the communities, as well as the affirmation of a certain conception of
Jewish identity, gave their movement a very different character from
the emancipation of the French or German Jews: confessionalism in
the west opposed secularization in the east.*[1] *This was the context for
a remarkable phenomenon, the flourishing of an original culture, yiddishkeit, which would be so brutally severed by genocide.*

These changes occurred very unevenly, however, varying with the

1. Rachel Ertel, *Le Shtetl*, p. 151.

groups and the places. Thus the eastern European Jewish world be-tween the two world wars presented an extraordinary diversity: or-thodox believers, Hasidim, more or less devout traditionalists, atheists, militants of several political movements (Zionists, Marxists, etc.). Not all of these upheavals are echoed in the memories we have collected, but certain critical moments resurface, and we can discern traces of them in the narratives.

EDUCATION

Memories relating to the heder are most often accompanied by a harsh judgment of the education given there. This is the traditional type of school where children from the most modest homes studied from the age of four or five: they learned to read and write and received an in-troduction to Hebrew as well as to biblical texts. School? That's a very grand word: the teacher (melamed) taught in one room, even a corner, of his small dwelling. Portraits of him are hardly flattering. They em-phasize his "primitive" methods, his brutality, and his ignorance, and gladly dwell on his more ridiculous characteristics. Just as our school-boys like to recall memorable escapades, former heder students still laugh about the tricks they played on their teachers. One of the jokes mentioned several times (another quasi-folkloric subject): those rascals attack the unfortunate melamed's beard, which they paste or cut or scorch!

Georges F.:

You came to heder if you wanted to learn. It wasn't compul-sory. In the room there was a big table and two benches, girls on one side, boys on the other. About ten families sent their children. It was the only way to learn to write because we didn't have the right to go to school. Indeed, there wasn't any. I don't remember seeing a school built in my village during my child-hood. A generation later, yes; that is, seven or eight years later, they built a school.

Me, I had a rabbi, a poor guy. He was nasty as a rash and beat the children like devils. That rabbi had a daughter and two boys. One boy was sick, with tuberculosis. He was there, lying there all the time, a young man of about twenty. He would spit. To bring children to that place, in the same room, with that guy with tuberculosis, you wonder how we didn't get it . . .

That rabbi was paralyzed on one side. He used to get so nervous and mad. With kids who were almost savages, he had good reason to get nervous. He stood behind the kids with his stick, and every now and then, with his good hand, he gave us a whack on the back because we didn't answer well. That wasn't so bad compared with others who had both their hands. But there were kids who got their ears pulled off, yes, he pulled an ear so hard he pulled it off. That's how he mistreated them.

Once we decided to revolt. You know what we did to him? He had a big beard. One day, he fell asleep on the table, like this. [*Georges imitates him.*] We glued his beard to the table and set fire to it. All the kids, not just me. The guy woke up smelling his beard burning.

The scene changes, however, with the Jewish school networks that developed in Poland between the two world wars. The diversity of their orientations reflected the heterogeneity of the population. The Agudat Israel *network (568 establishments for boys, in 1937, and 71,000 students) remained loyal to orthodoxy; that of* Tarbut *(267 establishments in 1935 and 42,000 students) was devoted to the teaching of Hebrew, in a Zionist spirit; while that of C.Y.S.H.O.[2] (170 establishments in 1935 and 15,000 students) was inspired with a Yiddishist and socialist ideal (which, in itself, had several political variants in the Bund and the leftist labor Zionists).[3] In the* Tarbut *schools, as in those of the C.Y.S.H.O., the curriculum included "modern" subjects (secular languages and literatures, the sciences, etc.), the use of Polish being limited to subjects like Polish history and literature. Pioneering pedagogical methods were practiced there (particularly in the Yiddishist schools), and our informers remember them with gratitude.*

2. *Agudat Israel,* a cultural and political movement that developed among Ashkenazi Jews and sought to preserve Orthodoxy against secularist and Zionist trends. *Tarbut,* Hebrew educational and cultural organization that developed in eastern European countries between the two world wars. *Centrale Yidishe Shul Organisatsie,* Central Organization of Jewish Schools.

3. R. Ertel, *Le Shtetl,* 253–264.

Lazare M.:

I went to heder maybe for a few weeks, until I learned the *alef bet,* being very small. You started heder when you were four, but the methods weren't. . . . The teacher, the rabbi, knew nothing of psychology or pedagogy.

Until the age of ten, I went to a modern school that was only moderately religious. You learned to read and write Jewish subjects. It was a private school, overseen by an association.

Then, in 1920, when I was ten, they opened a Jewish high school. My uncle, my father's brother, was a teacher in that high school.

"Is he the one who ran the heder?"

No, that one was my mother's sister's husband. He was an old man, with a beard, who barely knew how to write, but he did have a head for Talmud. The other one was a high school teacher who had himself finished school. So he said to my father: "Listen, give me your boy." And he took me into the high school, where I stayed until 1929.

Jewish subjects were in Hebrew; the others were in Polish. The first degree in Hebrew was granted in 1929. That was my class. Until the fourth year, the boys and girls were separate, and then it was mixed. They called it a coeducational high school.

I still remember what I wrote for my matriculation in Hebrew. My subject was Mendele and Sholem Aleichem. Mendele is satire; Sholem Aleichem is humor. Satire and humor aren't the same thing. Humor is gentle; satire is bitter. That's what I developed. My examiner became a very important man in Israel, Dr. Tartakover. He's a Jewish historian, a professor of history in Jerusalem or Tel Aviv. He's eighty years old now. He came to Paris three years ago. I have a friend here who knows Tartakover. I said to him: "Listen, I have to see Tartakover. I want to show him something." It's my Hebrew diploma. I still have the original.

You had to pay to go to that high school. The students were rich. I think I was the only poor one there, because of my uncle. There weren't any scholarships, but there was something called *fraternal* aid. All the students contributed every month. A little later on, I started tutoring. When I was in the sixth class, I could help the boys in the fifth and earn a little money. To get a degree was hard for a poor kid in Poland.

This year, on April 3, 1980, there was a reunion of the former students of the Jewish high schools of Kalisz. Two hundred people came. From Argentina, the United States, Sweden. From France, there was one person; I would have been the second. But at the last moment, I couldn't go. It still hurts me. I didn't go. Everybody was waiting for me. My classmates were there, or one class next to mine, a year more or less. And I didn't go.

Bernard P.:

I went to the Hebrew high school of Kalisz. Unlike the *Tarbut* high schools, the language was Polish but there were courses in Hebrew and even instruction in the Bible. Aside from that, it was a high school that conformed to all the same rules as at the state high schools in Poland.

In high school, I spoke Polish; with my friends I spoke Polish; I read Polish books. At home, I spoke Polish. My father generally answered me in Yiddish. But I didn't speak Yiddish. I spoke and read only Polish. It's not that I didn't want to speak Yiddish, but let's say that, in the generation of my friends, we all spoke Polish. My mother spoke Polish well, quite well, whereas my father had some difficulty speaking it. He preferred to express himself in Yiddish.

Helena G.:

When I think of the education I got in our school, I haven't yet seen a school that gives such an education. That's so even now, after forty years have passed. Back home, the teachers with the children, it was . . . you just don't see that today. Now, after all the years, when we see someone from our school, we're like brothers. We are brothers. We had a special education in our school. Maybe not everybody became a writer, but their behavior, their manner of being, was different. They always felt self-confident. First of all at our school, they freed us from our inferiority complex. If we didn't like something, we could say so aloud. They talked to us of hygiene, sexual questions—at that time!

In the Polish high schools, the number of Jewish students was limited in practice by a quota. The Jews often found themselves in a hostile environment. But there too the education seems to have been incomparably more interesting than that of the heder. Indeed, those high schools appealed to those who aspired to modernity. Many parents, eager for their children to climb the social ladder, made not only material sacrifices but also serious concessions with regard to religious principles (going to school on Saturday) in order to allow them to study within the state system. A typical example is young Julien K., whose father was director of a Yiddishist school in Chelm. He did not study in the latter but rather in the Polish high school.

A PASSION FOR READING

The thirst for learning is a subject that recurs in several memories. It appears frequently in the narratives of those who, being too poor, were forced to work from the age of twelve or thirteen, though they would have preferred to continue their studies. Traditionally, study represented one of the most highly valued activities in the Jewish world. But, henceforth, the thirst for learning went far beyond knowledge of the sacred texts and turned to secular subjects. It provided a vast audience for the fruits of Yiddish culture, broadly disseminated by newspapers, networks of libraries, and theatrical performances. The example of Julien K. seems significant here too. After studying in the Polish high school, he became a full-time radical and then learned to read Yiddish in order to study the works of Borokhov (who attempted to work out a synthesis between Marxist analyses and the Zionist ideal). That's not all. Several translations into Yiddish made known the great authors of foreign literature, notably such French writers as Balzac, Victor Hugo, Zola, and Jules Verne. This is how the adventures of Phileas Fogg came to play a determining role in the intellectual development of Yacob-Jaques L., whose conception of the world was suddenly turned topsy-turvy.

I went to heder at the age of four. First we learned the alphabet. I stayed there a year and a half, I think, and then they took me to another rebbe, who was already teaching a little bit of Bible. Then, when I learned almost the whole Bible, they took me to a third one, who started teaching Talmud.

I was the last of eleven children, and my mother wanted me to become a rabbi. OK, I'll be a rabbi. It went on like that until the age of fourteen. Then, I don't know how, somebody made me read Jules Verne's book *Around the World in Eighty Days* in Yiddish translation. You know, at the end, he says that Phileas Fogg was wrong about the day because he had traveled in the direction the earth turned. What kind of story is this? The earth doesn't turn—it's the sun that turns around the earth. You remember, when the Hebrews had to enter Jericho before sunset: it's written in the text. Moses stopped the sun. So I asked myself: "Who's telling the truth?" I knew that Jules Verne was a very good writer, a great writer. I said to myself: "It can't be, because Moses stopped the sun; he didn't stop the earth."

Two or three years before, they had established a modern school in our village. There was a teacher there, a young man of twenty-five. One day, I went to see him and I said: "Listen, this is driving me crazy. Help me. I want to know who lied to me. Is it my parents and all the Jews of the town who lied to me? Or is it Jules Verne who's lying to me?" He laughed: "Your parents and the others didn't lie to you, they didn't know themselves." And he explained the solar system to me: the planet Earth is only the third. He told me how it turns around the sun; he talked to me of Mars. Then he lent me an astronomy book in Yiddish. I didn't understand everything, but I read it.

Georges F.:

They sprouted like mushrooms; they were incredible. If they had had the opportunities we have now, geniuses would have come out of Poland. There were writers in our village. They sent for artists, great artists, from Warsaw. There was Schwartz, Maurice Lamp. There were great artists from Warsaw, the *summum* of the Jewish theater. They came to us and gave shows.

With the will to learn that the young people had, culture developed very fast. But in spite of all that, they really didn't have any opportunities. If they had been given greater opportunities, you would have had extraordinary children, geniuses.

MODERNIZATION, SECULARIZATION

This thirst for secular knowledge, then, led to doubts about the received wisdom handed down by tradition. From then on, the lost world assumed a more ambiguous aspect in memory. Nostalgia for childhood does not preclude a clear, even severe judgment of the poverty rampant in the shtetl as well as in the big city. Memories are registered within a global interpretation of society and history in which the notion of archaism, even primitivism, is logicallly opposed to modernity. The latter takes the form, first of all, of material progress, which for Georges F. corresponds to moving from the country to the city. The transformations of his childhood village illustrate the progress of civilization.

Then the village started to expand. There was a factory that moved in, a foundry, for stoves, which did very well. That attracted a lot of workers, and things improved. They started building a bridge to provide access to the railroad station. That was already technology starting to advance. The village was growing and even became a junction on the Polish railroad.

Little by little, a few more Jews came. Maybe eighty or a hundred families moved in, in all the trades: tailors, merchants, etc. And since the streets were beginning to be paved with sidewalks, they set up shops, little wooden huts. A baker went into business. He was a Jew and was already beginning to sell on credit. The village grew so fast that it almost became a center. Then a factory, a very big weapons factory, moved in and attracted a lot of people. But Jews didn't have access; Jews weren't allowed to work there. The factory was almost clandestine, with cellars. It brought a sense of well-being to the village. Little by little, it became a town like all the others in Poland. The tree trunks in the middle of the street disappeared; we had sidewalks, brick houses.

[. . .] One could find all kinds among those who came with the expansion of the village. All those who had known us from the beginning were friendly to us. They lived in harmony with the old-timers. But all those who came. . . . That factory brought some wealth and also the Polish intelligentsia. Since there were nice woods and magnificent streams in the woods, they moved into villas. They're the ones responsible for anti-Semitism. Otherwise, we lived very well. I don't know if it's wealth that brings anti-Semitism or something else.

The workers were Socialists but, in spite of that, they didn't like Jews very much. At the beginning, when socialism appeared, everyone was together. Then there was the Bund. You know what the Bund is? They were Jewish Socialists. That led to tension, separation between the socialists. It was the same idea but two organizations. Everybody was pulled to his own side. They didn't even let us demonstrate with them. There had to be a separate Jewish group, with the red flag, and the Catholics, the Catholic workers, on the other side, with the same flag and the same slogan. But it was no longer the same.

The notion of backwardness, however, is not limited to economic backwardness and poverty. It tends to include the whole of the traditional way of life, which forces Jews to distinguish themselves from the rest of the population by their language, their food, their appearance (caftan, skullcap, beard, sidecurls). Integration into modern society seemed incompatible with customs that were considered outdated. The next step was the questioning of religious practices and beliefs. The world of childhood thus appeared as a world left behind even before it was lost.

All variants and degrees are represented in this striving for modernity, from simple linguistic and sartorial acculturation to assimilation that is more or less complete. The evolution itself varies as a function of social status and geographical context. The Jewish communities of Poland and Russia, enclosed in their own particularities and composed of the lower classes, can indeed seem "backward," according to the criteria of acculturation evidenced by the French or German Jews, so proud of their integration into their respective nations.[4] Do these repre-

4. Cf. Jacob Katz, *Out of the Ghetto: The Social Background of Jewish Emancipation (1770–1870)* (Cambridge, Mass.: Harvard UP, 1973); Michael R. Mar-

sentations reflect a labor of memory, a retrospective judgment by people who have reinterpreted their past with the categories they assimilated after their emigration? This is only partially true, since these categories already conflicted with traditional values in the countries of origin. The memories collected reveal differences within families, cleavages between generations, even personal dramas. These differences, however, did not always take the form of sharp conflicts: some parents, influenced by their children, accepted half measures and compromises; sometimes they let themselves slip into the new habits.

Maurice N.:

My father dressed as a Hasid, with a caftan and a beard. He wore the Jewish skullcap . . .

Me, I already dressed like everybody else. But since I was at the yeshiva[5] in Warsaw for two years, my grandfather bought me a Jewish skullcap. It was round with a little border. I wore it, but I didn't like it. I didn't like to set myself apart with sidecurls. I didn't wear it for long, only for a year, I think. Then I took it off. I didn't want it. I didn't like it.

[. . .] My father was a total atheist. That started in Poland. But since he had a great respect for his parents (his parents had a terribly strong influence on him), he couldn't show it in Poland. He started by getting active in Zionist organizations, in Mizrahi,[6] and then in the Communist party. He had literature hidden all over the Gemore.[7] That's what led him to leave Poland and come here. You know, when a Hasid changes, he changes completely. It was something overwhelming, a revolution that took place, brutal, from one extreme to the other. But in spite of everything, until his death he stayed within the tradition. He often quoted what he had learned. He was really a

rus, *The Politics of Assimilation: A Study of the French Jewish Community at the Time of the Dreyfus Affair* (Oxford: Clarendon Press, 1971); Patrick Girard, *Les Juifs de France de 1789 à 1860: De l'emancipation à l'égalité* [The Jews of France from 1789 to 1860: From Emancipation to Equality] (Paris: Calmann-Levy, 1976).

5. Seminary of talmudic study.
6. *Mizrahi*: religious Zionist movement founded in 1902.
7. Or Gemara, "completion" commentary on the Mishnah, the code of the oral law (both together form the Talmud).

scholar, a learned man. There weren't many people in France who knew as much as he did about those issues.

Charles H.:

My mother even had her hair cut off before her wedding. It was traumatic for both of them. It seems that my mother had beautiful hair, and my father wasn't happy that they cut it off. But they did it. And I still remember my mother with a wig (what they call the *Yiddish sheitl*). It's a memory up to 1914, up to the war, because then, when my father was a soldier, my mother let her hair grow back and wore only a scarf. When my father came back home in 1918, after the collapse of Austria, cutting off her hair again was no longer an issue. So my mother got her hair back, but by then it had turned a bit white.

After the war, my father himself took off the *shtraimel,* the hat they wear on Saturday, a sort of velvet or silk hat, with borders of either fur or fur tails, depending on where a person is from, that go all the way around. In our village, it was fur tails, you see. Depending on how wealthy you were, it was otter or mink, a maroon-colored fur. It took the war to do away with the wig and the shtraimel!

Only on Saturday did my father go to synagogue in the garment they call in Yiddish the *jebetze,*[8] which comes from the Polish word *jupan*—a long garment, a sort of light overcoat of silk. It's rather strange because the pious Jews of that little town weren't aware that they were dressing like the Polish nobles of the seventeenth and eighteenth centuries. My father wore it on Saturday (in summer; in the winter, of course, he wore a fur coat over it).

Georges F.:

There were some who were already starting to open their shops on Saturday. Naturally, the finger of scorn was pointed at him. And no Jew went into his shop, only the Catholics. He opened his shop; he worked on Saturday. It was an incredible development. When we passed by, my father crossed the street

8. The *jebetze* and the *shtraimel* were Hasidic garments.

to avoid seeing it. Saturdays were really something—you couldn't even carry a handkerchief in your pocket. You had to hang it around your neck. That was observed in our house until I was twenty. But there was already a change in the village and a new spirit brought with it freedom of thought.

By now at home, my mother was also starting to understand, I don't know by what holy spirit, that it wasn't fair that there should be such poverty. Others were rich. There was no equality.

Yacob-Jacques L.:

Yes, I was dressed like my father at that time. I didn't dare do otherwise. My mother couldn't have stood it if I had dressed like the others, the goys. Oh, when I went to Warsaw, I dressed like them, with a vest and a hat, like here, yes, yes. But when I came home for the holidays, twice a year, for Passover and Sukkot, then I dressed like them, like the Jews, so as not to hurt my mother.

I had a brother in Warsaw. He had a watchmaker's shop. When I came to his house in a vest and a hat like everybody else, he said to me: "What do you know! I never would have expected it! There you are, dressed just like the goys. Who would have believed it?" When I stopped wearing a beard, my mother cried when she saw me. She cried for the beard.

You made a ghetto for yourself. For example, I have Christian friends here, and I'll tell you something, just between us, it seems to me there's a kind of wall between them and me. I'm wrong, maybe. Maybe I'm wrong. So, you see, when you came to interview me, it's not me who's doing you a favor, it's you who are doing me a favor.

Bernard P.:

I got through my bar mitzvah, but I don't think I prayed afterward. I pretended two or three times, but I never really prayed. I wasn't a believer, and that's stayed with me. I am deeply atheistic, although today I'm a little more tolerant toward religion.

At the age of fourteen, influenced by my father, I joined

Hashomer HaZa'ir.[9] My father had been a militant Zionist ever since his religious emancipation, because he himself came from a family of orthodox Jews. There were seven brothers. Three of them abandoned traditional clothes and were emancipated in a religious sense.

Encouraged by his own aunt, Lazare M. ate non-kosher food for the first time (not without an inner revulsion). Later on, his political involvement was aided by his mother's half-resigned, half-proud attitude. His trip along the path to modernity necessitated his first departure—from Kalisz to Warsaw—in order to study at the university.

You know, in Poland, in '20, '25, that was the time when things were starting to change. There were new ideas, Zionism, communism. In the high school in our town, which wasn't a religious high school, we ate without a hat, without a skullcap. But the food they gave us was kosher all the same. It didn't exist, the question of kosher, non-kosher. If you wanted to eat non-kosher, you had to go to the goyim on Yom Kippur. With us, everything was kosher. If I wanted, I ate ham, but not at home because I had to take my mother and father into account. For that I had to go to another neighborhood because, in our neighborhood, everything was Jewish, the meat was kosher, butter and milk were kosher. Non-kosher didn't exist for Jews.

But there were people, you know, who, when they started to change, were contentious, horribly contentious. They were very provocative. On Friday night, when people were coming out of the synagogue, they would smoke cigarettes right in front of them. What's the point? Or on Yom Kippur, they'd take a piece of bread and eat. There were people like that.

In my house, we respected the holidays, we were observant. But I myself didn't fast on Yom Kippur. I went to my uncle's to eat. My uncle and aunt weren't observant. But my grandmother or my mother, if they had heard that I ate on Yom Kippur, they would have said: "It's not true."

I'm going to tell you how I ate *hazer* [*pork*] the first time. My uncle said to me: "I'm taking the train to Cologne. You

9. "Young Guard," a leftist, Zionist youth movement.

and your aunt are coming with me. Let's say, about twenty miles. I'm going to buy you a round-trip ticket." I was his pet. And as for me taking the train, it was the second time. That was in '22, I believe. I was twelve. We went toward the German border, toward Poznan. Down there, everything had been German for two hundred years. It was altogether different. I was fascinated. My uncle went on to Berlin and we got off, my aunt and I, in a little town called Ostow. But we had to wait a few hours before going back. We visited the town and we went to get something to eat. My aunt took me into a restaurant and ordered something with port cutlets. She knew, she said to me: "It's pork rib, you have to eat it!" I was so scared. I ate, I ate, but I said to myself: "How can you eat that?" I ate it all the same. And I assure you, for a few days, I was sick. Not physically sick. But mentally, it hurt me.

[. . .] I was in the leftist labor Zionists. It turned out that May 1 once fell on the last day of *Pesah*. We had the meeting in a plaza behind the synagogue. It was city hall, let's say, that had authorized it. My mother knew I was to be the speaker on behalf of our youth movement. She wasn't happy that I was speaking, but she came to listen all the same, because it was her son who was speaking. My mother wasn't happy that I belonged to that movement but when they voted for parliament, she always voted as I told her. Because there was a Jewish vote, Jewish slates. "Mama, I voted for the leftist labor Zionists!" So she said to me: "But they're not religious!" "But, Mama, it's my party!" She always voted like her son.

[. . .] I went to Warsaw in '31. I stayed there three years. I was a leader of the youth movement and I studied, not at the university but in what was called a seminary, a Jewish teachers college. You can't imagine how a poor student managed to get by in Poland. To earn a little bit, I worked as a teacher in a Jewish school. Not full time. I had a few hours in a school where the language of instruction was Yiddish. It was from the C.Y.S.H.O.V., "Central Organization of Jewish Schools." All the schools of that organization had a leftist orientation. In Warsaw, there were four of them of the Bund and four of the leftist labor Zionists.

We shall not trace here the multiplicity of political movements that stirred the Jewish world of eastern Europe between the two world wars. Let us recall, however, that with their schools, libraries, youth groups, and sport clubs they constituted vast social networks of a totally new character, compared to those of the traditional religious currents (themselves very diverse). Although these narratives of activists sometimes seem stereotyped insofar as they endeavor to justify a past and a loyalty, they nevertheless re-create all the richness and vitality of the intellectual debates among the Jews of Poland in the 1930s. In the case of Marc B., political involvement sustained his thirst for learning.

I was born to a family of Hasidim. In my early youth, I wanted very much to read. My older brothers already had newspapers and books, and I always tried to read what they brought home.

I went to school until the age of thirteen, and then I became an apprentice (leather worker). Even at that time, I had such a desire for reading that every day I bought a newspaper that I sided with. I used to buy my newspaper on the way to work. There was also a library in Warsaw, a famous one, the only lending library. It was called Bressler. I enrolled.

It was the war of '14 that forced me to interrupt my apprenticeship, and I had to go without reading because my family was poor, and I couldn't afford to continue. But after the Germans occupied Warsaw, a canteen was opened. It was the union sponsored by the Bund that opened that canteen to give poor people something to eat. At the same time, they opened a reading room. There were newspapers, magazines, books. When I found out there was a reading room, I went there right away. I stayed down there. Several groups were formed. We argued. We discussed what we had read. We talked about events. I was young (I was fifteen) at that time, but I already had a few ideas. I went there every day for newspapers and reading. I didn't go to eat—I ate at home—but I went there because of the special reading room.

They also started giving lectures. Once they invited Medem,

who was a founder of the Bund.[10] He had been arrested in Warsaw, but they couldn't deport him to Russia. So he was freed by the Germans and he stayed in Warsaw.

At that time, the leaders saw that it was in their interest to make us join what was called *Zukunft*, the Jewish youth organization. *Zukunft*, that means the future. So I belonged to that Bundist youth organization. Every week the leaders came to teach us about sociology and economic life. It was organized in little groups, each of which had a name. I belonged to the Kautsky group.

The goal was also cultural. They started a little library. It was during the war, and they didn't have much money. But this group went to get books in private houses, from those who had them. It lasted almost two years. In 1917, instead of that canteen, they rented a big building we named Bronislaw Grosser. He was one of the leaders of the Bund; he had passed away in 1912. Later on, they founded clubs in his name in various towns of Poland.

Right away, when they saw I had a certain interest, I was one of those who helped out with running that library. It went on like that until the war. Life began again. It was all topsy-turvy. So they wanted to expand. They rented a bigger building and started buying a lot of books. At the same time, I was active not only in the youth group but also in the Bund party. I'm not saying I was a leader, just an active member of that movement in Praga. I was active in the Bund, but mainly for libraries.

Julien K. followed a more restless yet typical itinerary, going from leftist Zionism to communism, then to Trotskyism and later to Bundism. In each instance he based his choices on lucid analyses, while preserving intact the intense revolutionary faith that gave meaning to his life.

I started my political activity when I was in high school. I was always interested in the events that were taking place in the country, the world. I even remember the Pilsudski coup d'état. I was a very young boy; I was fourteen. He was supported by

10. Vladimir Medem, (1879–1923) was a prominent leader (not founder) of the Bund in Poland and Russia.

all the leftists, including the Communist party, which was clandestine. I remember the agitation in Cracow. Later on, let's say when I was seventeen, one of my pals, a little bit older than me, introduced me to Hashomer HaZa'ir, a leftist Zionist organization, where I fit in right away. The goal was *Aliyah,* immigration to Eretz Israel, to Palestine. At that time, I was a high school student; they said: OK, we can accept the high school diploma but, in principle, one mustn't study, except in special cases. We're going to work as simple workers in a kibbutz. At that time, yes, I planned to go to Palestine.

In that organization, there was a very friendly atmosphere, a great camaraderie. They organized parties, evening gatherings, celebrations, games. People had friends of both sexes because there were girls too. It had a very special spirit and you took to it right away.

There was a big controversy with Mordechai Orenstein, who published a very controversial article. In his pro-Communist zeal, he went so far as to justify the persecutions of the Zionists in the Soviet Union. He said that, until 1927, the leftist labor Zionists were legal there, which was true, and that all the Zionists who had been arrested hadn't been arrested as Zionists but as anti-Soviets. He also developed the theory that in the break in the labor movement the Communists were right, that their line was revolutionary and that the line of the reformist Socialists was false. So this engendered a great controversy. I stayed in Hashomer HaZa'ir until many of my friends left it to join the Polish Young Communist Movement.

In that organization, in Cracow, at least 80 percent of the members were Jews. Aside from a few mining areas where the Polish Communist party had a certain influence, it really didn't have much of a base among the Polish population. I think that comes in part (I see it now, but I don't know if I analyzed it in this way at the time) from the war of 1920 between Poland and Soviet Russia. Russia invaded Poland. There were strong anti-Russian traditions among the Poles. They were very passionate about their independence, and they thought the Communists were acting against their nation. And the Jews, in my opinion now—because that certainly wasn't my analysis at the time—

among the Jews, there was a kind of messianism. The Jews didn't find any place for themselves in society. Jewish workers were doubly persecuted, the intellectuals didn't see any opportunities before them, there was the *numerus clausus*. You felt that persecution.

There were several tendencies within Jewish life. One was to emigrate, to go to a state that would be Jewish; the other was to fight where you were, to fight to make the revolution that would save the Jewish people. At one time, I was tempted by the leftist labor Zionists. But there were also the Communists. We thought that was the radical solution. At that time, Yiddish literature was flourishing in the Soviet Union. The Yiddish language was recognized as an official language; you could speak in that language in the courts in the Ukraine. So, you said to yourself, there it is—liberation comes from there. One day I decided to make the leap and I got in touch with the Communist Youths.

I went to a meeting of Hashomer and made a declaration to explain why I was leaving the organization. But my comrades in the Communist movement didn't appreciate that at all. They were for the Trojan horse tactic: you had to try to stay inside Hashomer, to work to undermine it and win people for the Communist party. You had to play a role for a certain time and follow the instructions they gave you. But having made that speech and broken it off, I couldn't follow that tactic.

[. . .] I remember that I was already in opposition in the party. Once somebody came to our house, to my father, because he knew him. It was the famous historian Isaac Deutscher.[11] Now he's well known. He was a few years older than me and he was already one of the members of the Trotskyite organization that had just been created in Poland. He had been the editor of a Communist newspaper in Yiddish, *The Literary Tribune*. He had managed to put out a Trotskyite issue with some articles on Germany, on the greatest danger threatening the working class; all democratic forces should unite in a popu-

11. Isaac Deutscher, (1907–1967) was a Marxist historian and political scientist, born in Poland, internationally known for his works on Stalin, Trotsky, and the Soviet Union.

lar front against fascism. He was thrown out. Right then, I started reading Trotsky's pamphlets on Germany. I found very good things, especially on that issue of the Fascist danger and the popular front. He proved that the theory of social fascism was absolutely stupid: you can't call all non-Communists fascists. There are differences. Even if someone criticizes social democracy as being opportunistic, it really can't be put in the same category as fascism. For me, all those were quite convincing arguments.

At that time, a member of the Central Committee who had come to Cracow was staying in my house. A Jew, he read Yiddish. It was after the infamous March 5, 1933. Hitler had already come to power. Then, all of a sudden, there was an appeal of the *Komintern* to all Socialist parties to form a popular front. This guy from the Central Committee didn't know that yet but I did, because my father brought home the Moscow newspaper *Emes*. And that newspaper gave the text of that Komintern appeal. I was sly. I started by saying to him: "Comrade, don't you think we should appeal to all the Socialist parties in Poland to make a popular front? Maybe they won't agree, but then we'll be able to unmask their leaders." He answered me: "Why, not at all! You're really on a dangerous course. That would be to recognize them as partners, give them prestige. It's absolutely impossible. To address them means we become social Fascists ourselves. No, no way, we must never address the leaders of those parties. We want to make the popular front from the ground up."

So, without saying anything, I picked up the copy of *Emes* and gave it to him. He read it three times. He could read Yiddish. He read the text three times. Then he looked to make sure I didn't give him an issue that was ten years old, the date and all that. And when he saw that it was a recent issue of a Communist Soviet newspaper, that it was a genuine appeal of the Komintern—then, in a single stroke, but really without thinking, he said exactly the opposite of what he had said before: "Why, that's completely right! To unmask the social Fascists, you have to make the appeal." It really shocked me to see that mentality.

I was already under the influence of the Trotskyites when I

was arrested. I stayed in prison for a few weeks, that's why I didn't reach all the conclusions concerning what happened. But later I got in touch with the Trotskyite organization, which already existed in Warsaw. There was another small opposition group that went along with the popular front,[12] and later we united. I was one of the founders, so to speak, of the Trotskyite organization we created in Cracow. So I broke with the official Communist party. Naturally, all those who remained Communists didn't want to talk to me anymore. I had gone over to the enemy camp.

I had become a militant Trotskyite but it was true that there were certain things I didn't understand very well in Trotskyism because I really didn't know what was going on in the Soviet Union. All those problems of the struggle against the leftists, the ultra-leftists. But I did understand the popular front very well. Once Hitler had seized power, the Communists' position became absolutely absurd. They told us that there had been no defeat of the working class in Germany. We asked: "Why?" "Because there was no struggle!" "Precisely, defeat without struggle, it's even worse!" "Of course not, Hitler overthrew social democracy. After that we're the ones who will come. There will be a Red October after Hitler." Well, history showed what reality was.

12. The threat of fascism in France in 1934 led to the formation of a popular front between the factions on the left, which won the elections and came to power in 1936. See p. 181.

<table>
<tr><td>

┌─────────────────┐
│   │
│   │
│   5   │
│ *Metamorphoses* │
│   │
│   │
│   │
│   │
│   │
│   │
│   │
└─────────────────┘

</td></tr>
</table>

┌──────────────┐
│   5   │
│ *Metamorphoses* │
└──────────────┘ *IF ALL THE narrators born around the Mediterranean express a strong sense of belonging to the local community, if the local community was the center of gravity of their lives, they nevertheless also remember being at the junction of several cultures. The tale of their childhood and youth is generally the tale of a transition between an indigenous culture, natural as the mother tongue, and yet already a composite, and a culture acquired in their own environment or inculcated by school. They perceive that passage as a social climb, an escape, sometimes liberation. But, simultaneously, the impression pops up here and there of their having been a pawn in a game going on somewhere else: between the western powers, which were competing for new supporters (through the school, the press, the Church, music, etc.); between those powers and the indigenous states, which were not happy to see their subjects taken out of traditional frameworks and drawn irresistibly toward other horizons.[1]*

"AT THE CROSSROADS OF THREE CULTURES"

Georges X., born in Tunis in 1908:

Here's how it happened. Those who want exact information on the Judeo-Arab environment of Tunisia, particularly of

1. On the period and the processes recalled in this chapter by the Jews of North Africa, see André Chouraqui, *Between East and West: A History of the Jews of North Africa* (Philadelphia: Jewish Publication Society of America, 1968). For Egypt, see Jacques Hassoun et al., *Juifs du Nil* [Jews of the Nile] (Paris: Sycamore, 1981).

Tunis, must know that, for those of my generation, there was Arab, or Judeo-Arab, culture; there was French, or Franco-Arab, culture; and there was Italian culture. Now, because of my family, I myself was at the crossroads of these three cultures because my father was from Italian culture. My paternal grandmother, who lived in our house, only spoke Italian. She spoke only Italian or Arabic. She knew French, but she refused to speak it. It was a kind of madness about Italy. So, my father and I, we spoke to her only in Italian. And my mother, who was beginning to be emancipated—this was the first generation that was emancipated—she went to the Italian school and got a degree and it was only afterward that she went to the lycée.[2]

At home, then, until the age of ten, Italian dominated. Italian dominated even more so since my father was the correspondent of some sons of his cousins who were from Mahdia and were civil servants in Tunis. They stayed at our house on Saturdays and Sundays. And during World War I, they were Italian soldiers, with the Italian cloak. . . . Two of them died in the war, on the Italian front. They had . . . not a worship exactly but a kind of Italian impregnation that didn't go so far as worship. But, for me, it held a kind of fascination.

From a culinary point of view, for example, there was spaghetti and cheese in my house. And my father sent me to buy cheese at Cassar's foodstore. You don't know it? Cassar, they're Maltese. At the beginning of Rue de l'Église, there was a kind of courtyard and, there, there was a charming little foodstore, just like the ones you find in some parts of the Trastevere in Rome. It was exactly the same kind. And, of course, it wasn't kosher. My father wasn't religious. I used to go buy cheese there and then I'd come back to buy wine in a sort of wretched little Italian restaurant on the Rue des Maltais. My grandfather was connected to the Italian families by marriage, etc. But my father married a Tunisian, Sarfati, who was completely Tunisian. So when we went to my maternal grandfather, we changed worlds! That's true; we just had to go thirty feet and we were in another

2. The French lycée, that is. *Emancipation* is the word used at the time. The mother must have been born in the 1880s.

world. At my maternal grandmother's house, we ate *kamounia* [*cumin stew*] and we ate *mloukhia* [*stew of Jewish mallow*]. We ate all those whatchmacallits that we didn't have in my father's house. And there was the hubbub of Tunisian families—everybody talked loud. There was this kind of hustle, and even if the houses were clean, they smelled of onions. From Thursday on, they smelled of onions.[3]

My maternal grandfather was religious without being religious. He had already taken a tiny step toward emancipation, but he couldn't speak French. He only spoke Judeo-Arabic. He could write Judeo-Arabic. He was a grain dealer and, every night, when he came home, he did his accounts, standing up in front of a black cabinet. I can still see him. . . . Little pieces of paper, no ledgers, eh, little pieces of paper he stacked up like that. And I was always amazed at that writing I didn't know. I knew French. I had a vague notion of Hebrew letters because of the bar mitzvah; I had a vague notion of Arabic letters because of my Arab friends; but those letters—I didn't know what they were. He wrote Judeo-Arabic. The letters aren't the same as classical Hebrew. It looks a little bit like what's called Rashi's writing; it looks a little bit like that.

So he had a Judeo-Arabic culture. He didn't pray on Friday night anymore. The aunts told me he used to say *kiddush* [*blessing on the wine*], but I never saw him do it. He did do the whole Shabbat, that is, he had the Shabbat lamps lit; it was all quite proper. He didn't go to synagogue, and he didn't do the Havdalah either. I didn't learn the Havdalah until later.

He had taken a small step toward emancipation. But he was deeply Jewish, Judeo-Arabic. Because on Rosh Hashanah [*New Year*], he went to synagogue; on Kippur, he went to synagogue. Not only did he go there, but we went with him all the time. I remember perfectly hearing him chant all the prayers. It was a little synagogue next door, a family synagogue, private, which belonged to the Bessis. There were families like that [*meaning stuffy ones*], who were admitted to that synagogue of the Bessis.

---

3. The preparation of the Sabbath couscous began on Thursday. The two stews mentioned above also have a strong odor.

And I remember hearing him chant there every year in a very beautiful voice, a bit muffled, but very moving. That means that he had a deep Jewish culture. And for me, that was the Judeo-Arabic side.

At that time, we were introduced into French culture, step by step. We learned French, but we didn't rub elbows with them. We would go to the best one in the class to copy the Latin translation. As we came into a house, it smelled bad [*with a wrinkling of his nose, he recalls the smell of cooking with butter*]. What's true is that we didn't rub elbows with them. We didn't rub elbows with them because they didn't want to, because we were Jews. Besides, we didn't really push it because we didn't have the same games or the same ways of thinking. So we forced our way into French culture. We acquired the literary and scientific culture, but it wouldn't be true to say that we were assimilated at that time. We were able to take a few steps toward assimilation only here, in Paris. I lived in Lyon for a year. It was the same thing: I never saw the inside of one of my friend's houses. That began only in Paris. My problem is very special, in fact, because I married a Frenchwoman. She was a Frenchwoman from the provinces, and there I really was admitted. That's what encouraged my emancipation. So did my political orientation, which meant that a whole bunch of people were my friends. And of course, when I entered the families, I felt almost forced to be assimilated into them. The fact is that I came out of there reassured, which didn't happen to me with the Jews.

As for that French culture, we acquired it. It came later, whereas Italian culture and Judeo-Arabic culture are native to me. That's the difference. The others are native. The population of Tunis ran the gamut: there were those who were more consistently Judeo-Arabic in character, those who were more Italian, etc., a kind of melting pot.

And that's how we lived those marvelous years, rich years. It was a great experience because there wasn't any obstacle in the midst of the culture that was ours. We assimilated other elements coming from elsewhere, but they didn't assimilate us.

Of the component of his culture designated "Judeo-Arabic," Georges X. retains more than the strong odor of onion that prevailed in the house and the cryptic language of his grandfather's accounts. In other sequences of his biography, he also recalls two Jewish religious figures. One is negative: the ignorant rabbi who prepared him for the bar mitzvah without understanding anything of what he said or explaining anything he might have known. The other image that comes up, beaming in the twilight of a lonely room, is that of an old relative— an uncle or great grandfather? Who knows?—to whom the child brought his daily dinner, "an egg and an eighth of boukha" [fig brandy]. Characterized by asceticism, solitude, and mystery, the man was steeped in the study of the Zohar, The Book of Splendor, and it is this memory, a luminous point of childhood, that now seems to have led his descendant back to the study of Torah.

"At the junction of three cultures," he tells us. Looking at his statement more closely, the first culture corresponds to religious practices, to a scripture and to dietary habits. The second, connected with the memory of a language, Italian, and a diet of cheese, is also evoked by the newspaper an uncle reads and comments on in the evening. This culture is already part of the process of "emancipation" described by Georges X. But Arabic culture? Though it was the culture of the majority in the country, it is absent from the picture painted for us. Very present instead through schools, newspaper stands, and bookstores was French culture, dominant though the culture of a minority. Paradoxically, the living languages spoken since childhood seem to belong to a dying culture, whereas the printed language, laboriously learned, is the one that allows the narrator to pull himself up to modernity. A junction, yes, but all of its roads are not of equal value. Some seem henceforth to be dead ends while others are avenues of escape and social mobility. André A., born in Tunis in 1926, echoes him:

The Jews had the same habits, the same customs as the Muslims, yes! It's with colonialism that they played the French card. They tried to get out of their ghetto by adopting French culture—that's what it is. Previous generations had kept Muslim habits—the superiority of the man over the woman, etc.—and there was an inevitable development, a worldwide development, toward equality. But there was also the move, in Tunisia, of the Jews toward French culture, which happened because of colonialism. We are the products of colonialism. And finally, there were some of us who considered ourselves French. Like us: we're closer to the Martins than to the Muhammads. In Tunisia, I never read a single Muslim writer, a single Muslim poet. I read German philosophers; I read French poets . . .

Georges X. also describes this linguistic and cultural migration, which he calls "emancipation," as emigration. His early childhood was spent in a poor neighborhood outside the ghetto, but it is still presented as "a whole world," where all the components of the local society were represented: all, except one, for the narrative reveals that there was no French component. During his adolescence, the family moves—and the name of the street is indicative—to Avenue de France. This distance, less than half a mile, is remembered as a radical break. The grandfather will no longer return to Rue des Tanneurs except for Yom Kippur. For the grandmother, "there was no longer anything to look forward to, there was nothing." For the adolescent and his brothers, Avenue de France marks the coming of "culture." Later on, another move marks a new break. Georges X. leaves for France to study. He is "accepted" into French society and finally feels a sense of comfort he no longer shared with Jews.

The Rue des Tanneurs was an extraordinary street because it was an enclave. It was self-sufficient; there was no need to go outside the street for anything at all. There were butchers, vegetable merchants, doctors, restaurants, a printshop, a blacksmith, a carpenter, a baker. You just can't imagine all that was on the Rue des Tanneurs—a whole world. And that world had its peculiarities, because there was its own smell, and that is still in my nostrils.

The narrator then describes the tanners "at the end of the alleys," from which "a yellowish water flowed all day long." He discovered the innards of the earth one day when he had lost a ball, which wound up in the vat of a tannery:

I went to get the ball . . . and there I saw a sight I might describe today as infernal. Under a vaulted house, a rather low house, buried, half-buried, there was a tanner who had strung up some sort of thick leather aprons, slapping wilth a kind of wood shovel. I didn't see them. They must have been slapping on the hides . . . and I was scared. I ran away and left the ball.

But that wasn't all there was to the street—the street was where we lived. We were street children; the street belonged to us. There were grocers, who were Arabs. The baker—there was an Arab one and a Jewish one. The butchers were all kosher; people came from all over town to buy kosher meat on the Rue des Tanneurs. . . . In the alleys there lived many Italian families and many Maltese families. The Arabs were the tanners and some small tradesmen who were there. We lived in a community of Italians, Maltese, Jews, and Arabs, without any difference. The children played together without any difference. It was really a wonderful world.

Then, after the move to Avenue de France:

That was really another life. We moved on to high school. From the amusement of the street, we moved on to the amusement of the newspapers. The newspaper stands were closer. We threw ourselves into reading, culture. We went, my brother and I, to subscribe to the reading libraries. We had a completely different orientation. My grandfather didn't see anybody from Rue des Tanneurs anymore except on Kippur, when we went to the synagogue. . . . And that is where we lived until I left for school. And when I came back for vacations, my grandfather was dead and my mother had gone to live—taking her mother and one of her sisters, the youngest—on Avenue de Paris . . .

Ambivalent images combine here: the lost world was an infernal, archaic, visceral world, a world of dark alleys, dirty water, meats, entrails, and hides. But it was "whole," central (people came from all over the city to buy meat; the narrator also says that his street was "the industrial center" of the city). It formed a self-sufficient microcosm, rich in immediate and intense human relations: "The street belonged to us." By contrast, entrance through the front door—Avenue de Paris, the French lycée—to French culture leads to both emancipation and alienation: in France "I felt almost forced to be assimilated to them."

For Laure A., who was born and grew up in Istanbul at the beginning of the century, French culture was not only the culture of school and emancipation but also the culture of distinction, which placed people higher up on the social ladder. The westernization of the family had begun in the generation of her father, who was born in the last quarter of the nineteenth century:

At the age of twelve, my father spoke French as well as I do. At twelve, he wrote without any mistakes. He had learned French in a Jewish French school. Papa stayed at school until twelve or thirteen. Then his father died, and he had his four brothers to feed. He was the oldest; then there was Uncle Moses, Uncle Solomon, Uncle Raphael. . . . My father was the shrewdest, the most intelligent. He was called Jacques. The other one, Uncle Moses, he was a real Englishman, with a pipe, music. . . . The uncle from Berlin, Raphael, always had a monocle and a cane . . .

Characteristically, Laure A. gives her uncles' first names in the Hebrew version, but she frenchifies her father's name, which was Isaac. This game continues in the following sequence where, telling of the schooling of the girls of her generation, she persists in calling the schools of the Alliance Israélite the "Alliance Française," a name that serves here as a cachet of social distinction:

In my generation, there were schools in Turkey that weren't good; they had people who weren't from our social circle. . . . So my two oldest sisters went to convent schools—Christian, Catholic. Since there were a lot of us, Mama put them in boarding school. She was very happy with the education, with everything. Then a Jewish student there converted. That was a disaster for all the Jews—not only converted, but they made her a nun. She became Sister Something-or-Other. That she converted, that was nothing, but she became a nun. . . . Angela, I think. The Jewish community didn't accept that.

My two sisters M. and R. were in the French Jewish school. Teachers from the Alliance Francaise of Paris. They were Jews, but they had gone to school in Paris.

"So it was the Alliance Israélite?"

Yes, the Alliance Israélite Française, I think, in French. The *Alliance Française Israélite!* But later, that school was closed. The schools, they had children of butchers, of peasants. . . . You're going to tell me . . . Here . . . here, it's not like that. Milkmen are very respected. There, they were poor people—the baker, the one who sold meat, fish, all that—they were poor people. So to be in the same schools with them was to lower yourself a bit.

The three sisters then went to the German school, then the American College, and they spoke fluent Spanish, German, French, and English but not a word of Turkish.

"THE EXTRA MUROS"

Launched into European culture, its languages, its music, its styles, one had already gone without even leaving the ground on which he or she grew up. In Tripoli at the beginning of the century the school apparatus being yet embryonic, there were other strategies of social distinction than those recalled by Laure A. (Rather than going to school you had the headmistress come to your house for private lessons.) But just as inevitably, you became a foreigner—significantly, Camilla N. describes her family's move from the center of the city to an "extra muros" neighborhood—and you were transported to other shores: Constantinople, where Camilla N.'s father went several times? No, that is a dream long cherished but never realized. The father also had regular commercial relations with Fezzan and distant Africa. His daughter was fascinated by that. I ask her if she went there: "Are you kidding? Never, it was too far!" Instead the family went on vacation each summer, sometimes in Tunisia, sometimes in Italy. And once she got married, Camilla N. finally moved to Paris.

We spoke almost all languages, you know. That is, we spoke Arabic, but our friends were Syrians. There were state officials, functionaries of Turkey. They came from Syria, from Lebanon; they spoke Arabic, they spoke Turkish. Papa spoke Turkish very well, he was very assimilated with them. And those people were so nice! Such refined cooking! We had Turkish dishes that were really something!

And one of the things we had—this is to tell you about the mixture of our lives—was something extraordinary: we had, like many children, if you like, a kind of governess, a Jewish woman from Smyrna who spoke Spanish.

"So you also learned Spanish?"

A little. Greek, for example, we had Greek friends who came to school with us because there were things [*fisheries*] of sponges there, you know? It was small, small. I admit it was very small, but there were Greeks, there were Turks, there were English, the consuls, that is. So all those people saw each other regularly in the places called *extra muros* because they were outside the city.

You know, we spent much more time with foreigners. We were raised with foreigners, our family especially, because we were outside. The family, the cousins, had already gone to Europe. So they were very Europeanized already too.

There, I'm going to tell you, for example. There weren't so many teachers and schools and everything. My English teacher was the . . . priest of the Protestants, as it's called, he was the one who was Protestant. So I knew the whole Jewish religion explained in English because he taught me about religion. My Italian teacher was a defrocked priest. Naturally, there was a rabbi in the house every day who came for the boys. We had teachers for everything.

"You had private teachers?"

There wasn't anything!

"There was an Alliance school, wasn't there?"

Oh, yes, my French teacher was the headmistress of the Alliance school. But she came to the house only for us. There were the nuns; I spent a year at the convent school.

In Cairo, at the beginning of the century, Jews were also at the junction of three cultures but were attracted more by the French school—in either its secular or its religious, Christian or Jewish forms. People were proud of mastering so many languages, of bending to French school discipline, of having had to learn Arabic as a foreign language. At the end of the metamorphosis, Edmond H. means "the Jews" when he speaks of "Europeans." He is already posing as a Frenchman in his recollection of how the Egyptian elite was kept in a state of humiliation by British colonial politics. Native Copts and Muslims attended the same schools without being excluded from the Egyptian framework. For the Jews, however, frenchification by the school contributed to their marginalization.

Edmond H., Cairo, 1909:

It wasn't an Egyptian country; it wasn't the Egypt of the Egyptians. It was a *cosmopolitan* country. And that was our misfortune. Because if we had agreed to associate the Egyptian elite in what we were doing, we would never have had the troubles we had. Just like the French in Algeria. It was the century of British domination. So for all the formal papers, it was Arabic and English; for all the informal papers, it was French. In any store, big or small, you spoke French, and they'd answer you in French. Why? Because there weren't any Muslims behind the counter. They were mostly Jews, Greeks, Italians, Lebanese.

"What about the Copts?"

That's another category altogether. We'll talk about the Copts later. [*In fact, he never talked about the Copts later. Edmond H. goes on.*] In Cairo, any Jew who didn't speak three or four languages was an imbecile, pure and simple. You're going to ask me: "How can it be that he speaks three or four languages? He can speak four languages, without reading them, without writing them. Why?—Because he hangs out with, is mixed up with, all the others."

"So what was the most widespread of these three or four languages?"

French.

"Really? Not Arabic?"

No, Arabic was for the Arabs; not for us. My daughter finished her studies at the French lycée. She took her final exams: English, first part, Hebrew, second part. She never studied Arabic. My sister, who was in the American Mission, always had perfect English, perfect French. She couldn't read even one word of Arabic.

As in Tunis with Georges X., the indigenous language Edmond H. defines as "predominant" was really the language of servants and clients. How one used languages was one of the indicators of one's position in the social hierarchy.

FRENCH THEATER

After the school, along with the school, the bookstore, the theater, and the opera were other dazzling places in which one could enjoy the fascination of French culture.
Tunis. Élie B., born in 1898. As a child, he received two francs a week from his father.

I waited impatiently for Monday to go to the bookstore to buy a work for 1.25 francs. I spent eight pence on the movies on Thursday, with one penny at intermission for *kakis* [*salted crackers sold by peddlers*].

But it was during his first trip to France in 1920 that he discovered the world of books and ideas, the variety of the daily press and literary reviews, scholarly societies, and even some famous writers. His trip turned into a literary journey, an initiation into high culture, the measure of his divorce from the culture of his parents. While they visited the popular Parisian sights and stayed within Tunisian émigré circles, he crisscrossed Paris in the footsteps of his intellectual heroes.

[*In Marseille*], I was flabbergasted. I saw the open-air theater created by the Comédie-Française. That's where I bought my first books by André Gide, the books put out by the Mercure de France. . . . Then we went up to Lyon. In Lyon, I simply visited the Saint-Jean quarter. I visited Fourvière. I visited the old streets of the Saint-Jean quarter, and there too I discovered a secondhand bookdealer who sold cheap limited editions of great authors and authors I had heard of. . . . And then we went on to Vichy. Vichy was amusing because, I remember, I went to the Casino every afternoon to hear classical operetta. I visited the environs of the city, the Petit Palais. I went rowing along the Allier, and then I visited the women. . . . Then, we got to Paris. In Paris, we lived in Montholon Square. My father went to find the Tunisians who were living there.
"They were already in that neighborhood?"

When we left Tunis, we already had a plan. People said to us: "You're going to Paris, go see this one, go see X., go see Z." You knew that some guy was in some café. My parents went to the Folies Bergère, to the Concert Maillot. . . . I found out that there was a bus not far away that took me to Place Saint Michel. I went to the Place de l'Odéon. I went to theater shows at the Odéon. I went to see the publisher Figuière, who was publishing Brulat at that time. And I remember one day when I got my ticket to the Comédie-Française. It was September 18, I remember. *The Myth of Sisyphus*. . . . It was magnificent, that tragedy . . .

I remember my feelings in Paris when I passed Salle Marivaux. I often saw the great stage actor Gabriel Signoret go by. And I remember that, in Vichy, I went to the theater one day to see Ibsen's *A Doll's House* with Luc Népo [?] and his wife Suzanne Després. It was gripping. And in the orchestra seat next to me sat the great actor of the Théâtre Français, Léon Bérard. I looked at him with admiration, and he made a friendly little gesture to me, sensing that I was looking at him. I then asked to speak to him. I had seen him in so many films . . .

Another thing about Vichy was walking around the great avenues every afternoon, with the newspaper vendors who sold all the daily papers. At that time, there was a large daily called *Le Journal du peuple* [*The People's Newspaper*], edited by Henri Fabre, when Henri Fabre was at the height of his glory. There was also a weekly called *Les Hommes du jour* [*Men of the Day*], and all the leftist types contributed to it.

Back in Paris, I attended a conference of the Sociétés Savantes [*a cultural organization*]. I visited the Louvre. My parents had their pleasures, I had mine. They went to Chantilly two or three times to see the races because somebody had told them that that was a must. They went to the Folies Bergère and the Casino de Paris, but they didn't go to the theater even once. I saw publishers, bookstores. That year, at Figuière's, I met Count X., who was Huysmans's secretary. He took me to him and then introduced me to other writers. We'd meet in the Luxembourg; he lived on Rue Servandoni. One day, he said to me: "I'm going to take you to the teacher of us all," and he took me to Anatole

France. I made that little visit to the Villa Said . . . and when he asked me what I planned to do, I said: "My dear master, I'm thinking of devoting myself . . . I have parents who are well off . . . I'm thinking of devoting myself to literary pursuits." He smiled and said: "It's hard, you know."

Later on, Élie B. launched a little literary review in Tunisia, published his own poems, and opened an art gallery, all the while managing a pharmaceutical business. The review was titled Oasis: *"An Oasis is a place of concentration . . . a place of refuge [he hesitates, I am surprised, I think "ghetto"; then he goes on, more firmly], of encounters. . . . For us, it's a place of encounters."*

For Madame K., born in Tunis after 1900, Western culture also meant the stage.

Music? Every night, my mother sat down at the piano and sang: *La Bohème, Madama Butterfly, Lakmé.* . . . She played, and we put on our nightgowns. We went to see her, and then we scurried off to bed. And when we started learning the piano at the age of six, one day, my sister and I, we were stuck, we called Mama. "Mama, what's written there?" "I don't know." "What do you mean, you don't know?" "I don't know music, I don't know notes." She played by ear; she played very well. And Fernand, her brother, how he played the prologue of *Paillasse* and "The old man cursed me" from *Rigoletto!* You remember?

"But how did you learn music?"

Well, see. It was a culture of opera. My father had a very good position, he was rich. OK. My mother had her box at the municipal theater. She went to the evening performance on Tuesdays and Saturdays. We had three seats reserved for the Sunday matinee all year. We went with our maid. She was dressed up, wore a hat and a suit. She sat with us. On Sunday mornings, it was a ritual: my mother called us, my father got up, we sat at the foot of the bed. She'd tell us the story, sing passages to us, and when we went to the opera, we already knew what it was about. You don't have an inborn knowledge of music! And then, there was, I think, something in the family. We lived for music.

One more thing: My father couldn't study a lot because his father, as soon as he was grown up, said: "I'm not working anymore, you'll have to go to work." He took charge of his whole family. But when I started reading, I found in my father's room *all* of Racine, *all* of Molière, and *all* of Corneille in Old French, and *all* of Victor Hugo, the complete works of Victor Hugo. I remember, I was small, and I couldn't bear books in Old French! I was incapable of transposing, so I said "I wos." I remember Racine's *Les Plaideurs*—what I had to endure to read them.

I'll tell you something else. My mother always said that my Aunt Léa was very beautiful, a real beauty. She was sixteen years old when she got married. They called her the Rose of Tunis. She was extraordinarily beautiful. And she had been asked for by D. One of the rich D.'s. And my grandfather didn't want him because he wasn't educated enough. He preferred S.B. because he was educated! And *because he was French!* Because my Grandfather K. loved the French, while the D.'s were Tunisian and not educated at all. . . . My father wasn't handsome; he was dark. But he was French, and he was educated.

To be French was indeed the goal of that effort on the part of the Jewish bourgeoisie to adopt the ways of living, the provincial culture, that Tunis offered during the colonial period. You could be dark and even ugly, but education and French nationality gave you a mark of distinction. Nothing else, for in the gallery of characters presented by that woman, no "Frenchman from France," as they were then called, appears. You could read about France, hear about it, see it in the windows of the bookshops and on the school benches, but you hardly knew any Frenchmen. You were not close to any. Rather, to display a French personality was to distance yourself from the native culture, which was debased by the colonial situation. The same narrator adds:

My parents spoke only French at home. Even I have a lot of trouble speaking [*Arabic*]. When I got married, I was in Sousse, I had an Italian woman for some time. And when she left, I was forced to take an Arab maid. And that was quite a scene, we were like deaf-mutes, everything like that [*she gestures, mimes dialogue*]. I had to ask my sister-in-law.

Not all the Jews had access to the French school and some only passed through it. But, sooner or later, they were exposed to western culture styles and seized by them. Even Tita, who remained illiterate and Arabic-speaking, was glad when her husband adopted European dress. At the very least, others changed their names, and that already indicated a change in social station.

Tunis. In the last twenty years of the nineteenth century, Sarfati, a tailor in the souk, then a grain dealer, had six children, six daughters: Marie, Mathilde, Emma, Henriette, Georgette, and Olga. All the first names are western and were fashionable at their time. However, behind the facade, another first name was hidden, the one that assured continuity with one's ancestors. For children received the names of their deceased forebears, those of the paternal line having priority over those of the maternal line. So, Marie was Meïma, a diminutive of Miriam; Mathilde was 'Atu or Mes'uda; Emma was Meïha, named after her great-grandmother; Henriette was Shmana.

Meïha, 'Atu, Shmana—the etymology of these names is no longer known. You know only that someone in the family had already had them. When the stock of ancestors of the last two generations was exhausted, family memory reached its end, and the last born had only a western name: Georgette, born in 1899, the first to have a civil registration, had no other name; nor did Olga, born in 1900.

Naming the elders was the major concern; it took precedence over assigning a Jewish identity to the children when they were born. If all the Arab first names given in this family were used exclusively by Jews, only that of the oldest, Miriam, is from a biblical source. In the case of sons, the Hebraic tradition was stronger and combined with family continuity. Names from the Old Testament were then handed down from generation to generation. But sooner or later, westernization took hold, and the old names became middle names or were "translated" into a western language. A system of equivalents was set up in which Abraham became Albert, Haim was called Victor—for Haim is "life"[4] and there is the sound of vie in Victor—Makhlouf gave way to René, Judith slid into Edith. So everyone grew up with two, sometimes three, identities. One was for public and administrative purposes: in school, in various dealings with the bureaucracy, one used the western name.

4. Translator's note: In French, "life" is vie.

The traditional name, pronounced in the local language, was reserved for religious rituals, from circumcision to death. More private and for the early years of life, a nickname was used by parents, schoolmates, and relatives—Mimil, Dédé, Nani, Lulu. That diminutive concealed both the Hebrew name, which classified the individual as old-fashioned, backward, "Arabized" (m'arbi), and the western name, which thrust the individual into the "developed" world but which was somewhat embarrassing to use within the family and community group. The politics of the name follows and illustrates the westernization and secularization of the Jews from Salonika to Istanbul or Casablanca. Everywhere, a kind of Marrano-like[5] mechanism operated to conceal the Jewish identity, to confine it to domestic and ritual use. One sported a western name for public use.

Esther E. H., born in 1918 in Mogador, explains how her children's names were chosen: she was influenced by tradition as well as by recent history, that of the west, with the aspirations and illusions it aroused in Morocco.

[*The first is*] René, because my father-in-law's name was Makhlouf. René, that means Makhlouf, it's the same thing. If you translate, it's René. All Makhloufs are called René. That was my father-in-law who died. Because we can't give the name of relatives when they're alive. That is, the person is afraid he'll die; it's a superstition.

Yvette, she's called Zaïta, joy. Yvette, I called her, after a friend from high school whom I loved very much. We gave them two names but we always called them by the French one. [*Note that Yvette is the only French name; those that follow are Anglo-American.*]

Jimmy, his name is Haim: it's my grandfather, my mother's father; and Jimmy, because of the American landing. And we had a fellow, his name was Jimmy, he always came to our house. Robert, his name is Raphael. I gave him a rabbi's name. I said, if it's a boy, I'll name him Raphael. I don't know if I dreamed it or something like that. He's a great rabbi of Salé.

Lydia is named after Mama, Hanna. Mama, it was all the

5. Marranos: Jews who were forced to convert in Spain and Portugal were ostensibly Christian while maintaining secretly their Jewish faith.

same to her, when she was alive, she said, "It's Papa who was superstitious; he was afraid to die." Mama died at the age of eighty-five and my father died when he was sixty-four. So, you see, that's not what killed him. And Vicky, Victoria: "We're going to name her after Queen Victoria." It's whims. They came and you gave them names.

Laure A., Istanbul, about 1910:

My brother's name was Albert. Abraham, Albert. My brother was so simple! . . . I thought that Albert was common, so I called him Bert. It was funny, it was chic, it was English. He said to me: "If you call me that name again, I'm going to tell everybody that my name is Abraham. That'll teach you to call me Bert." He was capable of playing a trick like that on me!

Poor, less westernized Jews succumbed to the same attraction and followed the same politics of names. Yvonne A., the tenth child of a family in modest circumstances, born in Algeria in 1909: "My name is Ymouna, that means trust. It's a Hebrew name. But they called me Yvonne. It's more civilized."

A GAME OF CHANCE: THE IDENTITY CARD

In periods of stability, Jews did not ask themselves questions about their religious and political identity. They belonged to a family, a social milieu, a community, and did not look beyond that horizon. They lived an apolitical existence and were content to be citizens of their own microcommunity without bothering about national denominations. The "papers" that signified an attachment to some consulate of a European country were negotiated according to the interests of the moment and were subject to the policies and rivalries of the various powers. An individual who by chance, purchase, or favor obtained a European "nationality" did not really identify with that adopted nation. European nationality was considered an insurance policy rather than a testimony of identity.

When a political change occurred—legislative reform, a crisis in international relations, war—the question was then posed brutally and sometimes cruelly: Where to register? Where to find the protection of rights and agents who would defend "their" nationals?

This is the story of Edmond H. His ancestors, Ottoman subjects in Syria, had become French-protected Tunisians without ever seeing either Tunisia or France. In Egypt, Edmond H. lost that status without acquiring a nationality to replace it. He remained in that undefined— yet not uncomfortable—situation for a long time. It is in 1956, when he had to leave Egypt abruptly, that it became urgent to have an administrative identity.

M.S. had bought his nationality. Not his children, who were born in England. They became "British by birth." I'm going to tell you how he had obtained it. At the beginning of the century, the Ottoman Empire encompassed the entire Orient. In Egypt, the Jews didn't do military service. There wasn't any compulsory military service. There wasn't an army. On the other hand, in Syria, in Mesopotamia, in Lebanon, and in Arabia, the Turks had instituted compulsory military service. Now, military service with the Turks was very very hard, and the Jews tried to get out of it through any means. That's one of the reasons why the Jews of Aleppo, Damascus, and the Syrian towns escaped and came to Egypt, which, as I told you, became a land of milk and honey as soon as the Suez Canal opened. Some people left for Greece; others went to Europe; and the majority came to Egypt. That's why there were a lot of Syrian Jews in Egypt. Aside from that, they wanted to stay. They had their businesses; they had their houses. But they didn't want to stay as Ottoman subjects, so they asked the consuls to protect them.

Each one of the protected was granted the nationality of the country he or she appealed to without too many difficulties. Once it was given, the consuls of those countries saw that there were resources to draw on. Every time somebody came to ask them [*for nationality*]: "How much can you pay? You'll pay so much, they'll give you citizenship." And they found him some relationship with an Englishman, an Italian, a Frenchman. And, since the port of Livorno had burned down at that time, the *questura*—that is, the city hall of Livorno—had also burned down. So anybody at all could say "my parents or my grandparents were in the Italian papers." So the consuls used that over 150 percent, and distributed citizenship. In Egypt, the consuls told themselves: "Not only can you do something but you can make yourself some money." So, instead of addressing only the poor people, saying to them "Here's nationality," they addressed the rich Jews, saying: "There are mixed courts. If you have a bad deal, they will judge you in Arab courts." Now there weren't any Arab courts, that was a make-believe court. There were mixed courts, however. And if a native had a case with a European, he went to the mixed courts. It was not open to discussion.

So, those who profited most were the Italians because they could give Italian nationality after Livorno. Then came the French. They could also say: "They are Jews from Spain, who went down to the Basque country, to Toulouse, Bayonne, Bordeaux, etc., or to Algeria or Morocco or Tunis." That's how my grandfather, who was in Syria, was able to get Tunisian protection.[6]

"Tunisian?"

Tunis was a French protectorate. He preferred that because there was no military service. And we remained protected Tunisians ever since the beginning of the century. We had number 909 from the consulate. I still have the papers.

So how did we lose that citizenship? We lost it because, in 1940, Egyptian companies started rising. Now, the constitution of an Egyptian company provides for seven members of the council of administration. And it was stipulated that the seven members had to be Egyptians; they couldn't be foreigners. OK. I had an uncle who worked with my father.

Now, my uncle was a great poker player. One of his friends was Dr. Maher Pacha, who became chairman of the Council. He was assassinated in 1946. They played together at the Club. So he said to him: "Listen, my children need Egyptian citizenship." "What citizenship do you have?" "Nothing, French citizenship." Because they had a valid French passport, like all other

6. By then Tunisia was a French colony.

passports. Only, on the inside, it was written: "Tunisian French protégé." He said: "Go to the consulate, give up your French citizenship, and give me your paper of withdrawal. In two days, I'll give you citizenship."

He did indeed go there, he gave up his nationality, and they gave him the paper of withdrawal. In charge of this withdrawal, there was a secretary at the consulate called the Chancellor of the Consulate. This was one Monsieur A., a Lebanese: a Lebanese who was a 101 percent anti-Semite, not 100 percent, 101 percent. So he was fuming: "You want to withdraw? With pleasure, my boy, only we're going to convene the consular tribunal." [*The tribunal said*]: "Yes, we accept, but on condition that from Haim Michel H. on (my grandfather's name was Haim Michel), the whole H. *mishpahah*[7] gives up its French citizenship. A single individual cannot give it up. All or nothing." My uncle didn't give a damn. He said, all agreed. The decision was made: all the descendants of Haim Michel H. disappeared from the lists of the consulate. But he didn't mean us: we weren't the sons of the H. who withdrew. But the chancellor didn't give a damn. He mixed things up.

So, they got Egyptian citizenship and founded the Egyptian company. And we were stateless. Before 1956, you had to request Egyptian citizenship every five years. You paid for the right to request, and they still didn't grant us citizenship. They told us: "It's like this, it's the law. You have to make the request and we don't grant it to you because your name isn't Ahmed or Muhammad." "But we were born in Egypt." "Yes, but that doesn't mean anything. It's the law." In reality, you didn't need citizenship. Nobody cared about it. We never thought of leaving Egypt. What did it matter? You were there, so you didn't need papers.

Now we are in Tripoli. Camilla N., born Dutch in Libya, became Italian and then French. She also described these changes of nationality in which European powers played against weak states and to which the Jews adjusted more or less comfortably.

7. Hebrew word meaning family, which Edmond H. puts in the mouth of the Lebanese chancellor of the French consulate.

My father's ancestors had left Pisa at a time when there was a Pope who was very bad to the Jews. And they went to Tripoli. When they came, those unfortunates, to Tripoli, there were three or four families who didn't have a consul, who didn't have anybody. Since Italy was divided, there was no Italian consul. Italy wasn't yet formed. So Holland took those Jews under its protection and gave them Dutch passports. We stayed under that Dutch protection until the Turks woke up. Why? Because Italy had sent teachers, schools . . . not many schools, but elementary school anyway. She put out propaganda, and that caught on a lot with the young people. My brothers were absolutely . . . [*with a gesture, she suggests "inflamed"*]. They knew they were of Italian origin. And then Holland said: "Now that's enough, there is a time when everything has to be settled." So there was a very heated debate. My father had gone to Constantinople more than once, since the Turks had been really wonderful to him and he had friends there, he didn't want to do that. It bothered him a lot to make a choice. The Turks didn't give permission: "No, you've been here for I don't know how many generations, you'll remain Turks." Anyway, there was such a fuss that finally we were made Italians by royal decree. And that's how we came to be Italians.

NATIONALITY: SALONIKAN

A namesake of the previous narrator, Papou N., born in 1894, recalls the status of extraterritoriality from which the Jews of Salonika benefited at the turn of the century. He incorrectly attributes it to the intervention of Russia.

In 1878, the Russians forced the Turkish government to give up personal control over all the non-Muslim inhabitants of European Turkey. So someone who was, let's say, Orthodox belonged to the Orthodox patriarch; someone who was an Israelite belonged to the Israelite community; and, of course, someone who was French, English, Italian, German, or American belonged to his own consulates. . . . And for those of us who weren't Muslims, it was a dream. There was no tax. There was no military service. We weren't subject to Turkish laws. Someone who did something in the street would say to the policeman: "I'm not a Muslim." "So, what are you?" It depended on your community. OK, that's just to tell you how we lived without trouble.

But the vagaries of history put the Jews in prickly situations, which the hero enjoyed telling about and from which he always managed to escape unharmed. The Italian-Turkish war of 1912 forced the N.s and some other Jewish families to leave Salonika, some going to Brussels, others to Vienna, where our hero worked for six months. Then came the end of the war.

Meanwhile, the Turkish–Italian war is over, and we all went back to Salonika together. It was really a celebration because my brothers and sisters-in-law from Brussels came, and we all sailed from Trieste on a ship bound for Salonika. The trip lasted a week. It was really a celebration; my father was in seventh heaven. Besides, we weren't the only ones. There were at least three, four other Salonikan families in our situation, Italians like us, Modiano, all that, with their children. So, on board, it was one big party, so to speak. Everybody was happy and everything. And we get to Salonika—what misery!—just when the Greeks entered Salonika. They had finished one war, and already there's another Balkan war starting. So that was a disaster! But anyway, time passed, and afterward, everything returned to normal. This brings us to the end of 1912.

Our hero's tribulations started again with World War I and Italy's entry into the war, since the N. family is still "Italian."

Italy had entered the war with France and England against Germany. OK. She had appealed to all Italians who lived anywhere in the world to come join their homeland for military service, to enlist in the army. In Salonika, there were about thirty or forty Italians of military age. We said to ourselves: My word, this doesn't concern us. We never really knew Italy, so why go do military service? We're in Salonika, which was Turkish before and is now Greek. We'll wait. We waited.

But mobilization did indeed take place. Our hero and his brother were sent to France. This involved not just the two soldiers, tossed from camp to camp. Rather, it is the whole family that is mobilized to get them out of it: the mother and the aunt, who rush to Marseille, the father and a cousin to Paris, the brother to Salonika. A dialogue in Paris ensued between a politician and the father ("he was decorated with the Order of His Majesty King Leopold, he wore his medal proudly and his calling card was 'Dragoman of the Consulate of Belgium in Salonika'"):

"What is this story? I don't understand. Let's get to the point in a few words. You were born what?"

"Good, in Salonika, Turkey."

"So you're Turkish." (Then he addresses M. Longuet, the deputy: "They're Turkish, OK, what else?")

"Then, at the time of the proclamation of the capitulation in Turkey, we chose to be Italian protégés."

"Oh, yes, indeed, I know that. That does complicate matters. And now?"

"Now, it's Greek."

"But, you're not Greek?"

"Oh, no."

"And you're not Turks?"

"Of course not."

"And you're not Italians?"

"No, since . . ."

"Oh," he says, "what a story!" He addresses the deputy: "Monsieur Longuet, I am sorry, I don't understand. It's so mixed up, this Macedonian salad. I don't understand. In any case, there's nothing against them, is there? Good, since there's nothing against them, for us French, I'm giving the order in Marseille to set them free, to let them out of camp to do what they want."

In Marseille, at the prefecture, and after numerous tribulations, the whole family receives new papers and a tailor-made definition:

"As nationality, I put down 'Salonikan' for you."

"Fine, that's very good, Salonikan."

"You're satisfied?"

"Yes, Salonikan, that's very good."

Some summon up Pisan ancestors, others Livornese tombstones. M.S. (Salonika, born before 1900) claims to be from Spain and gets himself out of trouble twice: first, he avoids military service in Greece and then extermination by the Germans in France.

When the Russo-Turkish war broke out, we were old enough to do military service. So my family sent us to study at the university in France. We came to France, with my brother, and we reported to the prefecture. At the prefecture, they told us that we had to be in good standing at the consulate. At the consulate of Spain: "What? Foreigners, born in Turkey, you're Spaniards? How can that be?" They didn't understand anything at all; they didn't know history. . . . We went to see the ambassador, who told us that he had to consult with Madrid: "Excellency, we have to register at school, we need registration!" "I can't do anything. All I can do is to put an ambassador's seal on top." We went with our passports: "We're recognized by the ambassador." And the ambassador wrote to Spain and they confirmed that we belonged to the three hundred sixteen families who never lost Spanish nationality. You know about that? I'll tell you:

As Spanish Jews of Salonika, we needed Spain two or three times. The first time was when the Greeks occupied Salonika. We were under the Turks, under the regime that surrendered. The Greeks entered Salonika and said to us: "For us, there aren't any Spaniards. There aren't any foreigners. Either you're Turkish or you're Greek." "No, we're foreigners, we're Spaniards." So, we appealed to the Ministry of Foreign Affairs in Madrid, which filed a suit against Greece. That trial took place at the International Court in the Hague in 1916. They recognized a certain number of families—three hundred sixteen families— who had always been Spaniards. They added two.

When the Germans came here, we said: "We're Spanish, not Greeks, not Turks, who are the enemy, and we're not French either." We went to see the consul of Spain, who was a friend of my family, and I laid out the problem for him. He told me: "There's only one thing to do: go to Spain and explain your case." And he sent our request to the Ministry of Foreign Affairs while we went there.

During the war, people couldn't travel. But we were Spaniards. The Germans gave us safe-conduct passes, and I'll tell you something extraordinary: we went to Spain four times and came back. We crossed the border as Spaniards almost twice a month. It's unbelievable! Now, in thinking about it, we have to say we were unaware. *Con esta gente no se sabra nunca!* [8]

That identity document, meaningless in peacetime, was the last card you had to play in a crisis: sometimes it failed to save the game.

Three sisters were born in Istanbul. One, Claire C., married in France, was Spanish by marriage, and escaped Nazi persecution by leaving Paris. The second, who became French, also fled to the south. The third, Régine, of Turkish nationality, was deported to a concentration camp with her family. Claire tells:

My sister was in Bordeaux with her husband, because he was working there. They were with a very nice French family. So, some people said: "You know, there are Jews over there." The Gestapo came. My brother-in-law said: "But we're Turks!" But he had given his card to be renewed in Paris. They sent him to Drancy, and from Drancy.[9] . . . And it was absurd because my sister had written to me: "I'm afraid for you because you're French. . . . We're not afraid of anything because we're Turkish." And she's the one who was deported. Bad luck. She spoke Turkish. My brother-in-law spoke Turkish like a real Turk. That was very rare among the Jews.

Régine and her family did not return from the death camp. For years, her sisters hid the truth from the mother, making her think that Régine had immigrated to the United States.

---

8. With those people, you couldn't know!
9. Town near Paris where the French police rounded up the Jews in a camp before they were deported.

For a very long time, I was the one who wrote the letters. I said that they came from America. I said: "It's Régine who's writing." Then, with time, my mother also started getting old, it was already blurry. Toward the end, we talked as little as possible. She didn't talk any more either.

6
Wanderings

POVERTY AND ANTI-SEMITISM *are the*
most obvious and most often cited causes for leav-
ing. However, the emphasis shifts according to
circumstances and the generations of the emi-
grants. Those who left the Russian empire at the
beginning of the century were marked by the
memory of the pogroms (including the sadly fa-
mous one of Kishinev, in 1903), along with
the revolutionary troubles of 1905 or the effects
of the war against Japan. Nathan K., for example, drafted into the
Tsarist army and about to be sent to the eastern front, preferred to
desert: "I didn't have anything against the Japanese!" Right after the
outbreak of World War I, the renewed outbreak of anti-Semitism
produced a new wave of migrations. These included numerous students
who were prevented from studying certain disciplines (particularly med-
icine) by the numerus clausus. *Finally, in the 1930s, the economic*
crisis and wretched living conditions returned to the fore.[1]

DEPARTURES

Emigration follows a classic scenario. In most cases, a close relative,
an uncle or a cousin, has already gone. Sometimes his traces are lost,
and there is no more news. But most often, family networks are estab-
lished. The first emigrants give information and advice. They invite
the others to follow their example. Another member of the family then
leaves, settles in the new milieu, and is joined by his wife and children.
He sends money to his parents in hopes that they will come with his

1. Cf. Nancy Green, *The Pletzl of Paris: Jewish Immigrant Workers in the
Belle Epoque* (New York: Holmes and Meier, 1986).

brothers and sisters. Then the formula is repeated. Almost always, part of the family remains in Poland. And the litany recurs—they never again saw their relatives, left behind, caught in the trap, victims of genocide. The grief is mixed with a sense of guilt because they couldn't help them in time.

Robert S.:

It's especially Jewish education that cements solidarity in the community and love in the family unit: the father for the children, the mother for the children, the children for the parents, all willing to sacrifice for each other.

Being a student in France—how should I call it, a premonition?—first, I sent for my sister, the youngest, to get her out of Poland. I didn't want to go back there. I was afraid of returning to Poland. I wanted to bring my whole family. Since I couldn't do that, bring them all together, with the means at my disposal, I proceeded in stages. So in '35, I sent for my sister. And in '37, I sent for my brother. I arranged for him to work in the student union in Nancy. He waited on students in the canteen in exchange for his meals. That's how I got them out . . . because if not, they would certainly have disappeared like my parents. Afterward, in '38, I saw nazism: it was the *Anschluss* with Austria, the Sudetenland, and they were talking about Poland. I wanted to get my parents out and also my older sister, who had stayed with them. When I proposed that to them, my sister answered in a letter that my parents were afraid of coming to France because, at their age, they were afraid they wouldn't be able to get used to French life, not knowing a word. . . . As for her, she didn't want to leave my parents alone. So much so that when the Germans invaded Poland and started deporting the Jews—at a certain time, my sister was staying with a priest who had become friendly with her and who wanted to hide her to allow her to escape—she didn't want to leave our parents. And she knew she was going to certain death with them. That's what the family is, the sacrifice of the parents for the children, of the children for the parents . . . [*His voice breaks, a long silence, a pause.*]

With relation to other emigrations, the emigration of the Jews of eastern Europe has its own particular dimension. The touching quality of the departure does not result only from the fact that they were parting from loved ones. They were also leaving a cultural environment (language, food, familiar places, the celebration of holidays, etc.) that constantly maintained a certain consciousness of identity, even in the least observant Jews. Hence the fears of those who remained: once led astray in modern Babylon, won't the emigrants be forced to lead a life that was less Jewish, and even be tempted to assimilate?

Yacob-Jacques L.:

For parents, it was a tragedy when children left. They're going to go to America, and they're going to work on Shabbat! They knew that people work on Saturday in America. For example, when my older brother left for Switzerland, my mother wept for weeks and weeks. "He'll be a goy, what good is life: *wos teug mein lebn*, what good is my life? My son will be a goy."

For all the family networks and mutual aid, let us not paint an overly idyllic picture, however. The sense of solidarity does not exclude conflict, jealousy, or simply the exploitation of the newcomers, whose youth and inexperience often made them easy prey. Evidence of this is the case of Golda R., who made several departures. Coming to France for the first time at the age of thirteen, she was tossed back and forth between two uncles, who fought over her work. She then returned to Poland.

When my older uncle, the first one, left for France, I was six weeks old. He left and we didn't hear anymore about him. Thirteen years had passed. I went to another uncle, one of his brothers, who lived in Marseille. He and his wife did some business on a ship. That uncle wrote my parents to ask them if they wanted to send me to France. My father was sick and wasn't very keen about the idea. But, when I heard "Paris," I wanted to go. The uncle sent a contract, and my parents signed the authorization.

I got to Paris. The uncle from Marseille had sent one of his friends from Paris to meet me at the station.

[. . .] We had lunch and then he went out to send a telegram to Marseille that he was putting me on the train that night. While waiting, I asked: "I have another uncle here, Sam. Maybe you know him?" "Sam lives next door, in the hotel." "Since my Uncle Sam lives next door, I won't go before seeing him."

The wife told him in French, but I didn't understand, that he shouldn't go there, that he wouldn't let me leave because the two brothers were mad at each other. He didn't listen to her. When my Uncle Sam heard that a niece had come from Poland, that she wanted to see him, he rushed over with his wife. Seeing me, he took me for one of his sisters.

"No, I'm Golda, Brocha's daughter."

"My God! You were six weeks old, and now you're a beautiful girl. Where are you going?"

"Hermann brought me. He sent me a contract."

"Hermann brought you to be a maid in his house, to take care of his children. A girl like you can have a nice career in Paris. I won't let you go to him."

He came down and didn't go to work. He was a very good tailor. He took cloth and made me a beautiful velvet suit and a beautiful coat with a fur collar. Then he took me to his bosses and introduced me. The boss's wife told me that in Paris I could have a good career, that she would teach me to be a finisher.

Hearing all that, the neighbor felt sick. My God, I sent a telegram! He sent another telegram to the uncle in Marseille to say that I wasn't coming, that his brother was keeping me. And the next day, my uncle came from Marseille to Paris. Since he was mad at his brother, he sent that same neighbor to ask me to come down. My uncle went out on the balcony and called the other one, his brother. They made up. And the other uncle came up.

"Why did you bring Golda? What do you want to do with her? You want her to be a maid in your house. I don't want her to go to you. I'm going to teach her a trade so that she'll be somebody."

So the other one left. And what did he do? He went to the police and declared that he had sent me papers, that my parents had signed. The next day, we were eating lunch and chatting, when somebody knocked on the door: "Police!" A policeman entered: "You're Sam G.?" "Yes." "This is your niece?" "Yes." "She doesn't have the right to be there. You're not the one who brought her. She must leave for Marseille. If not, she must return home, to Poland."

The policeman explained that the brother was within his rights; he had sent a contract; my father had signed. Otherwise, she would have to leave and if papers were sent to her, she could come back later. My uncle said to me: "Don't worry. Return home, I'm going to send you papers immediately and you'll come back." So I returned.

But such trips were not made so easily. It was not until about ten years later that Golda returned to France (preceded this time by her own parents, who had decided to emigrate).

CROSSING BORDERS

Emigrants supplied with valid passports and visas could legally cross Germany, where they sometimes stopped before landing in French railroad stations in Strasbourg, Metz, Nancy, or Paris. Sometimes these passports were false or partially faked. And many journeys, particularly those of political activists, were illegal, punctuated by the most unexpected vicissitudes. The memories of border crossings and tribulations through the countries of Europe and even Asia thus represent one of the strongest points of the narrative: the duration seems to be magnified (events are told day by day, hour by hour), while the rhythm speeds up in a host of episodes and details. People pass spontaneously to the present, and they act out incidents and restore dialogues with an amazing precision.

The wandering often begins in 1914, with the first wave of refugees fleeing the theater of military operations. We recall that Hélène H. was living in Bialystok, which was then located about twenty-five miles from the German border. Her father, a businessman, "who had big ideas for big deals," had gone to Sweden to buy a wagon of hairpins to sell them in the Russian and Polish markets. He was held up there by the outbreak of the war. Hélène H.'s mother decided to leave Bialystok with her three children and join one of her uncles who with-

drew to the Ukraine, to Ekaterinoslav.[2] The family remained scattered during the war, until the Russian Revolution.

We (my mother, my two brothers, and I) were still in Ekaterinoslav. We didn't have heat; we didn't have anything to eat. We ate oats. My father finally found us in Ekaterinoslav. They decided to go back to Poland. They had come to get him: the *Tcheka* was already active. He had probably been denounced as a bourgeois. But there was still great confusion, a big mess. They hurried. They sold everything they had, the furniture, the linen. I remember that I went to the countryside with a sack to get bread for our trip. We left with that and a *tschainik*, a tea kettle. That was very important because there was boiling water in all the railroad stations. You could make tea. With tea and bread, you could survive.

We traveled in cattle cars, passing through the north of Russia, Lithuania, because there weren't any trains, you took the train in whatever direction it was going. I remember very well the train station of Kursk. It wasn't in our direction at all. We spent one or two days on the platform of the station waiting for a train. At that railroad station of Kursk, I'll always remember the people who were there, exhausted, waiting for who knows what.

Then we went on. We tried to get back to Poland through Lithuania. It was very hard because there were still skirmishes.

Another problem was that we had sold all we had, and Soviet rubles weren't worth anything. In order to travel abroad, you needed Tsarist rubles, only with them could you buy anything.

Finally we were close to the Lithuanian border, and we started looking for a way to get to the other side. You had to have a pass and you waited a good long time, at least two weeks, in order to get it. We lived there, on the border, in terrible conditions, in a peasant's house. We didn't have anything to eat; we ate grass that we cooked. There were soldiers wandering around there, digging up potatoes in order to eat them green.

Finally we found a peasant who agreed to take us to the other

2. Now Dniepropetrovsk.

side, for money, naturally. When we came to the border, the soldiers asked us for a pass: "Who gave you that pass?" "Don't know!" Because what one officer granted, the one at the border didn't recognize.

There was nothing to do but go back to the village. There we waited a while longer. The problem was to find another border runner. The second one was a Jew, a Jewish driver (not a cab, a sort of wagon): "I've got a son on the other side. I'm going to see him, so I'll take you." OK. We got on and set out again. Did they give us another pass? I don't know anymore. He must have chosen another crossing, another entrance. But we got lost. We spent the night in the fields, somewhere in a kind of racetrack. Neither we nor the driver knew where we were going. But in that place we met a peasant, for me the kind they talk about in literature, that old man with a beard, barefoot. And we asked him the way. So he said: "If you go that way, you're going to meet the Red Army, and if you go that way, you're going to meet the Lithuanians. So you have to go that way." That is, between the two, through the woods.

In fact, he gave us false information; I don't know if it was deliberate. We were intercepted by a patrol of Lithuanian soldiers: "What are you doing there? You're spies!" Can you believe it? In that cart, with all that luggage and three children. They took us to a village. They were on horseback, and we were in the cart.

And all of a sudden, from the woods, someone started shooting at the patrol, with us in the middle. The driver speeded up; my brother started shouting. We heard the sound of a bullet: "I got hit!" It was the driver who was wounded. And we, we ran, we ran in order to get away from the shots passing over our heads. My father and mother got out of the cart in order to calm the horse, and since I was the oldest, they made me get out too. And I was holding the tschainik, the tea kettle, because you couldn't let go of that for anything in the world. It was very important. I ran till I was out of breath and I shouted: "I'm going to drop the tschainik, I'm going to drop the tschainik!" You had to run fast in order to get away from the shooting between the Reds and the Lithuanians, and I dropped the tschainik. It was a catastrophe. There was no more tschainik!

When we came to the village (this time, we had crossed the border), we were thirsty. We asked for water and they wouldn't give us any. They wouldn't give us any water because we were Jews. They saw that right away. They put us in a kind of shed while waiting for the authorities.

[. . .] We went on, and we came to a little town, I don't remember its name exactly. I think it was called Souvarov. That's where my grandfather's brother F. lived. We went to them, they welcomed us warmly, and we ate white cheese. I'll never forget that cheese. It was something extraordinary, that white cheese.

Georges F. tells of his clandestine entry into France:

I crossed the border with a group. I was the only one, almost the only one who succeeded: out of fifteen, two stayed, the others were turned back. I passed through Belgium and I was arrested. They didn't mistreat us too badly. They asked us where we wanted to go. We didn't say we were going to France; we said we were going to Germany. And they took us to the German border. There, a smuggler was waiting for us, the same one who had taken us to Poland, in Cracow. He knew we had been arrested, the whole group, and he was waiting for us at the border. He had told us in advance to say that we were going to Germany and not to Poland or to France. He knew where they would take us. They left us at the border; they sent us back. Then this smuggler found us. He took us in a taxi and brought us to Gare du Nord. There were fifteen of us, a group of fifteen. Of all those fifteen, two stayed in France—those who could pass through the nets. They were hunting for foreigners. It was me and one other who had a deportation order. He hid. He stayed anyway, until after the war. He passed away not long ago.

Léon W.:

All my brothers left without passports, clandestinely, thanks to smugglers. Yes, they paid. My mother came to France later because her oldest son was already living in Metz. He sent her proper papers to make the trip as a visit. And when my mother was already in Metz, on a visit, my brothers said to her: "Mama, now you won't go back to Kalisz again. You'll stay with us." "And the children who stayed there?" "Don't worry, they'll come too." I was nineteen years old at the time, and they didn't want to let me leave because of military service. We found a guy at the prefecture, who said to me: "Don't worry, I'll get you a passport." And he told some story about my going to France for an inheritance. They made me sign a paper: "Once you have the inheritance, you'll come back to Poland to do your military service." Sure I signed, and I got the passport. Then I went to Warsaw for the visa, and with that I came to Metz. Two years later, I was summoned by the consulate in Strasbourg. I didn't answer, I didn't go, and they didn't summon me again. That's how it was left.

Here is how Louise M. succeeded in leaving Nazi Germany:

I was married in Berlin, five years before. I left Berlin with two children, a little boy of four and a one-year-old baby. It was a very difficult emigration because my husband had already left for Morocco to see if we could move there, and I was supposed to follow him.

All of a sudden, one beautiful summer day, the Gestapo came to my house. They wanted to arrest my husband. They thought he was involved in some deal of transferring money. But you can't talk to the Gestapo. Three men came at six o'clock in the morning. They searched everywhere, under the beds, everywhere, and when they saw that my husband wasn't there, they said: "You're coming with us." At that time, I had a girl in the house. I could leave her with the children. They took me to Gestapo headquarters, to an office where a man began shouting right away. But I said I didn't know anything:

"OK, we're going to take you to the cellar. Once you've been in the cellar awhile, memories will start coming back to you."

So I really thought that my last hour had come. He said to me: "Now, get out and wait in the hall." I sat down. There was someone else there, a man sitting next to me, who told me he was a Jew. "What are you here for?" "I don't know." "But you can tell me." I understood right away that he was an informer. And then I realized, without anyone telling me, that they put me face-to-face with someone who was supposed to recognize me, and since he didn't recognize me, the other one in the office had me brought back. All of a sudden, he became almost human: "I'm going to let you go," and he gave me an exit pass. You had to go through a kind of tunnel. I was sure that when I went through that tunnel, they were going to kill me. But that wasn't the case.

The next day, the men from the Gestapo came back: "Show us your passport." I showed it. "Do you have a bank account?" "Yes." We had an account, not very much, but they froze it even so. So there I was, with my children, no passport, and no money.

My parents took us in. I stayed at their house for almost a year. And my husband was in Spanish Morocco, in Larache, with my sister and brother-in-law. Almost the same day the Gestapo came to my house, the Spanish revolution had started and Franco left that little town of Larache.

Even so, I found a lawyer, a lawyer who was a member of the National Socialist party and who became a good friend. The Jewish lawyers I had appealed to at first really were good for nothing, nothing at all. They were liars and hypocrites. But him, after almost ten months, he succeeded in getting my passport returned to me.

It was first to go to Holland, and the permit there was for only four days. After four days, I went to the consulate and when I came, they looked at a list. In the meantime, my German nationality had been taken away, which I didn't know. And they kept the passport. Then, afterward, there were some fateful blows. My little boy, who wasn't yet two, caught typhoid, and while taking care of him, I caught typhoid myself. Finally, even so, they gave me a paper that would allow me to leave and go to Morocco.

Let us follow the odyssey of Julien K., arrested as a Trotskyite in Poland. His trial took place in Warsaw.

The trial lasted almost the entire day. There was a break at night. We weren't prisoners; we were provisionally free. But it took a bad turn. I thought: It's going very bad, I mustn't stay here. I told another one of the accused, the only one who was from Cracow, I said to him: "Come with me. Otherwise, we'll be back in prison." He didn't want to. But I left the court right after the indictment. I quickly got my overcoat in the lobby. I think I even threw a coin, and I left. I meet my own lawyer and I don't say anything to him. He asked me: "You're going out to get something to eat?" "Yes, I'm going out to get something to eat." And I caught the first streetcar that passed by without even knowing where it was going.

Julien K. was sentenced in absentia to four years in prison.

I stayed with that tailor for a few weeks. At first I never went out. Then, I remember I let my moustache grow, and I wore dark glasses—very classic! The organization decided that I should stay in Warsaw for a while. In the beginning, I was wanted. It wasn't the time to leave. I had to wait until things calmed down. Then they decided (my father was also informed) that I would go to hide in Czechoslovakia, going through the mountains.

They took me to the train at the last moment, with a ticket of course. It was the night before Pentecost, and the train was packed. A lot of people were going to the mountains. There weren't vacations like now, but there were a lot of people even so. I get on the train, and, by chance, I overheard two men talking, one saying to the other: "There are police everywhere, they're looking . . ." It didn't have anything to do with me, but I was scared. Then we got to a station and, as agreed, at such and such a depot, the guys came to get me. They gave me a card from the Alpine Club, and that card was valid to cross the border. I was on an outing in the mountains, with fine shoes and a knapsack. Finally, we got to a road, the guides left, and I went down by the road. I was already on the Czechoslovakian side. I went into an inn and saw a big portrait of Masaryk.

Then I got on a train, but it stayed along the border too long to be going to Prague. I was afraid the Czech police would send me back so I changed my plan and came to Brno, in Moravia, in the middle of the night. I ate something at the station and then took the train for Prague. The address they had given me in Prague was the office of the German Social Democratic party. Those who greeted me thought at first that I was sentenced to four months or four weeks. They told me that it wasn't worth the trouble. . . . I said: "No! Four years!" So they put me in a kind of house where there were a lot of beds and, thanks to their efforts, I obtained the right of asylum, the right to stay in Czechoslovakia.

I rented a room and wanted to study, but I didn't do very much. I visited people in different areas, Trotskyites, people who gravitated to the Communist party. Many of them were illegal, and that's what ruined me. I stayed in Czechoslovakia for eight months. Those illegals were known to the Czech police. One day, there was a big roundup, and I was arrested too.

They found all sorts of brochures, Trotskyite journals, and letters in my house. They kept me at the police station, in difficult conditions, then they sent me to prison with those who were forbidden to stay and common criminals. My father intervened through the intermediary of the Ministry of Foreign Affairs and the Czech Consulate. That happened after Bénès's election as president. Then a commissioner made me an offer: "We know from certain letters found in your house that you want to go to France. We also know that the Social Democratic Committee is interested in you. It will help you to cross the Austrian border. Sign a letter saying that you wish to leave Czechoslovakia. The police won't escort you to the border. You'll have permission to stay in Prague for forty-eight hours to arrange your affairs. The committee will take care of getting you across the border secretly. Then you'll get yourself to Paris." I accepted. It's true that I wanted to go to France; that attracted me more than staying in Prague.

I was sent to a town close to the Austrian border. I remember that they were talking about the Popular Front, about Spain. This was in '36. They helped me cross the border, and I was in Austria, very far from Vienna. I took the train—I had to change—and came to Vienna, where a friend of my father was waiting for me. I stayed there for three months, completely illegally.

Then I did something very stupid. I didn't know and I was so furious with the Czech police: I thought they had cheated me. I found that they hadn't treated me very well because they had put me in a more or less healthy cell, with common criminals. From Vienna, I wrote an angry letter to that commissioner. When my father's friend found out, he shouted: "What did you do? What stupidity! I know he would have helped you go to France. He would have given instructions for the Czech Embassy in Vienna to give you a Czechoslovakian passport. You could have entered France legally with the passport." Naturally, that was out of the question now.

Then I met a member of the illegal Socialist party (this was during the time of Schusnigg).[3] Meanwhile, my father came to Vienna, and we even went to my grandfather's grave. My father left me some money. Now, in Vienna, I had found a first cousin whom I knew in Cracow. She was a little older than me and lived with a guy who turned out to be a crook. I found them in dire poverty. They really didn't have anything to eat. I took them to a restaurant. I lent them money. And he told stories about his brilliant prospects in the movies, that he would earn a lot. In fact, he had already squandered my cousin's money, and he proceeded to squander mine. I finally wound up pawning a suit! The result is that I didn't have very much when the day of my departure came.

We still had to go through the mountains, on skis, skiing from the high mountains (we had to do this whole expedition in April). I had done a lot of skiing in Poland, in the Tatras, but I wasn't really a good skier. It scared me a little. I left with somebody who was supposed to show me, guide me, like an instructor. He himself was something of a leftist socialist and had decided to come to France with me. He perished later, during the war in Spain. So we left on that expedition with very little money. We got to the Tyrol, to Landeck, and we climbed the mountain to a shelter called Eidelberg. Normally,

3. Austrian chancellor at the time of Anschluss.

we shouldn't have stayed there, but he made me practice. He didn't want me to plunge into that expedition, all the way to Switzerland, without doing at least forty-eight hours of skiing exercises. It was very hot—I stripped to the waist—so hot in the mountain sun that I got sunburned. I got sick, my face was burning, I couldn't shave, and I had a fever, a very high fever. For about two days, I had to stay in bed. My companion also got sunburned. The result was that we used up our supplies. And we had to eat and pay for that mountain shelter, at very high prices. We spent almost all our money.

We finally made it to Switzerland. But during the expedition, there was another mishap. I lost a ski. . . . In Switzerland, in Susch, we went to a hotel, with the little bit of money we had left. We decided to leave the skis and to hitchhike. In fact, we didn't have enough money to take the train. We were in the canton of Grisons, not very far from Davos, and the railroad belonged to a private company and was very expensive; you had to make a long trip to get to Zurich, Bâle, and the French border. While hitchhiking, he even begged. A Swiss family gave us something. Naturally, the Swiss didn't understand that we traveled without money.

At Zuoz, not far from Davos, the Swiss police arrested us. And I remember that the police were especially outraged by the fact that we didn't have any money. My companion was all right with his papers because he had an Austrian passport; at that time, Austrians could enter Switzerland without a visa. But I didn't have any passport. If only we had had money! The problem is that we didn't have any. I remember that the police-man wrote in his report: *In Schrift und Geldslosen Zustand,* "without papers and without money!"

So, they put us in a kind of prison. There were bars and a very nice view of the mountains. We stayed there one night and, in the morning, the policeman announced to us: "You came from Austria; we're sending you back to Austria." My compan-ion answered that that was fine, he was an Austrian. But I said I didn't want to because I was a political refugee and I wanted to go to France. So the policeman said to me: "You can go to France if you have the money to pay for your ticket, and a policeman will accompany you." Since I didn't have any, there was nothing I could do. I had to go back to Austria.

We returned to the town where we had come down, to Susch. The Swiss police checked everything: such and such a hotel, etc. We left the skis; we couldn't drag them around anymore. And they took us to the border, to Martinsbruck on the Inn: on one side of the river was Austria, on the other Switzerland. There was a bridge. So my companion said: "I'm crossing the bridge," and I was tempted to do it, but he gave me this advice: "Don't do it. If you want to go to France, put up some resistance. You're staying!" That's what happened. I said: "I'm not crossing." I resisted. They really roughed me up. They took me by the collar. They led me by force and dragged me halfway across the bridge. And since the other half of the bridge belonged to Austria, they went back. I stayed on the bridge. Between Austria and Switzerland, in the middle of the bridge.

The weather was quite nice. It was April, the end of April; but little by little, it began to get chilly. I had a backpack. I took out a sweater and threw it on, as if I didn't mind. I stayed on the bridge. The policemen had gone. On the Swiss side, right at the border, there was an inn: a little boy sent by the hotel-keeper came up to me and asked: "Are you hungry?"

Encouraged by this gesture, Julien K. returned to the Swiss side; the innkeeper allowed him to call a contact in Zurich (for a delivery of money from his father) but refused to give him a room for the night and advised him to go to the inn on the Austrian side.

I listened to him. I crossed the bridge. On the other side, the Austrian customs officials, who had seen the whole scene, almost burst out laughing: "Why were you afraid to come?" [. . .] So I went to the inn on the Austrian side: "How come you stayed on the bridge?" They offered me a room and a meal, without asking for money. They said: "You know, we're having hard times in Austria. Ever since the attempted putsch against Dollfus, German tourists don't come anymore. It's a disaster. Anyway, we hope that someday we'll be reunited with

Germany. We're Germans all the same." OK, I didn't say anything. I slept there. The next day, I wanted to call Zurich again, so I went to the Swiss side; I went back over the border and crossed the bridge again!

On the advice of the Austrian innkeeper, Julien K. went toward Feldkirchen to cross the Swiss border in another sector. On the way, in Landeck, another innkeeper, a Rumanian Jew, came to his aid: Julien's clothes being torn, he offered him "some kind of golfing knickers with white socks; that's what the Germans typically wear (we were in the Tyrol)." Then he put him in touch with the border agents of a Jewish network. They made him climb another mountain and his guide left him alone, showing him a path that went down to Switzerland. It was night, and a storm broke.

The young man had shown me that road but I was completely lost. I had missed the path! I was exhausted, soaked. I kept on going down, dirty, soaking wet. By now it was morning, and I didn't know where I was. But finally it turned out that I was still in Austria!

I came to a peasant's house, and he gave me some milk. He let me dry my clothes, and I slept in his barn. I told him I wanted to get into Switzerland illegally, and he said: "I'm going to help you. I have a field that's right next to the border. I'll show you. One of my cousins has a hotel in Lichtenstein. You'll go to him. Then you'll only have to cross the old Rhine. But stay away from Buchs because that's a border station. The Swiss police check there. Go to Haag, an internal station. Take the train for Saint-Gall, and you'll get to Zurich."

But that's not all. It also turned out that this peasant was a Nazi: "You aren't the first one I've helped to escape Austrian tyranny. Others passed through my field, and by now they're all in Germany!"

Even so, I tell him I'm from Poland. It happens that he's got a daughter, and he introduces me: *"Ein Volksgenosse aus Polen!"* A fellow countryman from Poland!

He gave me a sickle. I pretended to work, and we crossed the field. He showed me what path to follow when night came.

I did as he said and I got to that hotel, whose owner was probably a Nazi too. Then I got to that station of Haag, I took the train, I changed at Saint-Gall, and I made it to Zurich.

I went to see that woman who sent me money; she welcomed me very warmly. I stayed in her house for a few days. She gave me a letter from a comrade in Cracow, a leftist Socialist, who advised me to appeal to a Polish Socialist association in Zurich. When I went to the building, I learned that the association had been there before the war of '14, but it no longer existed! They told me to go to the building of the Swiss trade unions. But there was a meeting going on—I should come back later, in two hours. So I went for a walk. I was still dressed like that, in my white socks. It was typically German, but I didn't know that. And the plainclothes cops arrested me: "You're German? Show your papers."

I told them I'm not German but, since my papers weren't in order, they arrested me, and I was sentenced to one day in custody for crossing the border illegally. Then they went with me to get my bags at that lady's house, and they put me in a train, in a barred car. "Where are you taking me?" "To Bâle. We're going to try to get you into France, since you have chosen that border. We're helping you, but be warned that if you don't succeed, if they send you back, we'll have no choice but to send you back where you came from, that is, to Austria."

I came to Bâle. I stayed one more night in the police station; it wasn't a prison. Besides, there's a policeman there who didn't understand. He thought I was being sent back to Germany. He makes a gesture like that: "What kind of blows you're going to get!" The next day, a Swiss agent took me: "You go down that street, there. There's a little field. You cross it and you're in France, in Saint-Louis. You go on, and you'll find a bus or a train station for Mulhouse."

I crossed. I went as far as the station. I saw that there was a train for Paris, but I didn't have much time. I changed Swiss francs into French francs, and I ate something. Everything was going fine until suddenly a French cop approached me and said, in Alsatian dialect: *"Sie san a Ditcher?"* You're German?

I said no, but since I didn't have a passport, he took me to the police station. The commissioner, a bearded man, spoke French: "Listen, they've been very strict about the right of asylum ever since King Alexander of Yugoslavia was assassinated. Tell me honestly, who sent you here to France? The International Red Help?"

"No, it's not the International Red Help."

"Search him!"

So they found the paper of the Swiss police.

"Ah! It's the Swiss police! We have to send him back!"

A policeman took me on the back of his motorcycle. He took me to the Swiss border station, holding the paper:

"Here, he's yours, take him!"

The Swiss police were furious. They were in a kind of barracks. They were very friendly, and they shared their own food, a very good meal, with beer. And they got mad: "Those bastards! In the country of freedom, after the victory of the Popular Front in the elections. They send you back like that, a political refugee. It's outrageous, scandalous!"

"You're right, but by the way, I'd like to ask you why I can't have the right of asylum in Switzerland?"

"Why, it's not the same thing. Switzerland is a little country. That poses problems. In France, there are so many foreigners, she can allow herself."

They took me back to Headquarters and explained to me: "We're not going to send you back to Austria again. We're going to try again. Since you went to the train station last time, don't go back there. Take the bus."

I felt uncomfortable because I wasn't shaved. I wanted to go to a barber, but the Swiss police wouldn't let me: "We don't have time!" So, on the French side, I went and got a shave. Everything went well, but all of a sudden, there was a scene like one in an American film I had seen, *I Am a Fugitive*. One of the station cops came into the barber shop! But he didn't recognize me. When I left I said: "Good-bye, gentlemen," and I remember the cop answered, "Good-bye, Monsieur."

I saw a bus and I asked if it was going to Mulhouse: "No, it's going to Belfort." "OK, that's all right." I spent a day in Belfort. I walked around and ate an excellent meal with so many hors d'oeuvres that I couldn't finish the rest of it. I thought it was very expensive. I remember what I paid: fourteen francs. Late in the afternoon, there was a train, and I got to Paris that night.

THE HOST COUNTRY

After arriving in France, time in memory passed faster; it flowed in rhythm with moving and changing jobs. Through the diversity of individual destinies, recurrent themes emerge here too: of work, tenacity, effort.

In the "Jewish" trades (tailors, tanners, furriers, etc.), the newcomers followed the network of relatives and immigrants who preceded them. Those who came to France at the end of the nineteenth and the beginning of the twentieth century ran little workshops or shops, and the influx of immigrants between the wars provided an abundant and generally submissive labor force.[4] The economic crisis emphasized the return to "Jewish" trades, organized according to the characteristic system of putting out work from patterns. Recent immigrants, often lacking a resident permit, subject to the competition of their co-religionists, and constantly fearing arrest (followed by expulsion), worked at home, illegally, for poor salaries. Home, for many of them, was reduced to one unhealthy room into which a half dozen people were crowded: freed to set their own pace, these homeworkers, in fact, imposed upon themselves a brutal work load.

Maurice N.:

I was living in that hotel [*in Belleville*]; there were only Jews there. There were six of us in one room. My father didn't earn very much. At that time, he was a deliveryman. So my mother helped him, with the four kids. But even so, she helped him a little, whatever she could do at home. And I gave a hand too.

As soon as I was thirteen, I went to work in the tannery. At thirteen. I had had only one year of schooling in France, but nevertheless I had to work. My father was then earning about

4. David Weinberg, *A Community on Trial: The Jews of Paris in the 1930s* (Chicago: University of Chicago Press, 1977); Cf. also Nancy Green, *The Pletzl of Paris.*

two hundred francs a week. I worked for a Jewish homeworker, as a tanner, which was eighty-eight to ninety hours a week. I earned a franc an hour, so I brought home ninety francs a week; that was an enormous sum. My father's two hundred francs and my ninety francs, that was a lot. And I went on working like that, all those hours, when there was a lot of work. When there wasn't much, you did fifty or sixty hours. And when there was a lot of work, you did as much as ninety hours.

My relations with my boss were very good. He was a very interesting man, who helped me in a lot of things. When I read a book, the two of us discussed it. He was a Jew from Lodz; he was deported later on. I stayed with him until 1936, the time of the Popular Front. He then proposed that I become his partner, but I didn't want to. I was already a radical and I left him. I went to work for another boss.

Several options developed outside the Jewish networks, however. The usual difficulties of every migration then stood out even more sharply: apprenticeship in the language, isolation in a foreign environment, adaptation to other customs. Certain subjects that were recalled in the previous episodes on departures recur, but with a new twist: people stressed the excellence of professional training acquired in the homeland and their passion for work as opposed to the norms of the host country. Furthermore, ingenuity took the more French form of resourcefulness. Henceforth, the notion of progress was confused with integration into the new milieu and a rise in the social hierarchy.

Yacob-Jacques L.:

They had given me a name of someone in the area of Montbéliard—a Jew who might help me. I didn't know a word of French. When I got to his house, he said to me, in German: "If there isn't enough work to keep my own workers busy all week, how can I hire you?" I asked him what I should do. "Go to the surrounding villages." I remember as if it were yesterday. When I left—I was already on the bottom step and he was on the top—he called me, came down: "Monsieur, here's twenty francs." At that time, that was money. But I was proud. That upset me: "Monsieur, I'm looking for work. I'm not a beggar."

I spent the whole day going from village to village. They didn't understand me, and I didn't understand them. I was so tired, so tired. What could I do? At night, I saw a café and went in. I spoke to the boss, but he didn't understand a word. So many years have passed and I still remember. So, I asked the girl who was waiting on me: "Do you speak German?" "Yes." "Oh, I'm saved." I told her that I was looking for work. They gave me a room and the next day, the boss said to me: "I understand now. I'm going to make a phone call." Then the girl explained to me: "They want you in Beaucourt, at Japy Brothers."

OK. I went to Beaucourt. The manager received me, but he didn't know what I wanted. Unfortunately, he didn't speak German. He called a girl who worked in the factory. She saw that I didn't understand. "The manager is asking you what you want." "I'm looking for work. Here's my passport, my visa, everything is in order." "Oh, yes, they called me. OK, what can you do? In our clockmaker's shop, the manufacture is divided into three parts: the first is apprenticeship, molds and wheels; the second is the escapement, the wheel that makes the watch go; the third is setting it in cases and putting on the frame and the hands." The girl asked me what I wanted to do: the first or the last part? She didn't mention the second part, the hardest. But I said that I wanted to do the escapement, to make the watches go. The manager: "Somebody who comes from Poland, who hasn't been to school, wants to do the hardest work?" "Yes, I can do it. I did it in Warsaw." "OK, I'm going to give you that work, but, note, if you can't do it, we won't change your job. We just won't hire you." "Fine, I agree."

So they made a place for me to work. The workers came to watch me. They brought me tools, if I needed this or that. In Poland, you don't see that. And the manager also stayed near me. So I called the girl over: "Tell the manager to let me work alone. I can't work when people are watching me." They left, and, of course, I did the job. The girl took it and brought it to the manager. I knew how it would end. The manager called me over: "What school did you go to?" "Yes, I went to school!"

"What school?" "Michel School." So, he loc
tionary of watchmaking schools and didn't fi.
explained to the girl: "Tell the manager he's w
father who's called Michel!" He shrugged, and, of c
hired on the spot.

[Two years later, Yacob-Jacques L. goes into business for h.

I saved up and I became a manufacturer. I brought independent workers. I always had four or five, sometimes twenty
workers, Jews from Poland. I lived in Beaucourt, a village of
five thousand inhabitants. Some said: "See, a Jew who can't
even speak French correctly and he's a manufacturer already.
And us, our great-great-grandfather worked for Japy." So,
what did I do? I said to them:

"Listen, gentlemen, what do you do at night?"

"Oh, at night, I go out, I go to a friend's house, play a game
of cards, or go to bed early."

"Me, at night, I work until midnight, you know? And on
Sunday? "

"I go fishing."

"Me, on Sunday, I work all day long. If you had done as I
do, you'd be a manufacturer too. There's no miracle."

*The language problem was posed most sharply for immigrants who
came to France to continue their studies. Their Polish diplomas were
not recognized, and they were forced to begin their entire course of study
all over again. Robert S. represents the typical case of the poor student
who worked at night to prepare for his examinations and in the day
not only to support himself but also to help his parents, who remained
in Poland. The trials he endured demanded great patience and an un-
common strength of character. Having arrived in France in 1928, at
the age of twenty, he could not pass his final examination until after
the war, in 1946, and finally set out on his own.*

I arrived in France, in Nancy, on October 28, 1928. I got off
at the train station with ten francs in my pocket. I went to see
a friend who had already finished school the previous year, and
who was living in a hotel. I didn't speak French; in Nancy they
spoke German. I said to the owner of that hotel: "Monsieur, I

. have ten francs; I'll give them to you to guarantee me a room for a week. Now, do you know anyone who might put me to work? I need to earn my living, I want to study, and I don't have any money. I don't want charity." And I told him that I was a Jew. "Well," he answers, "I just happen to know somebody who's a Jew." That was my future father-in-law, who had a little factory where he made boxes. No sooner said than done. He hired me. I prepared the boards in exchange for something to eat and pocket money, which I sent home. It wasn't much, but with the exchange rate, it allowed them to make do in Poland.

Unfortunately, my future father-in-law fell on hard times with his operation. I had to look for work and was one of the first students to come up with the idea of going to the streetcar company: I could work at the streetcar depot at night, which would leave me the day for my studies. So I worked from nine o'clock at night to five o'clock in the morning. My work in the depot consisted of washing the cars. At five o'clock, I went to bed; at seven, I was up. I went to school from eight o'clock to noon, from two to five. At five o'clock, I returned home, went to bed to sleep a little, and then started to study and review. I earned a good salary: a hundred fifty francs a week; that was six hundred francs a month. Of the six hundred francs, I kept a hundred and fifty for myself (for my room, my studies, food) and regularly sent home four hundred fifty francs a month, for my parents.

I emphasize that when I came to France, I didn't know French. So I started to work on grammar by taking time from my sleep. And when I finished work on the car, if I had an hour left, I hid so as not to be caught, and I crammed. I can say that the irregular verbs and so on gave me a rough time!

During the summer vacation, I didn't go back to Poland like my friends. I was afraid of getting stuck there for lack of money and not having any means by which to feed my parents. I was obsessed about it. I think that if I hadn't been able to leave again, I would have committed suicide.

So I opted to sacrifice my trip to Poland and instead to work to save enough money for my studies and for my parents' needs.

During the school year, I worked at night since I had to go to classes during the day. But during vacations and on holidays, I worked during the day, as a conductor. And even better: I did two days in one. How? Work on the streetcar was done from five in the morning to one o'clock—that's eight hours. And I started again at three o'clock until late at night. This worked out because the Frenchman took advantage of the fact that there was someone who could replace him. He said: "I want to go dancing with my girl," and it was Sunday, a holiday, or during the week. They knew I was willing to take the shift. At my age, I could work two shifts and, especially, by earning two days in one, I could reward myself with a meal, which, for me, was a real treat. What did it consist of? It's something extraordinary when I think of it now. I could pay myself with a steak, fries, and salad, a meal that was typically French, but for me, it was a royal feast!

I enrolled for the second year. I did it and when the vacations came, I asked myself again: "Am I going to Poland to see my parents?" I made an accounting, and, again for the same reasons, I deprived myself of the pleasure of that trip. I must add that if I had known how things were going to turn out, I certainly wouldn't have made that choice because I never saw my parents again.

For me, seeing how events were unfolding, there was never a question of my going back to Poland. At any price. I brought my sister from Poland, sending her money for the trip. At the outset, I got her hired as a cleaning woman at the cinema. She was a dressmaker. And little by little, she managed to find some customers; she made dresses, in secret, at home. [. . .]

My university diploma didn't give me the right to practice in France. There were two conditions *sine qua non* to be able to practice in France: to have an official diploma and, in addition, to be a naturalized Frenchman. For naturalization, you had to go through the union (of dentists), to get their approval, which they almost never granted. I remembered Député S., who had offered me his help. I explained to him: "I have to convert my diploma into an official diploma. I'll do that no matter how much time I have to devote to getting the French baccalaureate.

I'll slave away. But I can't commit myself as long as I'm not sure of obtaining French citizenship." He had me put together a file with all my work certificates. The whole thing didn't take long—he made me a royal gift. On the very day I received my diploma, in 1933, I received the order to pay the costs of naturalization, and I was naturalized. It was rare at that time, especially for a dental student: the union was vigilant in not letting anyone get through; you had to have a helluva talent to get their approval.

Thus, Robert S. set out to pass the baccalaureate. While he prepared for the examination, he obtained a position as attendant in a municipal library (where, despite his protest, they wanted to appoint him). Finally, the great day came:

So, I showed up for the first baccalaureate exam. I remember it as if it were yesterday. There was an open-ended topic: "Romain Rolland, in one of his works (I don't know which one anymore), says that he believes in the future of aviation. Say whether you agree with him and why." With my leftist leanings, if I dare say so, I defended the idea that if aviation could bring people together, contribute to brotherhood, I agreed; but if it had to serve war and destruction, no. And the inevitable happened, of course: I had the bad luck to fall on some turkey who gave me a low grade. By cross-checking, I was able to identify the teacher and I asked him politely to explain to me: "I don't claim that my essay was perfect, but did it really deserve that grade?" He answered me: "Monsieur, in our view the baccalaureate candidate is not asked to state what he thinks but what others, more qualified than he, have said." That meant you mustn't choose an open-ended topic because he judged that the candidate wasn't fit to deal with it.

After hearing this reasoning, what did I do? During the vacation for the second session, I took out of the library the four volumes of Faguet, the best critic of French literature at that time. And I memorized all the authors of the four centuries, Ronsard, Rabelais, and so on. I invested a lot of time, and more than once, I wept with rage; but without it I couldn't go any further. Came the baccalaureate exam, with the classical subject: "Which do you prefer, the theater of Corneille or of Racine?" Predictably, I grabbed Racine, and recited Faguet's reasoning (since they didn't ask me for my own opinion).

So I get through the first part of the baccalaureate, that was in '37, and started preparing for the second part. And there came the first mobilization, at the time of Munich. I couldn't take the exam. When I came back, I continued to prepare, and then it was cut off for good: the war began.

The epilogue of that "apprenticeship" came only in 1946:

We returned to Clermont-Ferrand, and I enrolled as a candidate for the second baccalaureate. I could have taken advantage of special arrangements, as a Frenchman who had fulfilled his military obligation during the war and who had served in the Resistance. But I didn't want to. I had the first baccalaureate, and I wanted everything to be equal with my French countrymen so that they wouldn't someday come accusing me of having taken advantage of war conditions. It was my right and my pride. So I passed the second baccalaureate, like all the others.

My naturalization, abrogated under Pétain, was now restored. I had only to convert my university diploma into an official diploma. At that time, the law demanded another five years, but in my case, they authorized me to present the five years in a single examination.

I came to Nancy. I worked in a garret (I remember the hotel) during the month of August. It drove me crazy. I knew my material inside out. Now, on the panel, there was one truly comtemptible individual, a pharmacology professor, an anti-Semite who was always picking on me: nothing I answered was any good. To make this clear, I have to point out that one of my buddies, H., who had gone to school with me, had become dean of the dental school. When I told him about my troubles, he himself went to the dean of the School of Medicine and it turned out that the latter was none other than the officer I had served with (as a medical orderly) throughout the war. So he sent for me: "What's this all about?" I explained that I had to convert my diploma into an official diploma. "In short," he said, "you had the right to get yourself killed for France but you don't have the right to live for France. That's not right and it can't be. Enough already. You've passed the exam. For grades, they'll take the file you had in 1933: you passed the exam once, that's enough. You did all that had to be done as a Frenchman. I can testify to it. Now, let's talk about something else."

And that's how, with the diploma, I could finally set myself up with everything in order.

NEW GHETTOS

As we have seen, in the "Jewish trades," the immigrants formed networks where they were among themselves, more or less isolated in the midst of French society. They certainly did not re-create the environment they had left: the demographic and cultural context turned out to be too different (kosher food or the rhythm of the Jewish holidays, for example, were no longer imposed with the same strictness as in Poland); and migration tended to accelerate the process of secularization begun in the homeland. But people did continue to socialize with Jewish friends, and though gatherings were henceforth held on Sundays rather than Saturdays, people still shared common memories, exchanged news, and were with their own.

Mutual aid societies, or Landsmanshaften, *formed by those who came from the same community, multiplied between the two world wars. At first essentially funeral societies, they expanded their activities little by little, eventually including social, cultural, or educational services. In the late 1930s, there were almost two hundred such associations in Paris, which embraced half of the Jews from eastern Europe (more than twenty thousand families).[5] They evidenced the vitality of immigrant Yiddish culture in the most varied forms: newspapers, libraries, theatrical and athletic activities. Very often, Yiddish continued to be spoken within the family circle, at least by the parents, even if the children preferred to answer in French. Paradoxically, in some cases, young immigrants did not really learn Yiddish until after they come to France.*

5. David H. Weinberg, *A Community on Trial.*

Bernard P.:

The Jewish community in Roanne then numbered about forty or sixty families, all from Poland, or more or less Polish: from Galicia, Poland, Lithuania, *Galizianer, Polak, Litvak*: that's who they are. Every Saturday, we got together. On Saturdays or Sundays, probably on Sundays. We gathered in a building that belonged to the community. We had meetings, we took excursions to the countryside. And we also danced; we got together to sing. We were young in those days. But that activity always took place with a Zionist background [. . .] We lived among Jews. My still rather imperfect knowledge of the French language would have prevented me from living outside that Jewish community. Besides, it's in Roanne that I really learned to speak Yiddish. I knew a bit; I could figure out the alphabet since I had learned Hebrew, but I learned to read and figure out Yiddish in my first months in France.

We lived essentially in a Jewish environment. Social visits, dates—we had them with the few girls from our own milieu. My wife was one of them (my wife here now).

Mathilde R.'s parents, however, decided that the only solution to the Jewish problem was assimilation. So they banished Yiddish from the house on principle and even went so far as to put their daughter in a Catholic school. Nevertheless, Yiddish cropped up in snatches, in the mother's words of affection to her daughter. And the family group preserved the culture of the homeland (Russia in this case) as a point of reference, as if, despite their integration into the French environment, they needed to recall their own distinct identity.

When I was born, my parents had the strange notion that the solution to the Jewish problem was assimilation. OK, they weren't the only ones. But for them, the solution was to play the ostrich, to put their heads in the sand so as not to be seen. So I wasn't supposed to be told I was Jewish. Which meant that I spent my childhood, up to '38, without knowing, consciously at any rate. Finally, there were strange things that stirred my curiosity. For example, my parents, who spoke Russian with each other when they didn't want me to understand, sometimes said: "They're one of us," speaking of people who were neither Russian nor Polish. I found that puzzling.

"They didn't speak Yiddish?"

No, not at all. They must have known it in their childhood, but they really forgot it.

The only thing is that my mother, in her moments of tenderness, sometimes said affectionate things to me in Yiddish: "*mein teures Kind.*" I remember that. I had no idea what it meant. Finally she told me what it meant, "my dear child." But in what language? I really don't know what explanation she gave me.

In any case, there was that puzzle: to be one of us, when you're neither Russian nor Polish, what does that mean? I had a vague explanation, consciously; that is, it spun around in my head. I thought that maybe foreigners were ours because they were foreigners. And sometimes they said it about people who seemed French to me and that must have complicated the puzzle even more.

So I lived in that kind of extreme ambiguity, both from the cultural point of view and from the religious point of view, with something nevertheless that was a unifying element, to a certain extent, because it wasn't just anyone who told me at that time that I was a Jew. It was my aunt, my father's older sister (who was deported in '42; I found her name in Klarsfeld's book not long ago).[6] And that aunt—I would say that in her house, it wasn't Jewish culture, although probably it was in the atmosphere and in the air. But it was a kind of Russian culture. When we gathered together, my parents sang with her in Russian or told me Russian stories. When I was still very little, I had already heard about Russian writers, Russian poets, or Russian composers. In short, Russia was a great magnetic pole. There was no talk of Jewishness.

POLITICAL ACTIVISTS

Political activists (Communists, Bundists, or Zionists, with their multiple shades and variations) also had their own mutual aid societies,

6. Serge Klarsfeld, a French lawyer who, with his wife Beatte, has been very active in hunting Nazis and collaborators.

youth movements, and cultural groups.[7] In their own way, these networks fostered a solidarity based on common culture and memory. Thus, the Communist activists, while preaching the dissolution of Jewish identity in proletarian internationalism (unlike the Bundists), were nevertheless grouped in the Yiddish language subsection of the Party. The fact of affinity and residence (the immigrant population being concentrated in certain quarters of Paris: the IVth, XIth, or XXth arrondissements) meant that activists of Jewish origin were grouped in the same cell.

Marc B.:

In 1925, I came to Paris. Since I had good friends who were tanners, I could get work right away. The same week, I got in touch with the Bundists in Paris. There was a café, 50 Rue des Francs-Bourgeois. All the Bundists gathered there, on the first floor, and they created the Medem Club. Because in the meantime, Medem, the leader of the Bund, had passed away in New York. We didn't have a building right away. We organized conferences, and we went on outings, to acquaint the new immigrants with cultural life in France. They put me on the committee of the Medem Club right away. In 1928, Nomberg, a great Jewish writer, passed away. They organized a memorial evening; the greatest writers—Sholem Ash, Schneour—came to that evening. They said: "We'll charge a fee, and whatever we take in will be used to create a library." We collected a certain sum and created that library, which was in that café. We bought a big cabinet, which still exists in the building we bought in 1928. Then, the first thing, we got offers from people who had books, and we bought them. I was one of the founding members of that library. In the Medem Library, there are still photographs of the first committees that created it. There are only two living members left from that committee, Monsieur W. and me. We went on like that. Then, when our movement grew, we rented other buildings, bigger, more comfortable ones. The last one was 110 Rue Vieille-du-Temple. We already had a big building; the library kept growing.

7. Cf. Nancy Green, *The Pletzl of Paris.* David H. Weinberg, *A Community on Trial*, pp. 51–62.

In 1932, we founded the social club Arbeiter Ring. The building, the entire building, belonged to that club. There wasn't a Jewish artist, a Jewish writer passing through Paris who didn't have a meeting in the building—110 Rue Vieille-du-Temple. Not only did we make an auxiliary of the Bund in Poland but also a Socialist movement, the Bund in France. We published a paper, the *Wacher,* the Awakening. I wasn't particularly one of the leaders; my goal was cultural, the library. In 1932, they also set up the mutual aid society. There were various categories of people who didn't have Social Security. They could enroll in the society and be fully covered. We also set up the community burial vaults in 1938. I wasn't part of that group at that time, but it existed! During the war, in the social circle, they set up a canteen to help women whose husbands had gone into the army as volunteers.

Maurice N.:

I became active in the Communist youth in '33 or '34. I was thirteen or fourteen years old. It was in Paris. First I was in the youth of the XXth. Most of them were French. There weren't many Jews, just a few. Right after, I joined the youth of the XIth because there were Jewish friends down there, so I changed my neighborhood.

In the Communist youth, they didn't label you a Jew or a non-Jew. At that time, they were seeking assimilation, like everybody else, like the French.

[. . .] I played football, did gymnastics. The Y.A.S.C. was a club that had five or six hundred members. Relations with non-Jews? You know, we didn't hang around together. We pretty much created our own ghetto . . .

Among leftist activists, Julien K. followed an original path, independent of the predominantly Jewish networks. We recall that he arrived in Paris after many vicissitudes, at the time of the victory of the Popular Front. After a few months, he decided to go to Spain to fight in the International Brigade with the Republicans. He was sent to the Aragon front.

It really was a strange war. We didn't have weapons, we did some exercises. The rest of the time we argued, we took sunbaths, and from time to time, we shot. The only expedition I went out on was at night. We went to the enemy trenches; we swiped a case of weapons from them. It wasn't a big deal. We had two or three wounded.

Among those who were with me, there was one—I learned much later who he was. He was the famous writer Orwell, the author of *Nineteen Eighty-Four*. He was wounded in my presence, right next to me. What was his name? Blair. I didn't find out who it was until years later because he wrote a book on Catalonia under his real name. Reading it, I realized it was Orwell. By then he was dead, because for a long time I hadn't known who he was. He was very tall and, once, when he stood up without thinking, a good shot on the Fascist side wounded him. We took him to the hospital in Barcelona.

OK, I stayed on that so-called front, I went on leave to Barcelona, I went back to the front, then again to Barcelona. There, there was the famous event of May 3, the civil war, the attempt of the Communists to liquidate the P.O.U.M.[8]

There was a big raid against the P.O.U.M., and that's where they arrested me. They took me to the police station, then to the passport office, Calle Corsega, which they had made into a kind of prison, an illegal prison, because it wasn't official.

At first, you had the impression that it would be terrible. We were four men, they locked us in a little room with no window, with barely any air, without anything: "You're going to sleep there, on the ground." There were also women, but they gave them a nice room, on the first floor, with beds. So, we revolted, we banged on the door, and, finally, after they yelled at us, we weren't locked up in that little cell anymore. We could sleep on a bench, and the lucky ones got a mattress on the floor.

One fine day, they said to us: "Get ready, you're leaving!" They put us in a truck, without telling us where we were going. We thought they were taking us to Carcel Modelo, but no, they

8. P.O.U.M. was a Trotskyite group.

took another road and we saw that we were leaving Barcelona. We were taking the highway. I remember that I was struck to see the inscriptions of the P.O.U.M.: "*Gobierno de la derrota que has hecho de Nin?*" We continued on. They took us in fact to the French border. We didn't have any papers anymore, nothing, because they had taken everything from us when they arrested us, even our photos, and they didn't return anything. So we wondered what the French would do with us.

LOVE AFFAIRS

Emotional life is recalled in the memories we have collected only with modesty and discretion. They do confirm that for the young immigrants of the 1920s and 1930s, even those who were totally cut off from religion, the possibility of marriage with a non-Jew generally seemed unthinkable. In fact, friendships and work relations, as well as the network of associations, favored unions between immigrants or between immigrants and the children of immigrants. This rejection of mixed marriage was already much less evident in the next generation.

The tale of Golda R. allows us to follow the lively and chaste love affairs of a girl who came to France in the 1930s. In its mix of sentimentalism, melodramatic situations, and theatrical strokes, the episodes she relates seem to come straight out of a popular novel. Despite loyalty to Jewish endogamy, doesn't this very "dated" style of amorous life indicate a certain form of acculturation?

When you're in Paris, you meet people. Matchmakers proposed marriage. They introduced me to a young man. In Poland, he had been a doctor, in Minsk Mazowieck. Here he couldn't practice. He wasn't allowed. So he made deals. He was very religious, very orthodox, but my father wasn't so religious. My mother was already used to Paris. She had to work on Saturdays. When he came, she hid the machine. She wasn't permitted to work. He was so religious! When he got a letter on Saturday, he wouldn't open it before night, before seeing a star in the sky.

"*Golditchke* (he was a Litvak), I want to marry you.".

"But I'm not religious. You're too religious for me."

We went walking on the Buttes-Chaumont. It was very hot, but he said that he was forbidden to go drink in a café. It wasn't allowed; it was Saturday. And he was very stingy. I didn't want a miser. Since he was a peddler, I said to him once, in a joke:

"You sell sweaters—bring me one, a white one."

Comes Saturday, he didn't bring me anything.

"But I would have paid for it! Go away and don't come back."

Still, he came back every Saturday. [. . .] At that time, my father died. He had a cousin, a woman, who lived near us. He came back, went to see his cousin, and then came to our house:

"My little Golda, I saw your father in a dream. He told me that we should get married, the two of us." "Listen, if my father had loved you when he was alive, and if he ordered me to marry you in a dream, maybe I would do it. But my father didn't like you. He didn't appear to you in a dream. Stop pestering me. Go find somebody else."

[. . .] In the shop where my mother and my brother Leibl worked, there was a presser. He said to my brother: "It seems you have a sister. I'd really like to meet her. Why doesn't she come?" As soon as I heard there was a young man who wanted to meet me, I didn't want to go there. My mother said: "Come help me turn one or two coats." I didn't want to.

One Sunday when my mother was out walking with my cousin, she met him, Chil. He came up to my mother and asked her: "This is your daughter?" "This is my sister's daughter." "Will you allow me to walk with you?" "Why not?" They continued walking, and they arranged that the next rendezvous would be at our house. Chil began coming to our house; he came every night. Once he said to me: "No luck. I talked about you and now I meet you. Why didn't I meet you sooner?" "What difference does it make since you're going out with my cousin?"

He visited her for maybe six months. I said to my cousin: "Rosette, how long are you going to drag on with Chil and work for nothing for your brother? You can get married. You'll work, you and Chil, you'll be able to live." She answered me: "You're right." She went back home and told her brother that she was dating a young man and wanted to get married. Her brother started roaring: "You want to take a presser! You wretch, you'll die of hunger!" Another imbecile would have answered: "What more do I have in your house?"

So, this Chil was a presser. He didn't have any money, no house. He slept in a hotel. He didn't squander his earnings; he kept it to take her to the movies. When Rosette came to us for lunch, we told her to bring Chil: if there's enough for three, there's enough for four. Let him eat with us. My mother said: "Listen Rosette, I'm going to rent you a room. Don't work anymore for nothing for your brother. Get married."

So, they decided to apply to city hall. Rosette had trouble getting a birth certificate, but her mother sent her some sort of certificate from Poland. When her brother Max learned that she had been to city hall, he made a scandal: "Your cousin convinces you so that you'll be miserable. They want to bury you!" It was Saturday night, the brother came to our house, and they started fighting, her brother and her fiancé. Tables and chairs were flying, a disaster! After such a battle, there was no more talk of marriage.

Chil kept on coming to our house. He had become my brother's friend. He liked it at our house. If he didn't show up one night, he missed our home. He came every night. Once, something happened. It was maybe eleven o'clock. I was already sleeping, but my mother had brought some work home from her boss. She was still up. The windows looked onto the street; he saw the light and came up.

My mother looked at Chil and realized that he hadn't eaten all day; his veins were blue. She came to wake me up:

"Golda, come do a good turn. Give Chil something to eat; I don't dare invite him."

I got dressed; I went in: "Why have you come so late?"

"I was coming from my sister Esther's, and I saw the light."

It was winter. We had pickled herring, jellied calves' foot. There was always something to eat in our house. "Chil, do you want to eat something?"

I served him, he ate. My mother went to bed, my brother was sleeping, and I stayed with him. So he said to me: "Golda,

I want to tell you something. Fate wants you and not Rosette to be my wife."

"Chil, that's impossible. Since you were going out with Rosette, I can't go with you."

I knew everything that was going to happen. Chil started to talk. He didn't stop talking, all night long, until it started to turn light. He talked so much that I finally said yes. I gave my word. And he: "I swear to you that Rosette is nothing to me. She's not the one I have in my heart. It's you that I love, but I was wrong, I did everything wrong."

My mother had heard everything. Just imagine. In the morning, when she came in, he rushed to her and hugged her: "I was supposed to become your sister's son-in-law; I prefer to be yours."

No sooner did I say yes than I regretted it. The neighbor came in, Roïsse. We were all from the same shtetl, Otwosk. When she heard the story, she said: "Golda was for you, not Rosette!" And my brother: "Since that's how it is, Chil, don't stay in the hotel, with all the expenses. I sleep alone in my room. Come, you'll stay with me."

But things turned out badly. A few months later, Golda and her family discovered that the "fiancé" had returned to Rosette and her family. They threw the traitor out.

And Rosette took him back. But a little while later, her brother told him that he had no more work for him.

"If that's how it is, I'll take a gun and kill myself. I'm going to kill Rosette, and I'll kill myself too. I shamed Golda, and she was dearer to me than anything. You won't get away with this."

Max was scared, and finally they got married. What kind of wedding did they make? They bought two slices of ham. There wasn't anybody there, and they called in a kind of Jew who blessed them. And they went to live in the hotel, in that "fine hotel."

We were mad. I had sworn that I wouldn't talk to my cousin anymore. Then, thank God, she got pregnant, she had twins. And the two children died. A while later, she got pregnant again, and that child also died. They said to themselves: Our children are dying because of our guilt about Golda. She must forgive us or we'll never be able to have children. I didn't know anything about all that. One day, my mother met my cousin in the street. Rosette came up and kissed her:

"Aunt, dear aunt, I have already had three children who died. Golda must forgive me; everybody says that Golda must forgive me."

"I myself forgive you right away," said my mother. "Golda also forgives you. Have children who live with your husband to be a hundred."

But I didn't want to see them anymore, not her and not him.

[. . .] I was working in a knitting shop as a winder. The boss's wife had a sister, and we became friends. The poor girl also had two children, and she got sick. She had cancer. We got along very well, the two of us. When I finished work, I helped her, I bathed the children. She knew she was going to die. She had a very good husband. One day, she said to me:

"You know, Golda, when I'm dead, I want you to marry my husband. My children love you. You see that he's a good husband. Promise me to marry him."

"How can I make you such a promise? You're going to get better. You'll raise your children."

I didn't promise her, but she died. The children loved me very much. The little boy was already four years old at the time; the older one was six. He said to his father: "Papa, I'd like you to marry the lady who works at Madeleine's." Avrom also wanted to marry me; he didn't want anybody else. He came to our house and stayed until two o'clock in the morning, talking with my mother. He had a big knitting shop, a cottage at the Porte des Lilas, but he went bankrupt. His wife's illness had cost him all his money. One day, he came and said to me:

"Listen, Golda, now I am poor. I don't want to drag you into poverty. But promise me that you won't take anybody else."

"I can't promise you."

So he went to work in Alsace, in partnership with his brother-in-law. They worked in metals; they bought cars.

Avrom made a fortune as a scrap dealer and returned for Golda. They married in 1937 and moved to Elbeuf.

Already in the old country, a gap had appeared between a generation of parents bound to a set of traditions and the generation of their children attracted to "modernity." Yet another gap separated the generation of immigrants and the generation that grew up in the host country. A series of contrasts would manifest themselves, for example, during the immigrants' periodic trips home to visit parents who had remained in Poland and to introduce them to their grandchildren who were born in France. These migrants find a different but familiar world, religious practices they have abandoned but that they pretend to resume, so as not to give shock and out of respect for their parents. Their own children, however, discover a strange, totally unfamiliar world, where they themselves become objects of curiosity for their cousins from Poland.[9]

The gap between the generation of the immigrants and the generation of their children is therefore defined, essentially, as a function of the familiarity each of them maintains with different cultures. The immigrants had come out of a world in which Yiddishkeit was a fact of life: whatever their ultimate development, they preserved its imprint and often felt nostalgia for it. They judged contemporary life and, more particularly, their children's behavior in reference to values they received from that lost world. Conversely, in spite of their integration into the host society, they maintained a sense of distance from it, sometimes quite minimal, but irreducible nonetheless. Their children were impregnated by French culture, which was for them another fact of life. There resulted differences that affected not only language or tastes but also spontaneous reactions, life-style, and, finally, the consciousness of Jewish identity itself.

Robert S.:

It's a terrible thing to ask a person who was born in one country and who immigrated to another to adjust to the soil, the language, the environment, the conditions, the life of that new country. It doesn't matter how much you try to learn a language: what is ours to determine, we manage to do. But what is not ours to determine, that's what you take from your

---

9. This is one of the subjects recalled by Maurice Rajsfus, *Quand j'étais juif* [When I Was a Jew] (Paris: Mégrelis, 1982), pp. 102–113.

homeland. You can't be a Frenchman or a Pole just because you want to. At a certain age, to try to adjust to the life of a country that you don't know from Adam, that's something else. Especially when you want to possess the language and its refinements.

It wasn't enough for me to read the articles in the *Temps*. I also wanted to understand the jokes in the *Canard enchaîné*.[10] If you have to explain a witticism, it loses its charm; it's not a witticism anymore; it's detracting from something beautiful. On the day I could finally grasp the nuances of the *Canard enchaîné*, I said to myself: you have only barely begun to taste the richness of the French language. Still, I could take heart. I was no longer that ignoramus who had to ask what they're talking about and how this is eaten. I could follow when fireworks erupted at the table with the children, who handled the language correctly because they were born in France. I didn't want to seem inferior to them; it was my vanity. I'm the only one who knows the price I paid to obtain it. But I did it. Nevertheless, in spite of everything, I have the sense of having achieved only partial success. Not because I didn't want it, or because I didn't pay the price. But because it can't be had. There is something that is not determined by you, and that makes you what you are. The native ground—I don't have it.

[. . .] There is something that predisposes every Jew in certain ways, especially when he comes from those countries where Judaism was at the base of life. There's no other life possible. The Jew is marked, whatever he does. Even if I had wanted not to be, I couldn't not be Jewish. In my soul, I think, I feel like a Jew. I accommodated myself to the demands of social life in France. But if I had to choose, if I have the possibility of going to a meeting or a ball with French people or a Jewish meeting or ball, I wouldn't hesitate: my heart pulls me there, I feel better there, I'm with my own.

If I could have opted for a double nationality, things could have fallen into place more easily at least. That would have

10. A satirical weekly.

made my life less complicated. It's a line of argument I can't use in talking with a Frenchman; it would shock him, right, because he wouldn't understand. I'm not complaining. I have shown that, among civilized people, you can find a *modus vivendi*. For example, with Monsieur M. [*his daughter-in-law's father*], I would much prefer to talk about literature, but we can't get together, because if you let him talk, it would be Maurras or Déroulède,[11] and I wouldn't touch that subject. But he wouldn't come to me and talk about my authors. So we meet on the ground of wine and cheese. And there I'm ignorant. Anyway, I had to learn, not because I learned to like them, but because I have no choice when I'm in a group where I can't raise other questions.

With all that I have seen, I must conclude that I haven't changed one iota on the Jewish level. I have remained just as I was, minus religion, because I thought that that wasn't the essential thing. The essential thing for me is the culture that is transmitted by Judaism, by the writers and by the religion.

The difference between me and my father was that of one generation that gave life to the other. The difference between me and my sons is a leap of two or three generations. It's impossible to adjust to it. Yet I know, God knows, the pains I have taken to try to follow my children, to understand them. But there are moments when I don't understand, things escape me. Do you feel the soul of a child?

The lack of connection with the generation born in France is manifest particularly when the problem of mixed marriage is posed: even with the most open-minded parents ("I want his happiness above all"), there is a sense of a private reticence. When they express their regrets more openly, they find consolation in the notion that their children, in spite of everything, still feel Jewish. By what criteria? In this respect, the State of Israel sometimes plays a paradoxical role: Robert S., former Communist fellow traveler, like Maurice N., former Communist, converted subsequently to a certain solidarity with the Zionist movement. Both declare their pride in seeing their children share those feelings.

11. Maurras, Déroulède, symbols of French right-wing nationalism.

Robert S.:

I couldn't leave my children and settle there, in Israel. In spite of my sorrow about it. I saw that the children wanted to stay in France even while my heart was drawn there, there, there. . . . I had everything to make me happy, in France, but there was an element of dissatisfaction. I missed the essential. Because if you had to choose between the two, I was more Jewish than French. Let's say the word, let's not be afraid: I was a Jew.

By what criteria did I raise my children? Judaism: I have an awareness of having done the job of passing on what I received. I told my sons the Aggadah[12] as well as the Jewish past: the destroyed Temple, all they have suffered, the wanderings through so many countries, the Inquisition, and so on. That they know. But they haven't lived like me in the milieu where the same thing, when it's told, weighs more. A history told in its context weighs differently from history taken out of a book. I told them a page taken out the context of life. Take a book, no matter how interesting it is, read a page from it—what does that give? It gives what it can give. I did my best, but I was aware that never (and for good reason, it wasn't possible) will my children be what I am, that is, an uprooted Jew. But still a Jew.

So I brought up my children with the idea of Judaism. When Israel was in danger, they were on the list of those who wanted to go as volunteers. So both of them remained Jews in their soul. Of that I'm proud.

Maurice N.:

My son has his own opinion. I don't want to influence him. We talk, we talk a lot. . . . He supports Israel. When there's a demonstration for Israel, for the Jews in Russia, my son is there. He doesn't miss a demonstration. But he's not committed politically. I think he's very disappointed by all the parties, like me, maybe. But when there was war—every time he wanted to enlist. He went to the embassy to enlist.

12. Moral precepts and parables of the Talmud.

He has two children, a boy and a girl. They got a liberal education, without religious beliefs; but they know what Judaism is. They're beginning to know. They know they're Jews. They're for Israel. Especially the little girl—she's very Jewish.

PART THREE
The Others

7
Around the
Mediterranean

THE MEMORIES OF *the past revived a dense world, marked by a wealth of communications and "the polyvalence of relations."* [1] *For better or worse, the relations between neighbors, friends, relatives, or in the economic sphere wove a network of relations among members of the Jewish milieu. But what about non-Jews? What trace did they leave in memory, with what features do they appear in the picture? These are delicate questions, for it is painful to talk of tensions and unresolved conflicts. Recalling a lost world, people would like to describe it as harmonious and to expel discordant notes from memory.*

"We" vaguely indicates the family circle and the whole Jewish population to which one belonged. Beyond that circle, conceived as a totally natural unity, one recalls other ethnic and religious groups. Individuals are not generally designated by status, occupation, personal qualities, but first of all by their group affiliation. While many narratives affirm the friendly tolerance that prevailed between adjacent groups, subtle and multiple signs reveal a more equivocal reality. It seems rather that misunderstanding, even mutual distrust, often separated the various "communities"—taken as a whole, despite the clear social distinctions within them. School, the neighborhood, work could bring individuals together but not the groups to which they belonged. Besides, the various components of the population were not perceived and presented as equal. On the contrary, one senses gradations, a hierarchy, and, consequently, the

1. I take this expression from Joëlle Bahloul, *Parenté et ethnicité: La Famille juive nord-africaine en France* [Kinship and Ethnicity: The North-African Jewish Family in France], Report to the Ministry of Culture, Mission du Patrimoine ethnologique de la France, 1984.

search for appropriate means to avoid the lower orders or to climb to higher levels. So behind the peaceful coexistence lay the tacit competition that set the various groups up against one another.

A MUTUAL EXCLUSION

Istanbul in the 1920s. Laure A. recalls both her friendship for an Armenian schoolmate and the collective antipathy the Jews felt toward the Armenians. She literally could not stomach them, she could not swallow their tea:

Not everybody could go to the school I was in. It was very expensive. As a matter of fact, there were only two Jewish girls, me and one other. The others were either Russians who had scholarships, Bulgarians and Rumanians who were very rich, even some who had scholarships, or Armenians who had scholarships. The Americans protected the Armenians, and we hated them. We Jews hated the Armenians. We didn't trust them. I don't know why. But when I was very small, about eight years old, I had an Armenian friend who was very nice. I had been in her house. She had a splendid house, white, much nicer than ours, with a big garden. She didn't have a mama, she had a grandmother. I admired that house a lot. So the grandmother said to me: "Tchai, tchai." In Turkish that means tea. I didn't know that. We never drank tea at home, except when we were sick. It didn't exist. So I said: "Thank you, Madame." She had given me tea. As soon as she turned her head, I threw it into the flowers. I couldn't swallow it. Later she said to me: "Another cup of tea?" I said: "OK." I did the same thing. I couldn't bear it. It was the custom of the Armenians.

But that Armenian girl was so nice, with big black eyes. She had been with me in the German school. That's where I knew her from. And I remember, we were very, very good friends.

In the picture of manners described by Laure A., her father, a rug dealer, was a big businessman with an international reputation. He was honest and generous. His Armenian colleague had to bow, "kneel," to such virtues. Thus is history turned into a parable.

My father had a large fortune. He had a factory near the customs house. There were girls who worked for him. It was a big enterprise. But it was all wholesale. Papa didn't sell retail. He exported. For example, there were customers who came from Germany, Vienna, who knew my father's name. They came looking for him. Once they had come to buy some things. My father said to them: "I'm sorry, I don't have that item, but go next door." Because my father was like my brother, very generous, very grand, not petty at all. "Go next door." "But that's your competitor!" "He's not my competitor, we don't deal in the same thing. Go next door, you'll find everything you want." That was an Armenian. And that Armenian was under the impression that my father hated him. Jews and Armenians weren't supposed to get along. When he finished his business with that Viennese, he came to kneel at my father's feet. He said to him: "Monsieur A., I didn't know you were such a fine person. You know what golden business I did thanks to you?" I said [sic]: "It's nothing special. Since I don't deal in that, you should take advantage of it." "But I, myself, wouldn't have made such a gracious gesture. And I had no idea that the Jews were like that."

Istanbul, former capital of the Ottoman Empire, was still the capital of Turkey after World War I. Would Laure A. talk about the Turks? They are almost absent from her memory. Yes, thinking about it again, she remembers dancing with one or two of them but somebody had immediately recalled the rules of the game. In the summer, in Moda:

Down there, there were dance halls. And we danced with Turks. We danced wildly with Turks, Muslims. There was a Turk who was crazy about me. That Turk wanted to kiss me on the mouth. I knew nothing about that. That disgusted me. So after he touched me, I wiped my mouth: "Ah, you're wiping yourself, you're disgusted with me and that's why you're wiping your mouth!" "No, I'm just not used to it." "You'll get used to it. You're going to kiss me." So I told my brother-in-law. He said: "Listen, Laure, never with Muslim Turks. Pay attention. You can go around with them but don't get close to Muslim Turks. It's very dangerous. They can make you pregnant. They can do a lot of things to you, and you can't do anything to them. They're the masters here."

The anecdote speaks of a mutual exclusion. On the one hand, the Jews did not have access to political power, which the Turks remained masters of; on the other hand, they roundly rejected this system because it was considered inferior to that of the western powers. Laure and her kind didn't talk to Turks and studied only in foreign schools in Turkey. She insists that she did not want to live or get married in Turkey. At the end of the 1920s, the family moved to Milan. Laure finished school in the American college, joining her parents only during school vacations. After two or three of these trips:

At customs, they said to me: "It can't be true. You're not a student. You're trafficking in clothes. At your age, so young, to go to Turkey to study—that can't be."

"But I'm not going to Turkey, I'm going to an American college!"

Laure finished our interview with this nice formulation, which recalls Renaissance travelers describing the Ottoman Empire: "I don't think I was much help. You didn't learn much about the customs and manners of the Turks."

Tunis between the two wars: Madame K. remembers her childhood in the nice neighborhoods, her Muslim girlfriends and classmates. She recalls the prohibitions—you must never play with boys—and today she defines that spirit of the times as "regressive."

Well, the spirit we had! Next to us, on Rue Ismaïl-Dupont, there were two Z. brothers, Nourredine and Tahar, who became a doctor. They were handsome! But since we were Jews and they were Arabs, we took the streetcar together as if they didn't exist and as if we didn't exist. We didn't say hello to each other, nothing. In 1972, in Hamilcar, I met a blond gentleman with blue eyes—Nourredine. He looked at me, I looked at him, and he said [*murmurs*]: "Why, it can't be, it's her, hello." And I said [*long murmur*]: "Hello." There, now we said hello to one another. . . . After fifty years, we said hello to one another. I thought that was funny. That story, the Arab, you didn't see him.

"You had no relations with the Arabs?"

With the girls, yes. But the men, we took the streetcar together and we didn't see one another. What a spirit we had, regressive. I remember that we had a neighbor, Lalla Fatha. We went to her house. So my father made a rule that we must never play with the little Arab boy. So the poor kid, he said to us: "Can I play?" We said: "No, you aren't to play with us." Later on, he became a member of the High Council!

"WE ARE NOT ARABS"

Tita S. no doubt never knew that nice quarter of Tunis, but her vision of the Arabs remains what Madame K. denounced as regressive. For her, it was the humiliations the Arabs once made the Jews suffer that led to the French occupation. Thus, two poles emerge in her representation of the society: on one side, the Arabs, threatening, unfair, dangerous, opposed by the French, on the other side, who had come to restore justice. In her narrative, in fact, these French remain a kind of inaccessible abstraction.

When the situation was straightened out, when the French came, they [*the Arabs*], didn't bother the Jews, no. The situation calmed down. Before, who went out at night? Nobody. Because the Muslims weren't scared of the Jews. The Jews didn't feel confident about it because, at first, they would harm them. The others weren't good, weren't nice. When the Arabs were told that what they were doing wasn't good, they listened.

"Did you spend a lot of time with Arabs, your father, for example?"

No. Papa didn't work with them. He knew them, sure, but he didn't spend time with them. He had a shoemaker's shop. Why would he spend time with Arabs?

We didn't associate with them. We weren't friends with the Arabs, no, since, as I said at the beginning, they frightened us. We remained frightened. I had a brother, Amos, who went with the Arabs to Sidi Mahrez when he was young. He was a bum. There were Arab cafés there, and the Jews used to sit in them. When he grew up, he brought his friend to my mother's house. Who was his friend? An Arab! He brought him and said: "Please give him something to eat, Mama." They were like brothers. But me, I didn't want to. I said: "May you have bad luck! You could only find a Muslim for a friend!" And what did he say? "On Mama's life, he's gold! He doesn't hurt anybody, he doesn't bother anybody!" Before, the Arabs were a little. . . . Later on, they got to know the Jews and saw the type of people they were. They went and drank together in the café.

The father was a shoemaker; one brother was a bum; the other was a stevedore. Even at this level of the social scale, Jewish identity implied that one kept the Arabs at a distance, that one looked down on them.

"How did your mother dress?"
Like the Arab women, with that kind of dress and a *sarwal* and a handkerchief like mine.
"The veil?"
No. We're not Arabs!

Then, recalling the gatherings of women in the courtyard of the house:

"So, you stayed sitting on the ground, talking in the court-yard?"
Standing. We didn't sit down. Are we Arabs?

A barrier also separated the Jews from other segments of the colonial population: a linguistic barrier, a status barrier. Tita, who did not give the Arabs names, uses titles when she recalls the French, "Monsieur," "Madame," "the boss."

"And the French, you knew them?"
Never. I didn't know to talk. Later, I knew, when I worked in the hotel. With Madame Anna, a Frenchwoman, no, an Italian woman. It's the same thing. She taught me a little.
. . . I knew French people, but I never talked to them. The boss of the hotel, Monsieur Armand, who could talk to him?

In her long biography, Tita did not name, did not mention any other individual belonging to the non-Jewish population.

SALONIKA: BROKEN HARMONY

Greece, between 1910 and 1920. Reality, like memories, is full of contradictions. In everyday life, Ida O. recalls Greek and Armenian friends, shared discussions and plans, the attraction she felt for Greek religious practices.

As for me, my girlfriends were Greeks, not Jews. We lived among Greeks, in mixed neighborhoods. Clashes? Yes, there were some, but it was a fair fight, for you gave insult for insult. The Greeks sometimes got excited. Coming out of school, they called us *tchiufuti*.[2] They threw stones. But it wasn't serious; we called them something else.

Ida O. recalls the gifts she brought to the Greek workers at Easter time, the processions she participated in, but also the distrust that existed even between friends. The accusation of ritual murder returned every year.

The most tragic night was Easter night, Greek Easter. Always the Jews killed a child; they put blood in the matzah. Every year, it was the same drama. You could see that the young people were in a bad mood. On Easter night, the Greeks, they were really worked up. For all eight days—no matter how many friends you had; no matter that throughout your youth you went out with Greeks, had discussions. Who knows, someday you might even marry a Greek. And on the eight days of their Easter, it was the end of the world. And on Easter night, on the street where we lived, on all the streets, they passed by with the Virgin Mary in some thingamajig they held by the hand. And all of them with candles behind. There was a procession that went to the church. And me, I stood in the middle. What could happen to me? I liked it a lot.

2. *Cifuti,* jibe frequently used in Turkey as in Greece with regard to (or concerning) Jews.

And that night, all the neighbors didn't talk to us. The next day, the young people who didn't talk to us at night, they came with boxes to make a collection. "Christianetsi, Christianetsi."[3] That means "Jesus is resurrected." It was magnificent. And as for us, my father took us to the Greek workers. We dressed to the nines, with little baskets. We went to visit all my father's workers in their homes. We brought them lots of colored duck eggs. That's how customs were. It was marvelous.

Ida O. describes the situation from before the 1920s. The Jewish population of Salonika was the most numerous and, socially, in a strong position. In the 1920s, anti-Semitism broke out. Like Ida. O., Gabriel D. (Salonika, about 1910) attributes the tranquillity the Jews enjoyed to their favorable social position. With the arrival of the Greeks from Asia Minor, those "sub-Greeks," the two groups experience a change in relations.

We were living harmoniously, Greeks, Jews, Turks. In Salonika, we lived very, very, very, very, very, very well! In 1912, the Greeks returned, but we also continued to live with the Turks because it was the Ottoman Empire. When Venizelos came to power in 1922, there was an exchange of populations, which, in Greek, I call the *abalai*.[4] All the Turks in Salonika went to Turkey or Asia Minor, and all the Greeks from Asia Minor and Turkey came to Salonika, and they made an exchange. After that exchange, anti-Semitism started in Greece, you understand? . . . We were living well because almost all the Jews of Salonika were merchants . . . plus a few craftsmen and a few construction workers, and all that. . . . We were living well until anti-Semitism started. Anti-Semitism started in Greece with the people from Asia Minor, not with the Greeks! . . . But the sub-Greeks!

3. *Christos anesti.*
4. One hundred fifty thousand Orthodox Christians from Asia Minor were "exchanged" for four hundred thousand Turks deported to Anatolia. Venizelos, a "liberal" leader, defeated in the elections of 1917 by the party favorable to King Constantin, returned to power following the defeat of Greece by Turkey (1921). Greece then experienced several years of political instability.

In Salonika, as in other parts of the Mediterranean basin, the Jews who went to schools set up by the western powers were attracted to England, France, or Germany. In this case, confronting the rise of Greek anti-Semitism, it was to Germany that one looked for salvation! Ida O. again:

We had the *fraulei*, German women, nurses. We liked the Germans very much. I remember my father in Salonika. After Greece began to humiliate us, he was always praying to the Good Lord for the Germans to come.

I had girlfriends who were musicians, who had come back from Germany. They were thrilled with Germany. . . . They told us: "Let the Germans come to Salonika!"

However, they finallly found salvation in emigration. Ida O., who couldn't bear a first trip to France in 1924, returned there for good in 1929. A half-century later, she proudly retains Greek nationality:

With the Greeks, we were very happy, very, very. When they told me that the Jews were deported in one day, I couldn't even imagine such a thing, never.

M. M., also a Salonikan, attributes the break with the Greek population to a strategic error on the part of the Jews in their participation in the elections. Implicitly, two subjects intersect in his reading of the past. First, there were the contradictions inherent in a political system based on a general election combined with a society divided into clearly separated ethnic and religious groups. Individual choices inevitably impinged on the community; collective preferences involved the risk of reprisals. To this conflict of allegiance, to this insoluble tension, M. M. opposes and prefers the status quo ante. *Then the second subject emerges, the contradiction between the century-old presence of the Jewish community in Salonika and its situation of quasi-extraterritoriality. The community benefited from a kind of internal autonomy; it did not have to take a position on issues that went beyond its own boundaries. Integration into a broader political whole was not desirable—for the reasons already indicated—and when it was imposed, Jews got out. This same speaker, who fled Greece to avoid military service, fought in France to obtain his naturalization and then to serve in the army and do his "duty."*

When I was in Greece, there was no war, no family spirit, no spirit of a country that welcomed us . . .

"You didn't have any attachment to the country?"

Yes, I loved Greece and I continue to love her. But it's perhaps unique in the annals of history: people who live in a country, who have never done military service—they're independent. We were left to ourselves. . . . While here, it's completely different. Once you set up a home, you've got children, there's no reason why a Frenchman would go fight and, me, I look on.

This situation of extra-territoriality is not "unique in the annals of history." Converging memories come forth from Istanbul, Tripoli, Alexandria: excluded in fact, if not in law, from the political scene that involved the majority population but not the Jews, the latter took advantage of the situation to exercise their rights and duties within the confines of the community. So one felt at home in his homeland but on condition that he was with his own people. If this isolation was threatened by anti-Jewish violence or by political changes that imposed new obligations on the Jews, they left. Ironically, they were ready to accept wholeheartedly the obligations imposed by the new host country,[5] for there they had access to a political body that ignored differences of "race and religion," at least in principle.

From Tripoli at the beginning of the century, Camilla N. reports memories like those of Ida O. in Salonika. She also brags of having grown up outside of the confines of the Jewish milieu. Her family had contacts with the ruling circles, first Turks, then Italians, after the establishment of the colonial regime. And the father rivaled the Turkish dignitaries. Thus, he "inherited"—at his own expense, to be sure—the carriage of the governor who was recalled to Istanbul.

Our friends were Syrians. There were—how shall I put it?—state officials, functionaries of Turkey. They came from Syria, Lebanon, they spoke Arabic, they spoke Turkish. Papa spoke Turkish perfectly, he was very assimilated with them.

5. We have previously seen other aspects of the attraction exercised by France.

[. . .] It was very funny in our family, there were seven of us. There were the believers, the nonbelievers, everyone was a type. My oldest brother was religious but didn't learn Talmud; he was very, very liberal. Because we were raised with priests. When the Italians came there was an archbishop, the Archbishop of Tripoli. He preferred my brother to all the others, and the Catholics were furious.

Governor Redjeb Pasha had to leave. We liked him a lot, and he liked us a lot. He used to say: "You are my children." He called my father and said to him: "Listen, N., I must ask a favor of you." "Ask me whatever you want." So he said: "Listen, I have to go—it's really a coup—but the one who's replacing me is my worst enemy. I adore my horses, my carriage, my driver. I don't want him to get them. I don't want him to sit there in the carriage where I sat. I don't want him to have anything of mine. So, it would give me pleasure if you bought it." My father said: "I would be delighted to do it and am very unhappy about your departure." So we inherited—Papa bought—that carriage, with all the gilding, the victoria, the horses, marvels. The coachman was over six feet tall, with the bearing of a nobleman of Constantinople.

When the other Pasha came, he sent an emissary, one of Papa's friends, called Muhammad El Jamal. Muhammad El Jamal really was a very good friend of the family. He was often there. He came and said: "N., I have bad news for you." "What's up?" "I was with the governor. OK, well, he's very upset about the carriage and the horses. Well, the horses, that's all right. But he can't find a driver to suit him." You bet, the coachman had an unbelievable style! "So he asks you . . . if you would give him your coachman." OK. So my father says: "Just imagine, to give the driver, the horses, and all that? What happens to me? Listen, tell him that he's the master; that not only if he asked for things, but if he asked for my son, I would give him my son as a driver if that's what he wanted. Because it's fitting that one shows him respect. Really, tell him that I am at his complete disposal."

We were all around there. We didn't know what was going on, but we saw that something very dramatic was taking place.

Muhammad said: "Calm down, calm down." He left and, later, he said to that governor: "You know, not only would N. give you the carriage and the driver, he'd even give you his son because he can't refuse you. But I went there and the children surrounded me and said: 'What! You're going to take 'Abdu away from us, you can't!' They were crying. Really, I think it wouldn't be good to take 'Abdu . . ." So the governor answered: "Tell N. that I thank him very much for everything and that I accept his driver, but me, I give him back to his children."

Camilla N. had almost nothing to say about the native population except once, to describe a religious procession with a combination of fascination and fear. Like Ida O.'s parents, hers are presented in the role of benefactors, patronizing the other religious group. Further on, the Libyan population will be recalled, in association with another instance of intolerance.

What did they call Arab fanatics? Those who make *jihad* [holy war], what are they called? They had a name. . . . At certain times, when they had a celebration, there was the *zawyia*—you know what a zawyia is? It's an oratory. OK. Each zawyia had all its followers, and the young ones especially, who did what corresponds to Christian things, when they go in the street with the Virgin Mary, a procession, eh? So each zawyia lined up to make jihad. They went to the city, they were all very worked up, because for the eight days before, in their zawyia, they drank very stimulating things, they shouted, they talked.
"These were the 'Issawa?"
The 'Issawa! Then they came out. It was something very impressive. You know, all the consuls advised all the Europeans to lock themselves in and not come out on those days because you couldn't know what might happen. It was extraordinary because our house was on the sea, on the main street, and they all passed by us because it was on the way to the home of the Turkish governor, and they were going to pay homage to him. It was really spectacular. But we, we weren't afraid, because they liked us a lot. First Papa, every time a zawyia needed money, he gave it to them. Every time a mosque fell down, he had it rebuilt. So they liked him a lot. And they passed by with

camels and children and banners in two parts: instead of having a flag with only one wing, there were two wings. There was the guy who holds the pole and the banner covered all those who make the 'Issawa. Those 'Issawa, with a drum, they were actually in a trance. They shouted "Heia, heia, heia," and they started like this, like this, like this [*movement of the head*]. Then, I don't know if you've seen that Arabs leave a braid in the middle of their head. So, on the day of the 'Issawa, they undid that braid. Yes, they undid it and it made the movement with their hair that falls like that and like that [*waves her head*]. I remember that, when they passed under the house, you know, down there, we distilled orange blossoms, roses from the country. We had flasks, and we sprinkled all the flower water we had on their heads. They did something special for us; it was an homage. That's to tell you. . . . When I think that there are hatreds, it sets my teeth on edge, it really irritates me, it breaks my heart.

"That's to tell you . . ." What are Camilla N., Ida O., other Salonikans trying to convey when they recall both the good relations between the groups and the anti-Jewish demonstrations? If they remember acts of violence—verbal or other—it is to take objection to them immediately. Sometimes they assert that the incidents had no consequences; sometimes they distance them by locating the victims in communities they didn't frequent or by putting the culprits on a social level that allowed them to view these events "with contempt." Sometimes, the clashes are imputed to foreign elements. This defensive attitude has often been observed in French Jews, who resort to the same mechanisms to banish painful memories from their minds, to shroud a phenomenon that they are unable to explain.[6]

"LITTLE THINGS"

For Camilla N., anti-Semitism is not a fact of experience but a fact of discourse, reported by a history book (which reveals to her that the evil was rampant very close to Tripoli, in the small communities of

6. Dominique Schnapper, *Juifs et israélites* [Jews and Israelites] (Paris: Gallimard, 1980); André Harris and Alain de Sedouy, *Juifs et Français* [Jews and the French] (Paris: Le Livre de poche, 1979).

Libya, those "little things" she never saw) or by an anecdote she heard
from a poor mattress maker. Like Ida O., her social position sheltered
her from hostility, but others told her that in the city itself, where she
never went, poor Jews had to respond with patience or trickery to the
daily harassment to which they were subjected.

So me, in my delusions—since we were very spoiled—that
we were very friendly with the Arabs—and, really, when I was
small, I had never heard that there were any troubles. Troubles,
little things, yes, little things. . . . But then I read that book
they sent me,[7] and I saw what horror, how many times they
were massacred by the Arabs. It's something that really hurts
you.
"In the ghetto?"
Yes, But no, not those of Tripoli, but there were Jews all
around, like Tanjura, you know, and other such small places.
There, from time to time, massacres were committed. It really
hurt me because it took away many of my illusions.
I'll tell a little story—of how they hated the Jews. There was
a *madrasa* [*school*], you know what that is, there, next to the
ghetto. And once a year, we had a mattress maker who came
to wash the wool and redo the mattresses. He came to the house,
of course, since everything was like that. His name was Hamini.
He was a Jew and so [*laughs*] he said to me: "I'm always working, and there I am, working in the door [*gesture of her lowered
head*] of my shop, and all the kids coming out of the madrasa
came over. They knocked me on the head. They said, 'here,
ged bouk ou jeddek' [*here, for the grandfather of your father and your
grandfather!—an insult accompanied by blows on the back of the neck.
The narrator's explanation is not clear.*] So, what did he do? He
was very silent, like that. He was an old man. For me at least,
at that time, he was an old man. So he said: "One day, I couldn't
take it anymore. I had a headache. What could I do against that
rush of kids. I couldn't. I took a pile of pins, a lot, and I stuck

7. R. de Felice, *Ebrei in un paese arabo: Gli ebrei nella Libia contemporana tra
colonialismo, nationalismo e sionismo (1835–1970)* [Jews in an Arab Country:
Jews in Libya in Modern Times between Colonialism, Nationalism, and
Zionism (1835–1970)] (Bologne, 1978).

them [*laughter, indication that the pins were lifted*]. Here came the first one, came the second. They didn't come back anymore." You could always get them with trickery.

"BUT WHAT IS IT, THESE JEWS?"

The sense of superiority that some felt with respect to the Armenians, others with respect to the Arabs, could also be felt with respect to other Jews. As for Ida O., she did not even suspect the existence of other communities. In the 1920s:

I didn't even know what Poles were. When I came here to France, my sister said to me: "A friend's coming here, and she's a Pole." "What's a Pole? I thought we were the only ones alive!"

I never knew anti-Semitism. I didn't know what it was or about German Jews. There was only us. I said to my sister: "But what is it, these Jews?" "What do you think, there's just you?"

In Salonika, I thought it was just us, that there were no other Jews. But that's too stupid because my husband had two movie theaters in Salonika. He showed films from Poland, from Russia: the pogroms they had there, terrible! And we thought that it was all just stories.

Salonika again, at the beginning of the century:

The first time I saw an Ashkenazi is when I started school and needed a hat for school. My mother took me to the hat-maker. I saw this gentleman who spoke a very bad Spanish with a very thick accent, and I said to myself: "This isn't a Jew." I asked my mother: "What is that man?" She explained to me that they were people from Poland. But we never considered that they belonged to us. We knew nothing about each other. There were some who became Sepharadi because we were the majority. You recognized them by those names, the name Ashkenazi. Everybody with the name Ashkenazi is Sepharadi.

In Salonika, there were very few Ashkenazim. They were small craftsmen, especially hatmakers, things like that, and we didn't have anything to do with them. They had their own

synagogue. They had one synagogue, we had thirty-six . . .
[*H.S.y B., born before* 1900]

Istanbul, Milan, Paris: about 1930, in Milan, Laure A. met a
young Viennese Jew whom she wanted to marry.

He came from a very rich family. I was at their house with
Mama. They had big dinners. As for me, I was almost engaged. . . . He was quite a man, you know, athletic, skiing,
tennis—all that. He was completely my type, while the others
were old hat.

When we got to Paris, my father met this young man's
father. And they didn't get along. Because we're Sephardi, he
was *eshkenaz*. So, we had a kind of . . . [*pout*]. They, for their
part, considered themselves superior, and we, in Turkey—it's
dumb—we considered the eshkenaz inferior. So, once, when I
told him that, he burst out laughing. I said: "At home, the
eshkenaz were dirty." "For us, the Orientals, the Sepharadi,
were dirty!"

She finally married a Sepharadi from Salonika who was living in
Paris:

His first language was Spanish, like us. But he also knew
Greek. He didn't like Greeks, but he spoke Greek.

IN ALGERIA: THE FRENCH MIRAGE

As with their Tunisian neighbors, the Jews of Algeria have
memories that reveal misunderstanding and fear of the Muslim popula-
tion, of those who are indiscriminately called "the Arabs." Inversely,
the valorization of the French goes hand in hand with a distancing that
is both suffered and desired. Suzanne T., whose tribulations and social
rise we have followed (p. 39, 50), regularly inserts French people into
her narrative. They emerge at key points to resolve crises, settle difficul-
ties, bring decisive help. She places them in a relationship of patronage,
presents herself in a position of deference, also emphasizing the contrast
between their attitude, which she judges positively, and that of the
Jews, who are seen to have no respect for principles. Fairness is on the

side of the French. So, it was a young French captain who addressed her husband in the familiar form at their first meeting and got him his first contract; it was a French bailiff who took the side of the law, whereas his Jewish colleague gave in to personal interests. In Algiers, a French confectioner, "a good-hearted man" who understood "the drama of the common people," rectified an injustice and opened the vast perspectives of the Rue d'Isly for the husband. It was a French midwife who saved her life during a difficult birth.

With the declaration of war, the husband went off to the front, leaving Suzanne with but a few pennies.

Then I thought about how I was going to feed my children. So I went to see my neighbor. She manufactured clothes. I asked if she could lend me her permit so I could get some work. She gave it to me. I explained to her that I couldn't work outside, that I had to find work to do at home while taking care of my children. I left the baby with her—he was barely two months old—and I went to town. There were two factories that did work for the army: that of L., a Jew, and that of Essartier, our new mayor. I started with the Jew because his place was closer to my house. When I introduced myself, the forewoman sent me to the office. There was a woman. I later found out that that was Madame L. She started asking me questions: whether I had a sewing machine, what I could do. I told her honestly that I had never worked, that I had small children. She answered that she didn't want a beginner and that she wasn't interested in taking care of those details. I went to the other factory, which was much farther from my house. What could I do? I had no choice but to go to that factory. A woman said to me: "What do you want?" I answered: "I want to see Monsieur Essartier." She asked if I had an appointment. I said no. So she answered that he was busy, that he couldn't see me. I said to her: "Tell him that I'm from Bouzarea." She went to see him, and she told him. He opened the door and told the clerk to leave us alone. He had me sit down and started asking me questions. I told him that we lived in Frais-Vallon. I told him everything. When I finished talking, he said: "Come with me." I showed him my neighbor's pass; she worked for him. He answered: "No, I'll give you work in your own name," and he went with me to the cashier. He told the head of the office that whenever I came for work, I was to be paid right away without any questions. I left my name and address and he told the cashier: "Give Madame T. ten francs." I told him: "Monsieur, I asked for work, not charity." He answered that he would take it back little by little. He never did take it back. For work, he gave me army shirts to put the buttons on: five pennies a shirt. I left with work, and he gave me money. I started that very day.

If the French were the patrons and protectors, they could not be the alter ego. *That function was reserved for Spanish friends. Associated with images of happiness and abundance, they were so dear to Suzanne's heart that she named her daughter Hermine, after the wife of her husband's worker and friend. The rest of the population remains virtually invisible. No Algerian appears in the picture, except in the form of a threatening crowd of Arabs descending from the douars to stir up trouble in Sétif or Constantine. On one occasion, an anonymous "old Moorish woman" saved her daughter from a disease the doctors were unable to cure, while another "old Arab woman" helped her sister give birth. On another occasion, the blacksmith neighbor protected the family against rioters. He too remains nameless and Suzanne sometimes describes him as an Arab, sometimes as a Berber.*

Suzanne had begun her biography with her birth, immediately followed by these words: "My grandfather fought in the war of 1870."[8] *A claim to glory: she not only received French nationality like all the other Jews of Algeria, following the Crémieux Decree (1870), but also, as it were, on the field of honor. That her father returned wounded and an alcoholic from the war of 1914, that her son was killed in a French uniform in the Algerian war of independence has no effect on her pride of being French. On the contrary, that pride was nurtured by the trials she had to endure: today, two portraits hang in the apartment where she lives—those of her dead husband and son—and there is a frame containing her son's citation, his war cross, and the military medal.*

8. The Franco-Prussian War.

Two moments are engraved in the memory of the Jews of eastern Algeria: the riots of 1934, during which Algerian Muslims pillaged shops and massacred several scores of Jews; and the period of the Vichy government, which expelled the children from the schools and excluded Jews from the administration.[9] Yet, that Jewish couple from Constantine, married in 1938, describes the riots as a fleeting episode and even disguises it in a narrative of friendly relations, illustrating how difficult it is for people to admit acts of violence.

She: We were fine. We always had very good contacts with the Arabs and the Christians. There was no racism like we find here.

"So, you never saw riots?"

He: There were riots in '34, but it was no big deal. There were some who were attacked, but they weren't from Constantine.

She: No. We had very good contacts.

"But they were important all the same, the riots of '34?"

She: Oh, yes, they were important.

He: In '34, yes.

She: They looted all the stores, killed a lot of Jews.

He: But you didn't take that into account.

She: It was settled right away the next day.

He: They apologized, and that's it.

She: The town stayed under siege. For how long?

He: It must have been quite some time . . .

9. On these two periods, see Michel Abitbol, *Les Juifs d'Afrique du Nord sous Vichy* [The Jews of North Africa Under Vichy] (Paris: Maisonneuve et Larose, 1983).

She: My parents had a farm. We lived off of that farm. The gardener [*an Arab gardener*] would bring us fruit and vegetables. We shared some with the neighbors. The soldiers who guarded us during those riots knocked on our door with their rifles to ask for something to drink. That frightened us; we screamed. Since we had a lot of plums, I gave them the basket. That pleased them. We gave them whatever bread we had. I had my gardener come to bring us flat bread from home. His mother made it and he brought us a pile of flat bread, since we weren't allowed to go out. Everything was under siege. I gave some to the soldiers who were guarding the entire neighborhood.

With all the other witnesses, these riots left bitter memories. It is an event that people cannot erase; it inevitably returns in the narratives.

Gillette F., born in 1927:

I can't keep from remembering August 5, 1934, when they broke into our store, my father's. I was seven years old. I remember that story very, very well. The night before, or rather two days before, my father had gone to Constantine to buy merchandise. They started throwing stones at the store because it was in an Arab neighborhood. And a young man came to tell him: "Deïdou, pay attention, I think they're going to rise up against us." And in fact, the next morning, the milkman came, an old man, you see, I remember very, very well, you see, it's funny. He knocked softly on the door and we were afraid: "Don't go out. Don't go to the store. They're ransacking the store and all the stores nearby, Guenoun's, Guedj's, Uncle Alfred's." And we saw—since we were living on the first floor, Avenue Magenta—from the window, whose shutters were closed of course, we saw my father's fabrics going up to the Arab village, along with the mattresses from the houses they had looted. That's a thing that marked me. And since then, the poor man [*my father*] never got over it. Six months later, we decided we didn't want to stay in Aïn Beïda anymore, because it was impossible to live like that. In '39, we moved to Constantine.

Aïn Beïda again. Claire A., born in 1916, narrates:

The riots of '34—that was the catastrophic time for us. I was a girl. I was seventeen years old, and my mother made a decision that very month to leave Aïn Beïda because we were surrounded by Arabs. And you know what happened. They looted our store; they set fire to my father's store. They looted our beautiful house. We had a marvelous house, and they set fire to our house. We were left without anything.

It's very simple. When the Arabs came into the courtyard, we had some amazing luck. Just at the moment—after a whole night of having stones at the doors and windows, they couldn't get in, and by nine o'clock in the morning, they smashed in the door. They grabbed on to Simone, my sister. She was little, maybe two years old. She had a knife at her throat, Simone did. She was at death's door. At that moment—since we lived near the railroad station—the legion arrived. They came into our house. So the Arabs ran away. Two of them were killed in our courtyard by the Legion. Otherwise, the whole family would have died.

We made it through the riots. That's why Mama didn't want to stay anymore. First of all, we didn't have a house anymore. We didn't have anything. On the morning it happened, my grandfather, the poor man, came, Grandfather Aouzi, Mama's father. . . . He came to take us to his house. Well, we left barefoot—no shoes, no clothes, nothing. They took us like that, with a whole army. An escort, so that we could leave our house and go to our grandfather's. You know, that story has remained engraved on my being. We could never forget it. . . . And we stayed with my grandparents while Mama went alone to look at an apartment in Constantine. And that's how on that same day, she found an apartment on Rue de France, and a week later, we were all in Constantine. There we had to begin from scratch all over again. It wasn't easy.

[. . .] We were doing very well in Aïn Beïda. We had lived very, very well. When those riots took place, all the stores were destroyed. There was a fire, and then it was all over. All the Jews suffered. Overnight, they were barefoot and naked.

"What caused these riots?"

You certainly know that the Arabs were against the Jews. That's how it was. The Arabs who came down from the mountains didn't know for whom or why they were killing, that's all. Let me tell you something even better. I had a girlfriend. We were never apart. She was the daughter of a forester, French. She came to my house. She was Catholic. She ate at my house; she slept at my house. It was mutual. I also went to her house. On the day of the riots, she herself was the one who pointed out my house. And when they smashed in the door, I saw her, her, in front. She was saying to them: "Here it is, here it is. Get in, kill!" It was awful. Well, ever since then, I haven't trusted anybody anymore. It was over. I was really cured of it. That's something I'll never forget—she was the one who pointed out our house, because how would the Arabs, who came from far away, know our house? And then we started all over again there. We were in Constantine, and, believe me, it didn't go well.

Constantine, in fact, had the same troubles. But being in a larger community offered some protection, not only from danger but also from close relations with "the Arabs." Returning to Aïn Beïda in 1939, five years after the riots:

It had become too. . . . There was too much . . .

"The Arab community, that is?"

That's it, yes, too, too. . . . I remember Yvette. Someone had sent her a love letter, a marriage proposal, so you can imagine! It was a panic.

Raoul was going to the Arab cafés. You see what a mess it was. [*Gillette F., born in 1927*]

In Constantine, that promised land, the riots were even worse. Suzanne T. reports facts and dates, with the explicit desire to offer testimony regarding that traumatic event.[10] *Correctly—for the chronicles of the period confirm her tale—she emphasizes that the colonial authorities didn't do anything to prevent the troubles and that help was*

10. In the same spirit, she had earlier recalled riots in Sétif in the 1920s.

late in coming. In a revealing slip of the tongue, she says commiseriat *to refer to the police station, where the Commissioner did not show any commiseration.*

On August 2, 1934, a Friday night, my husband came home as usual, with a melon and a watermelon. He told me that things weren't going well in town, that the Arabs said that a Jew had pissed on the wall of the mosque. We ate supper and went to bed.

Every Saturday morning, my husband's friends and their wives used to come pick us up to go to the swimming pool, not far from where we lived. While I was dressing the children, my husband had taken out the picnic basket and was waiting for his friends in front of the door. The closest neighbor came back from town. He asked my husband what he was doing in front of the door so early in the morning. My husband answered: "I'm waiting for some friends to go to the swimming pool, like every Saturday." The neighbor, a blacksmith, had two sons—grown men—two daughters, and his wife. So he said to him: "Your friends won't come. You'd better go back inside. It's very bad in town. Most of all, don't go anywhere." My husband came back in and told me what the neighbor had said to him. We believed him because a sixty-year-old man wouldn't make up things like that. About ten o'clock, we saw my father-in-law coming. Thinking that we didn't know anything, he came to warn us. But when he left, he couldn't make it through the city anymore. Soldiers had to escort him home. From our house, we heard noises and shouts from the city. By evening, we went back (from the courtyard to the apartments) with the children. I had three children of my own (the baby was six months old), my husband's young sister, who had come in the morning with her father and who didn't want to leave, and the famous Joel. My husband was keeping guard. The children had fallen asleep. But neither my husband nor I closed our eyes.

Early in the morning, the neighbor came to do errands for me. I'll always remember: I had made noodles with tomato sauce, fried fish, pimentos, a salad of tomatoes and cucumbers. My husband and the children were sitting, waiting for me to give them something to eat. Just as I was going to put the pot on the table, I hear a noise I had never heard before. So I asked my husband what it was. He answered: "It's the alarm." The town was on fire, in flames. People were screaming. My husband put a ladder against the roof and he had us climb up, one by one. We hid behind a chimney. Next to the roof was the balcony of someone named Rougie. We went down to that balcony: the woman went to open the door to let us in. Her husband came and he said to his wife: "We're not going to get ourselves killed by the Arabs for Jews." His wife wept, begged him to let us in for a little while. But he wouldn't hear of it. He opened the front door and threw us out. It was Sunday, August 4, and it was almost 11:30. All the Arabs were gathered to kill the Jews. He closed the door behind us. When they saw seven people coming out all at once, they were stunned. At that time, the blacksmith neighbor opened his door to us and let us in. He stood in front of the door with his two sons, his two unveiled daughters, and his wife. It says a lot for an Arab to unveil his wife and daughters. He said to the Arabs: "You'll have to kill me and my family before you kill those people." He also had the Guedj family in his house, and the Melki family—many families from the area. There was my uncle, my father's brother, who was the guard at the powder factory, and another guard who lived on the other side. The neighbor went out and phoned the police. He told them: "Several families are in danger." The police told him that they were coming to get us. It was two o'clock in the morning when the police car pulled up in front of the door. With their weapons in their hand, they made us get in. The place was full of Arabs. From there, we went to the powder factory to pick up the other families. When we got to the Place de la Brèche, they had us get out to take shelter in the commiseriat. That's where I realized I was barefoot. There was glass on the ground. I walked on it and slit my foot.

The other families were able to stay with relatives. For us, with my uncle and my husband, they found us a place to live. We weren't about to make trouble. We lived through some very difficult moments, the time when everything calmed down.

Thank God, we got out of it alive, but we didn't trust anyone anymore. For the sake of the children, we found a place to live in town, and that's where we stayed.

[*Later on:*] My husband went to see the commissioner. He told him how that Berber had saved several Jewish families. A little while later, he was decorated with the medal of bravery for his courage.

After telling what she and her family suffered directly, Suzanne T. assesses the riots for the Jewish population as a whole.

Within a short time, the town was fire and blood. Rue Nationale was the street most seriously affected. Rich Jews lived in that neighborhood as well as on Rue Caramoun and Rue de France. The Attali family lived there; the father was a printer. Their daughter had just gotten her diploma as a midwife—in Algeria, there was no school for midwives, you had to go study in Montpellier. The parents had waited for Sunday, the very day of their daughter's return, to celebrate their son's communion [*bar mitzvah*]. The party was to have been that very evening. But the Arabs let loose. The girl was downstairs with her brother. They started by raping her, torturing her right in front of her brother. They cut off one of her breasts. Then it was the boy's turn. He was barely thirteen years old. In Rue Nationale, the family of Alphonse Halimi was killed. The little servant, seeing how they killed the masters, took the two-month-old baby from its cradle and hid with him in the attic. She saved the baby's life, but he was completely orphaned. Later on, when help finally arrived, she was absolutely hysterical. At the end of the Rue de France, it was a family of butchers, Taieb . . .

There were others who were killed—in all, a collection of thirty-three coffins. The whole town was in mourning that week. All those corpses were gathered together in the cemetery, and all the shops closed that day as a sign of mourning. The French had stirred up the Arabs against the Jews. They had waited for the month of August, when everybody was on vacation. The mayor, Morineau, the prefect, all the notables were absent. They left the Jews at the mercy of the Arabs. There was an assistant to the mayor: what could he do after the town and its inhabitants were massacred? He called on the Senegalese riflemen stationed in Philippeville.

The town was never itself again after that—what with the unemployment, the unease. People were scared. Everybody was scared at the sight of most of the Jews in mourning. Constantine had been known for its gaiety, but nobody wanted to laugh anymore. You had to go on working to live; you really had no other choice. But something was missing. You lived in the fear that it would happen again. And that's how the year '34 ended.

In the memories reported from eastern Algeria, no one mentioned the riots of Sétif and Constantine that took place in May 1945 and during which several thousand Algerians died, victims of ruthless repression. People weep only for the dead of their own community.

FAR FROM THE FRONT:
ANTI-SEMITISM AND THE WAR

In the interval, World War II had taken place. In Tunisia, it left memories of the fear provoked by the German presence between the autumn of 1942 and the spiring of 1943. Everywhere, the memory remains of the shortages and the ingenuity necessary just to survive. In Algeria, there is also the memory of the shock at the anti-Semitism of the colonial population and the anti-Jewish laws imposed by the Vichy government.

Suzanne T.:

One day, in 1941, I had sent my two children to school as usual. An hour later, they came back crying. I asked them why and they answered: "They sent us home from school. The principal told us that school is for the French, not for the Jews." And with the other students, he sang them an anti-Jewish song. And, of course, misfortune never comes alone. We heard on the radio that all Jews had to appear with the family passbook on Rue d'Isly in order for all to register. With my husband (meanwhile demobilized), we went. There was a line and we stood at the end of it. I had my last baby, who was four months old, in my arms. All those who passed by wondered what it was. They looked at us like we were strange animals. In front of us, there was an abbot, Abbot Stora, and his sister, a little mendicant nun. A policeman came up to them and said: "Father, Sister, you don't belong here." The abbot answered: "We're Jews." Then our turn came. They gave us the blue papers—I still have them—for the whole family, even the four-month-old baby. Along with these papers, they were supposed to give us the yellow star. Thank God, they never gave them to us. They had even planned a concentration camp to lock up all the Jews in El Biar.

Later, on the radio, we learned that all the Jewish students could return to school. But the children never wanted to go back. Life became impossible with the alerts and the bombs.

Gillette F., Aïn Beïda:

I didn't want to go to school anymore because of the status of the Jews. You mustn't forget that, unfortunately. And since they had shoved us aside we didn't have any desire to study anymore. They shoved us aside: if you were a native Jew, you were this, you were that. The French came first and then us. We were part of the natives. We weren't part of the class anymore. They put us in another school, which was in the *midrash* [*the synagogue*], a Jewish school. We could continue our studies, but I know that I lost all interest in it. It was over, and I just let it drop.

Manou B.:

There was racism there, but we didn't give a damn. It wasn't really a problem. We did suffer from it in '42 at the time of Vichy, but that didn't last long. I was sent home from school in '42 with my little brother, and I started working in the barracks right away as a secretary.

[*Speaking of the Jewish neighborhood, she continues*]: Anyway, even if you wanted to live farther away, you weren't allowed to. People wouldn't let you in as soon as they knew you were a Jew. They refused to give you a place to live. When I got married, I had found an apartment in the Saint Jean section. I went to see it. My husband didn't look Jewish at all. He was blond with blue eyes, he didn't look at all like that . . . not even like a pied-noir. We went and saw the apartment, and we were ready to negotiate. And when he gave his name, Cohen-B., the guy said: "Listen, mister, there's somebody ahead of you." So we didn't get the apartment. I got married in 1945, right after the war.

Other Jews of the Mediterranean basin were already in France when the war broke out. They shared the tragedy of the Jews of Europe and the unspeakable memories it left behind.

8
In Europe

IN SOME MEMORIES of Poland or Russia, the figure of the Other at first seems absent. The memory of the shtetl, with its warm community, passes over the Christian part of the village in silence. The Jewish world seems to be a self-enclosed entity.[1] When the Poles or the Russians inevitably burst into the narration, they simultaneously shatter that isolation and the earlier happiness. Then hatred and violence well up: in the memories of childhood, the Others are associated with anti-Semitism.

THE OTHERS IN POLAND

Handed down from generation to generation, historical memory in eastern Europe has preserved a long series of misfortunes, from the massacres of Chmielniecki, in 1648–49, to the waves of pogroms in the 1880s and then in the beginning of the century. Individual memories dating from the interwar period, in newly independent Poland, are a continuation of this collective past.

In this context, the case of Élie E. is distinguished by its originality: So tiny was his shtetl in Galicia that the Jews (two or three families) had no alternative but to live in economic and social symbiosis with the Polish peasants surrounding them. He explains how his family escaped the flood of pogroms around 1920.

1. On this "erasing of the *goyim*," see also Annette Wieviorka and Itzhok Niborski, *Les Livres du souvenir: Memoriaux Juifs de Pologne* [The Books of Memory: Jewish Memorials of Poland] (Paris: Gallimard/Juliard, 1983), p. 138.

My father owned lands, which he cultivated like a peasant. He was a very pious, very religious Jew. My mother, who was from Rumania, came from a great family of rabbis, *mitnagdim,* learned men who criticized the romanticism of the Hasidim. We lived in a tiny, very isolated shtetl in Galicia, in the sub-Carpathian Mountains, set in a magnificent landscape, with beautiful curtains of trees. To get there, you had to continue by cart, after the last station of the narrow-gage railroad.

There were only two or three Jewish families in that shtetl. I liked the Polish peasants all around us. I played with their children, except during the days of the pogrom. Then they told me: "Tomorrow, we won't play with you—they're going to saw the Jews!" What did that mean? They put a Jew between two boards and they saw!

Right after the Great War, there were peasant uprisings, first against the landowners; then there were pogroms and, finally, a series of acts of marauding. During the pogroms, we saw the peasants leaving the surrounding villages in carts, heading for a shtetl. The returns were especially painful. They came back dragging Jewish women—we heard the cries. First one shtetl, then another. We waited for our turn. My family escaped the pogroms because, every time, something happened that allowed us to be spared.

I remember, one day, I was in the kitchen with our stableboy and some peasants from the shtetl he had gathered to protect us. They were standing guard. Since I was a young boy (about ten years old), they didn't pay any attention to me. And I overheard our stableboy say to the others: "If there is a pogrom against them, we're the ones who have to begin. They're ours!"

There was also a carpenter's son who had come back from the war after traveling a lot. He had acquired nice manners. To us, he was brilliant. We admired his fine appearance, his elegance. I remember that he had a magnificent butterfly collection. He paid court to my older sisters with a perfect correctness and propriety. So, he often came to the house, stayed late; he became a sort of regular. He and his companions would protect us. It was during the banditry, which could strike anyone, not only the Jews. And that friend, who often came to our house, was arrested. He confessed to twenty crimes and was sentenced and then executed. That's how we learned that he himself had been the head of a gang. He came to our house just so he'd have an alibi.

Is there some sort of paradoxical mutual attraction combined with anti-Semitic violence? The narrative of Georges F. (committed, as we have seen earlier, to the ideas of modernity and progress) indicates another type of ambiguity. His shtetl had been transformed, with the establishment of a munitions factory; it took on the proportions of a small town. Georges F. states that, with the economic development and the increase of the Polish population (composed of workers, engineers, and members of the intelligentsia), anti-Semitism was considerably aggravated: it seemed to result ultimately from the process of civilization itself.

Then the village grew. It attracted a lot of people. They built a bridge to provide access to the railroad station. It became a railroad junction for Poland. [. . .] A factory, a very big armaments factory, was set up. It attracted people, but the Jews weren't allowed to work there. None of that was done for the Jews; the Jews were pushed to the rear. They started building houses for the workers, the Catholics, since the Jews couldn't get into the factory. When all those workers came into our village, racism also came, anti-Semitism. While the Catholics were gathered in church on Sunday, the Jews were afraid to go out into the street. We hid. There were times when we just didn't go out into the street without being accompanied by someone.

Racism was a by-product of civilization and kept us from living normally. [. . .] By 1933–34, the situation was becoming intolerable. In the streets, they constantly taunted us: "Just wait till Hitler comes, he'll take care of you!"

One felt sorely betrayed and bewildered to discover this anti-Semitism even among those considered to be friends.

Léon W.:

I told you about the May Day demonstration. That was in 1922. I participated in that demonstration. We paraded with the red flag; they had deliberately put us in the middle. Then, right in the midst of the demonstration, somebody shouted: "Down with the Jews!" I got hit with a stone in my leg. They were socialists who were shouting, workers. Even in the Socialist party, there was anti-Semitism. I never understood why.

The hostility of the surrounding world did not always assume the exacerbated form of the pogrom. It was manifested, more or less sharply, in the banality of everyday life as well.

Bernard P., born in 1922:

One problem concerned the high school [*the Hebrew high school of Kalisz*]. Since school was six days a week, we didn't go to school on Saturdays but on Sundays. And because of that, as a small child, I had the opportunity to experience for the first time the effects of anti-Semitism, for, often, while going to school on Sunday, I had to protect myself from stones thrown by the non-Jewish boys who didn't accept the idea that you could go to school on Sunday.

Maurice N., born in 1920:

Anti-Semitism always existed because we were separate. The Jews were on one side, the Poles on the other. In school, we weren't mixed, and there was antagonism. There were often wars between us, between Jewish kids and Polish kids. We used to fight a lot.

Robert S., born in 1907:

So I went to high school, and as far as I can remember, it was there that I had my first contact with anti-Semitism. Every week, we had a lesson in Jewish history, Judaism, an hour a week with a Jewish teacher. That is, every year, there were three series, A, B, and C, like today. We divided up: the Jews of the three series formed a group with the Jewish teacher, and the Christians gathered with their priest. And we found that every time we met again after the religion class, the behavior of the Christian students toward the Jews was abominable—as if somebody had incited them against the Jews. At first, we didn't understand. We were just kids, eleven years old. We didn't really grasp very well what was going on. But I remember that they spit in our faces and treated us as dirty Jews.

Charles H., in his small town in Galicia, also went to the Polish high school. His memories echo the preceding ones though they paint a more subtle picture.

In the Polish high school, we were in contact with non-Jews, who were in the majority. To begin with, there were two of us Jews in a class of twenty-two or twenty-five students; that is, we weren't even 10 percent. Sometimes, a certain camaraderie developed. I used to go to the homes of non-Jewish friends where I was accepted, or they came to my home. But I don't remember eating a single time in the home of a non-Jew in eight years of high school. And they didn't eat in our home either. We lived separately, side by side.

It's rather strange, it will give you an idea of the relations we had. I must have been fourteen or fifteen years old. I started the first soccer club in our town, me and a non-Jewish friend who came from Cracow. We became friendly because we were among the best students in the class. He told me that in his old high school he had played on a soccer team. In our little town, people didn't know what soccer was, neither the Jews nor the non-Jews.

So the two of us decided that's what we would do. I remember that we collected money for a year to buy a leather ball. We took it from our allowances: try talking to parents about a ball! First, they didn't even understand what we were talking about! We talked it up with our classmates, and I was the treasurer. A few months later, we finally collected enough money and, on a trip to Cracow, we bought a ball. Afterward, it wasn't a problem. There was a big field in the back of city hall. We marked it out, we drew lines, maybe not exactly according to the dimensions, but we began practicing. Then, we managed to form two teams. Soccer had caught on. There were matches, and people came to watch. Nobody paid, of course, but people came to see. My friend was the president of the club, and I was the treasurer.

Two years later, once it was already established, the teacher of our class started to get interested and he took charge. Since it was his class, he took over and started coaching us. It was then that there started to be a hostility toward the Jews. I, along with my pal, was the founder, yet he gradually pushed me out. I was one of the founders but I was a Jew, so the teacher took over as boss, and I found myself out. They couldn't eliminate me as a player, but I was no longer one of the leaders of the club. Now that the club was organized and was successful, that teacher turned it into a patriotic and anti-Semitic glory.

So, since there were quite a few Jews who came to watch the games, we created a Jewish athletic club. Like all Jewish clubs, it was called Maccabee. We created our own club. When there was a match against my class, I played with the Maccabees.

[. . .] I was the best student in the class and, in particular, I was the best in Polish. One day, to give you a sense what it was like. . . . It was the last year, we were already preparing for the baccalaureate. Our Latin and Polish teacher was very friendly with us. One day, he gave an assignment: we each had to make an oral exposition on the influence of the uprising of 1863 on Polish literature. He started with one student, then a second, then a fourth, a fifth: they talked, let's say, two or three minutes, or they didn't open their mouths. After half an hour, tired, he called on me. He called me by my first name: "Haim, do you want to speak about that?" And me, I spoke for an hour and a half! I had read a lot of Polish literature (and not only Polish literature). So, the remark the teacher made at the end of the class:

"And it has to be a Jew who tells you about that!"

That's the remark. And he wasn't an anti-Semite. He was friendly . . .

My friends needed me. Sometimes there was a problem or a composition to do at home. About ten of my classmates came to my house to ask my advice. I was very much in demand, for no other reason than that they wanted my help. Except for one girl. I was in love with her.

She was the best non-Jewish student in the class, so we studied for the baccalaureate exam together. It just happened that this girl was the best. And she was good-looking, with her black hair. I had been very friendly with that girl for two or three years by then. Many years later, in Jerusalem, I learned from an aunt (the only one who survived because she had been in Siberia; one day she talked to me about that when I found her again in Jerusalem)—I learned that my parents had been afraid of a mixed marriage. I didn't know, I was so absorbed in preparing for the baccalaureate exam. I was working hard. We worked together; we were good friends. Anyway, I probably was in love. I don't know exactly what her feelings were. But we did kiss each other. In those days, to kiss a girl was a big deal! But neither of us, not me and not her, thought of marriage.

So there were Poles who were close and even friendly. There were also those who played a role in the life of the Jews: caretakers, shabbes goyim *(who took care of the fires and the lights during holidays). Precisely this involvement in the Jewish world reduced their otherness. Those Poles not only shared the joys and sorrows of their neighbors but they also spoke perfect Yiddish. Sometimes this proximity gave rise to mix-ups, later jokingly recalled. Léon W. lived in Kalisz in the house described earlier by Lazare M.*

The caretakers spoke Yiddish just like me. I'm going to tell you a story that illustrates this. It was during the pogrom. The caretaker of our house lived in the cellar. It was a basement. A Jewish shoemaker also lived in this basement. During the pogrom, they beat up the Jews. They came into the courtyard—we lived a little farther away, on the first floor. They came into the courtyard and started smashing all the floors. They thought they were in the Jews' houses, but it was the caretaker's! So [laughs] the caretaker came out and scuffled with them! Such stories.

It is as though the Other could only have brotherly feelings if he were drawn into a condition of sameness. A tragic case bears this out: reverse assimilation led to sharing the fate of genocide.

Georges F.:

Yes, I had friends who weren't Jews because our village was so small. We knew each other, and we ran into each other on the square. Personally, I was well liked by my Catholic pals. We lived so close together that we didn't learn much Polish but they learned Yiddish. Really. There were kids who lived with us, Catholics, who spoke Yiddish like me. There was one who got himself deported, a Catholic. He got himself deported just because of his language. He spoke Yiddish, and nobody ever believed he was a Catholic. He went up in smoke like the rest.

THE WANDERING JEWS

Conversely, however, mastery of the Polish language was not enough to ensure integration into the national community. We recall the difference that existed for Robert S. between the Polish he used with his parents (although they spoke to him in Yiddish) and the French he learned later on (and which, despite all his efforts, still put up resistance to his eagerness to master it). The complicity that bound him to another Polish speaker could not, however, substitute for a homeland. With his fellow citizens, he never found the emotional warmth or the bonds of solidarity that united him with the Jewish community. Quite the contrary, he felt persecuted and rejected by the Austrians as well as by the Poles. Deciding to leave his homeland and to live in France, he moved into a situation of total and utter uprootedness. His life unfolded against a background of insurmountable otherness, for he would always miss that familiarity with a native land that one usually acquires only in one's childhood. Ultimately, in attempting to define himself, Robert could only turn to the millennial figure of the Wandering Jew.

I think that a person's baggage begins with the years of childhood, when everything is stored away like a treasure you draw on in hard times. Now, as for me in that period, I myself didn't store up anything. Why? Because the behavior of the citizens of first Austria and then Poland kept me from getting what I was entitled to expect. I was always beyond the pale, I was always marginal: in Austria, in Poland, and later in France. In spite of all my efforts to try—I don't say to assimilate (for that's not my goal)—but to integrate into that society where I was destined to live, without offending it, I have always felt that people considered me different. I've tried everything. I've done everything, but I haven't really succeeded. I see that whatever we do, we're strangers wherever we go: the Wandering Jew.

I can reassure myself, being a French citizen, naturalized, having filled all my obligations—I say it honestly: I have never suffered from anti-Semitism in France, because here it is latent. For the moment, I feel relatively calm. But if you ask me whether I'm sure that those things, anti-Semitism and all the rest, won't come back, I wouldn't swear to it.

Here I am, this uprooted Jew. I would have liked to keep up with my high school friends. I've always missed them. In short, I had to pick up twice and start out all over again in a new society. Now, the connections that bind young people in school can't be compared with those you create later on. Memories of childhood are of a certain sort: "You remember that fight, that joke?" It's all there, moments of pain, tears, and joy. Later on, you can't allow yourself that luxury (for it is a luxury); and that's the essential point.

Louise M. feels a similar sense of uprootedness and finds that the same holds for her friends, in England, Holland—everywhere.

It's no fun, you know, to be . . . to lose your roots. It's no fun. My best friend lives in London, my best friend since Frankfurt, a long, long time ago. She's an art historian, and her husband was too. She never completely put down roots in England. Her relatives, most of them, also came from Germany. She always says that her nationality is British but that she isn't English because that's only when you're born in England. Otherwise you're *British*.[2] So, she remains a foreigner. Maybe it's different in America. But in a country of tradition, it's hard. In Holland too. I have a cousin in Holland. I have gone to visit her many times, and who are the people around her? They're always people who came from Germany.

THE OTHERS IN FRANCE

In France, these immigrants are marked by a double otherness: of the foreigner and of the Jew. Aside from administrative and police

2. The word is given in English in the original.

annoyances, they inevitably find a certain anti-Semitic hostility. But in this country of the Dreyfus Affair, anti-Semitism appears much more "moderate" than what they knew in Poland. At least up until the war. In fact, their memories are divided by a new gap, this time, a chronological one. Although the memory of the 1930s, for example, dwells on the difficulties connected with "permissions" (or "refusals") to stay, it is often expressed with humor and does not fundamentally question the hospitality of the French.

Georges F.:

Life in Paris wasn't so happy for those who came. You had to hide, not go out at night. The police were after us. It wasn't all that great. For example, one night, despite the problems, I went to a class on Rue de Lancry. There were classes for immigrants, but we were afraid to go because they could pick us up coming out. We were illegal.

Bernard P.:

It wasn't simple. France didn't give a visa. But finally, with the help of relatives, we passed through Italy. We stayed there three weeks. In Italy, we got tourist visas (that was one of the last visas), tourist visas for France. And that tourist visa could be changed in France into a permit to stay that could be extended from month to month. Until the Liberation, I had no papers but the receipts of extension from one month to the next (aside from the period of hiding, of course).

Julien K.:

When I came back to Paris, I tried to legalize my situation. But since I was returning from Spain, I didn't get a real permit to stay. They just extended my receipts until, finally, they gave me a refusal to stay. That was a valuable paper. With a refusal to stay, you could stay until a particular date, at which time the arbitrariness started. Sometimes it was for two months, sometimes three months. And once they extended me for three days. When I went back to the prefecture, they said to me: "Bring certificates from three consulates, saying that they refuse to give you a visa!" I don't remember anymore what consulates I went to. They gave me certificates easily enough! And that's how I managed until the war, with the refusal to stay.

We remember that Mathilde R., by contrast, was born in France and was even brought up not knowing (in principle) of her Jewish origin. She therefore could not make sense of the way the others looked at her in the Catholic school and the meanness of some of the teachers.

First, I had a schoolmistress who twisted my name in a horrible way. I didn't understand why at all. I just thought that my name was particularly difficult to pronounce and strange, one that made my little classmates laugh a lot. For a schoolmistress, every time, she kept harping on it. I can't say that she was really unfair because, frankly, I had come to be second or first, but she was always very nasty, very harsh, while she was generally nice with students who were well behaved.

I also remember (that must have been the next year) that, in gymnastics, there was a teacher who also made a point of systematically messing up my name. I was very good in gymnastics, but I remember that, one day, there was an unusually difficult competition. That is, she had us do increasingly complicated movements, and she eliminated those who failed. Then there were two of us left. She knew that there was one movement I did badly and that's the movement she chose to decide the winner. Anyway, it would perhaps oversimplify to say it was only because of anti-Semitism. But that doesn't keep me from being convinced of it today.

OTHER JEWS

The Others are not only non-Jews, Poles, Russians, or French. There are also other Jews. Certainly, in France—and especially in Poland or Russia—the immigrants were familiar with the extreme diversity of the Jewish world, from the most religious to the most assimilated. But it is significant that the discovery of other Jews, who are Jewish Others, took place during trips and migrations.

When Robert S., coming from Poland, arrived in a big city in eastern France, he found a category he was ignorant of until then, the Israelites.

Their integration, even assimilation, into French society did not sur-prise him at all. But he was astonished by their indifference to the misfortunes striking their co-religionists in central and eastern Europe and by their hostility toward the immigrants.[3] He was stunned and shocked by the absence of solidarity among Jews, which was inconceiv-able to him. His clash with the rabbi of the city marked a break in his life: he lost his faith.

When I came to France, before I found work with my future father-in-law, I went to the rabbi, as a Christian would go to his priest. I went to see the rabbi because I had been raised in the spirit of Judaism and I was a believer. At least I was when I left home; it was only later that I became the infidel I am now. So, I went to the rabbi's. He was Alsatian, the chief rabbi H. I knock on the door. He opened it but didn't invite me in. He asked me what I wanted. So I explained to him, in German, that I wanted to work to put myself through school, that I wasn't asking for charity. I made it very clear that I wanted to work. And what did the rabbi, chief rabbi H., answer me? "Young man, you should know that you don't come to France to study if you don't have money!" He was about to slam the door. I had just enough time to put my foot in and stop him, and I said to him: "I'll meet you again in five years. I'll prove to you that one can study when one wants, even if one doesn't have any money." And I left.

However, thanks to a subterfuge, Robert S. benefited anonymously from the Jewish community. We recall that, in 1933, after five years of study, he received his certificate as a dentist.

I devoted the first money I earned to paying back my debt. This time openly. I went to see the Secretary of the Faculty.

"Sir, I now have the money necessary to pay back the com-munity. If you will be so kind as to give me the acknowledg-ment that I have signed, I will take the sum to the rabbi."

3. On the relations between French Jews and immigrant Jews, cf. Paula Hyman, *From Dreyfus to Vichy: The Remaking of French Jewry, 1906–1939* (New York: Columbia University Press, 1979). Also David H. Weinberg, *A Com-munity on Trial*, pp. 95–132.

I knocked on the rabbi's door. And that time, he invited me in, for I was speaking proper French.

"What's this about, young man?"

He had obviously forgotten me.

"Chief rabbi, in 1928, I came to you. You received me at the door. I made myself very clear, at the door. I asked you to help me get work and not money. I didn't come to beg for charity. And you answered me: 'In France, you don't come to study when you don't have money.' I, in turn, set a meeting for 1933. Here I am. This is to prove to you that when one wants to, one can study. And here is my diploma. That's not all. We aren't yet even. I contracted a debt through Monsieur T., the Secretary of the Faculty; you advanced a sum that helped me at a critical moment. That allowed me to continue my studies. I am grateful to you for that. I thank you for it. Here is the money I owe you."

He took the money and stared at me.

"Young man, I must tell you that this is all to your credit."

I laughed at what he told me. I thought that, if I hadn't had the will to study, he would have ruined my future. And I couldn't forgive him for that.

"All the same, I would like an explanation, chief rabbi. I was raised in a house where religion counted. The world claims that the Jewish community is distinguished by its solidarity. Jews are supposed to support one another. You didn't give me any evidence of that. Why did you refuse when I asked you for work? I was only asking for work, not money."

So he took a key, opened a drawer of his desk, and took out a pile of passports.

"There, young man. All those passports are pledges for the money your studious comrades have borrowed."

"Is that a sufficient reason to refuse me? Why did you put me with them? In the Bible, in the story of Sodom and Gomorrah, Abraham haggled with God so that He would forgive: "My God, if you find only fifty righteous men, will you forgive?" And he came down to one. If there was only one righteous man, God would have forgiven. He didn't find any, and God didn't forgive. But you? You didn't know if I was upright or not! Why did you judge me without knowing? You failed in your duty and you have lost a Jew. I succeeded in finishing school because that was my will and my ambition, but you don't have any share in it. You failed in your ministry."

If I had given him a couple of slaps, it wouldn't have been more effective. He got the little lesson he deserved and I left.

For Robert S., other Jews weren't limited only to French Jews; he also included the children of immigrants, born in France, who, in their arrogance and blindness, thought they could escape the dangers of Nazism. He repeats the reasons why he is cut off from religion.

I understand, one could argue that it is man, not religion, that is sinful. When a priest does his holy office badly, he is removed. Now, I talked about it with the Jews of the community: they liked that Alsatian whom I detested from the depths of my heart. Because he had all the typical Alsatian traits. I become almost racist as regards those Alsatians. I was able to observe them during the war, Jews and Christians. It's really something to see: they're more French than the French. Alsatian Jews are just like the *Yekes,* the German Jews. They thought: "It can't happen to me, a Jew who has been here for one, two, three centuries. It can't happen to me."

I'm going to quote one case. In Nancy, there were two boys who rose up from the ranks. They were of foreign origin, but born in France. The rabbi pushed them. One, named D., went to the Polytechnic school[4] and then had an important position in the Socialist party. Another one, B., became a lawyer. At present, he's in the consistory. They were that kind of French Jew who—with regard to us foreigners who came from Poland and central Europe—kept us at a distance. No mixing, if you please. You mustn't mix napkins and washcloths. Yes, I had a rough time of it. When I met guys like that, it made me sick. I couldn't foresee that, unfortunately—I really mean unfortunately—the future would undertake to show them that, although they were born in France, they wouldn't be spared any more than we foreigners who came from somewhere else.

4. One of the most prestigious French schools for engineers.

Life takes funny turns. Sometimes it corrects injustices. I was in Montpellier, at my oldest son's. I went out to the avenue and sat down in a café to read my newspaper. All of a sudden, I felt somebody tapping me on the shoulder. I looked up and saw my B., after thirty some years, lawyer B., the one who was so aloof, as if he had been born in France because of some personal merit. Of course, I invited him to join me for a drink. I invited him to sit down at the table, and he actually did. I had the sense while we were talking that something was bothering him. He was ill at ease. I was too, but it was more obvious with him. He was very fidgety. Something was wrong. And then, at a certain moment, he came out with it: "Monsieur S., I owe you an apology."

Yes, after some thirty years. I said to myself: So that's it. He's got it, he's finally understood. I knew what it was all about. I was sure it was going to be that and that was that. I listened to my Lawyer B., after so many years:

"You can believe me or not, but for years it's been haunting me. I was unfair to you, thinking it wouldn't happen to me."

"Yes, Counsellor, I think you were unfair and, morally, you hurt us a lot with your behavior. You did just what the Yekes did when people talked to them about their situation. Up to the last minute. However, we had already seen what Hitler was capable of."

The memories of the Jews of central and eastern Europe virtually ignore the Sephardic Jews. These latter were occasionally mentioned in historical contexts, when the various misfortunes of the Jewish people were recalled: the expulsion from Spain and the harshness of the Inquisition have entered a common memory that stretches from the Mediterranean lands to Russia. But Sephardic Jews appear physically only in the course of the itineraries followed in migrations. Thus, we have seen Louise M. escape from Germany to Morocco (by way of Amsterdam). There, Moroccan Jews emerge as fundamentally different and "backward." She then experiences a total inability to communicate.

In Morocco, naturally, our life was completely different from what it had been in Germany. It was something else altogether, to such an extent that the Moroccan Jews sometimes didn't want to recognize us as Jews. They just didn't want to: "Because you don't know this, you don't do that, so you're not Jews." In general, we were extremely well received, but there wasn't . . . there were very few points in common between their life in general and ours. Naturally, that changed, when we came it was still very backward. You can't imagine the women there. The women were still in a condition that was really . . . characterized by great intellectual poverty. Those women didn't understand that we were Jews. We didn't have anything in common with them.

With the men, it depended on the generation. Those who went to school and became teachers or . . . That made an enormous difference. But mothers didn't speak French. Fathers maybe knew it, but mothers spoke only Arabic with an unbelievable speed, unbelievable.

Mathilde R., then about ten years old, took a trip to Poland with her mother, to visit her grandparents and other members of her family. She was still ignorant about her Jewish origin (although certain signs had aroused some puzzlement in her). For her, this trip was the occasion of a double discovery. On the one hand, the anti-Semitic hostility of a Polish child made her suddenly aware "of what she had always known." On the other hand, she met Jews who were unknown to her until then—Hasidim—at whom she looked with condescension (while warning us, clearly, that she no doubt adopted the assimilated, upper-middle-class opinions of her uncle). Mathilde R.'s story in fact unfolds on several levels. She reenacts the events intensely, in slow motion, to such an extent that the image, rich in detail, seems frozen, as if speech were attempting to restore the moment when the scene was engraved in her memory. At the same time, in a complementary movement, the narrator flies over the years, establishing relations her contemporaries could never have suspected. Both a remembrance and a reflection on remembrance come into play. Finally, with an almost timeless serenity, in her retrospective commentary, she puts in the same category ("there was no longer any difference") all those other Jews of Poland, in whom she has found her own identity.

There was the daughter of the caretaker of the little building there. One day, she started dancing around me, dancing on one leg and singing: *"Kocher Zyd! Kocher Zyd!"*[5] On that day my eyes were opened. I absolutely . . . That was really the way they describe . . . the way we know it happens when children discover. . . . They are told one day how children are made and they know they always knew it. Really. In short, I understood everything all at once.

I also understood that it wasn't nice. It didn't seem to be all that bad, what she said to me, but I understood very well that she wasn't doing it to please me. I ran to my aunt, my mother's brother's wife. She was an intelligent woman, very sweet and nice, who disappeared with her husband during the war, in the Warsaw ghetto. She consoled me, saying: "You know, being Jewish is very good, very noble. We're a very old people, a very noble people." I still remember the words she used, in Polish, even though I never speak Polish anymore and I never did know it well. I still hear her words. Probably from that moment on, I began to notice quite a few things, unless I have reinterpreted them since.

During that short trip to Poland, that stay which lasted one or two months, in the summer of '38, I remember walking down a street in Lodz. There was a big banner across the street, with a brush attached. And it was marked: *Bic Zydow.*[6] I asked somebody to translate it for me: "Get the Jews!"

I also remember my uncle, the middle-class uncle. He also practiced the policy of assimilation in Poland. I still see him, wearing gaiters, pale yellow gloves, a cane with a handle. It must have been a Sunday, a Saturday, in any case, a day when they didn't work. And the Hasidim passed by, in long coats, with *payes.*[7] They didn't look very clean. Maybe it was because I had already adopted the prejudices of that side of the family, although I was fairly neutral about all that, I watched them. But I had the impression that they weren't very clean. They went by and shouted to my uncle: "It's because of you, people like you, what's happening to us!" And my uncle answered them: "It's because of people like you!"

5. Kosher Jew, in Polish.
6. "Beat the Jews." The narrator's translation is softened.
7. Sidecurls.

That's something that stayed with me like a kind of symbol: you could have put that in a film and seen them together, at the end, in a concentration camp, reconciled the following year. There was no more difference.

I see it all again, there. Absolutely. I think that if I went back there, I would find the house and the exact place where my uncle was standing when those Hasidim passed by.

PART FOUR
*Exile and
Mourning*

9
A New
Diaspora

In the camp, I had this idea of coming to France. In the camp at that time, you couldn't have anything in your pockets because there was a search every other day. If they found a piece of paper, anything, they beat you. My cousin [*met for the first time in Auschwitz*] gave me his girlfriend's address: "I can't give you my own address because I don't know where my parents are." And there it is, that address. I still remember it: Thérèse Levère, 17 Rue des Fleurs, Paris XVII. And every morning, when I got up, I said my prayer: Thérèse Levère, 17 Rue des Fleurs, Paris XVII. . . . Well, when I was liberated, in Sweden, he [*the cousin*] was already in Paris. He was a survivor. I wrote to his girlfriend. She went to his house and told him: "I got this letter from Stockholm." He answered me right away. We got in touch and he told me: "If you don't want to go back to Salonika, come to France." And that's how I came.

[*On his arrival in Paris*] My uncle said to me: "Come to us to eat whenever you want." And I went to eat at my uncle's house every day.

Then later, I met Salonikans who were there from before the war. One day, they introduced me to a lady: "You like her, that lady? She is also a stall-keeper. Her husband was deported. If you like, I'll put you in touch. See if it suits you. If not, you needn't do anything. If it does, we'll introduce you to her." It worked out, and I'm still with that woman. [*Gabriel D., Salonika, about 1910.*]

In the cohort of Jews who have told us of their youth here or there on the shores of the Mediterranean, a first group came to France between the two world wars, those of the eastern Mediterranean. In North Africa, the colonial regime appeared firmly established and destined to last. Social mobility, westernization, and secularization reached new strata of the Jewish population. Those who left for France went for a little adventure and stayed only temporarily, returning with some new asset, a university diploma, for example. In Egypt, the formal independence the country enjoyed since 1922 opened new vistas to the most enterprising. In Greece and Turkey, by contrast, political conditions became unstable. The revolution of the Young Turks, the capture of Salonika by the Greeks in 1912, the arrival in Salonika of more than one hundred thousand Greeks from Asia as one of the population exchanges following World War I affected all elements of the population and upset relations between religious communities. First, the Jews wanted to evade military service and conflicts that were none of their business—the Italian-Turkish war of 1911–12, the Balkan wars of 1912–13, and finally, World War I. A few years later, they had to escape anti-Semitism, which began to rage more openly in Greece. As Gabriel D. tells us, some left Salonika for Palestine. He was one of them. He participated in the construction of the port of Tel Aviv but did not stay there. Some went to the United States, and others, finally, chose France.

Why? Explanations have already come up in the memories we have read: all western countries enjoyed great prestige, unlike the local sociopolitical systems in which people calculated that the possibilities of making their way were limited. Through school or other means, they had acquired French culture. But the lever of history they tell us about, the decisive element that loomed to set them in motion was a relative who had already taken the plunge and moved to France. Someone from "home" was already there; "home" had moved to France and was waiting on the other shore. An unconvincing explanation, for somebody had to make the break in the first place. But people don't want to dwell on the driving force. They just assume that once the community of origin had set foot in France, France was no longer a foreign coun-

try. The connection with France can be so tenuous that sometimes it sounds like an incantation: "Thérèse Levère, 17 Rue des Fleurs, Paris XVII." Gabriel D., who saw his wife and daughter die in the camp, thirteen members of his family deported from Salonika to Auschwitz, recited like a prayer the name of that girlfriend of his cousin, who grew up in Paris and whom he met in the camp. In Paris, a newfound uncle fed him, and other Salonikans married him off.

"THE SAME GROUP"

Let us listen now to one of the pioneers of the migration to France (at least in our group),[1] Papou N. We left him in Marseille during World War I, where the authorities had created custom-made national identity for him: he was declared a "Salonikan." In Marseille he was no longer alone; indeed, he never was. His brother Henri had been inducted into the army at the same time as he. Their parents, informed of where their children were, immediately joined them, accompanied by one of their daughters. With this first movement, the family network reconstituted itself in the host country. They moved to Rue Paradis. The process continued: thanks to cousins from Paris, our hero was released, and the family obtained identity documents. A third brother, who had left Salonika for Athens during the war, also arrived in Marseille as did a sister, already married. The family network was further reinforced by the marriage of the brother of a sister-in-law with the hero's sister:

Aunt Sophie's brother, who had already known Aunt Mathilde in Salonika, also came to Marseille on leave, because he was in the Serbian army. He was a colonel or some pretty important rank. And we entertained him in our house, etc. . . . with my sister, who knew him . . . so well that three days later, a week later, he asked my father and mother for her hand. So my father and mother agreed, because they knew the family, since the sister was already my brother's wife. Aunt Mathilde got engaged and he went back to the army. They waited until

1. The Jews of the Ottoman Empire had begun to settle in France as early as the nineteenth century. See Paula Hyman, *From Dreyfus to Vichy*. More particularly, two of Papou N.'s uncles had emigrated to Paris.

the end of the war to get married and, in fact, when the armistice came, it was a time of great rejoicing. He came to Marseille on a regular leave and right away moved in with his fiancée. And they set the date of the wedding.

Simultaneously, a second process was operating, with the same success: the family network functioned as an economic network. From 1916 to 1918, the Marseille branch of the family supplied the brother, a purveyor of the army in Salonika. When the war was over, Papou N. persuaded his father to let him go to Paris to open a branch of the Marseille business. The new brother-in-law, barely demobilized, returned to Belgrade and was also ready for merchandise:

When he got back to Belgrade, he opened the shop he had with his father, and he needed merchandise. I was working as an agent in Paris for cloth, velvet, whatever he wanted. And from there, he sent me other customers. So it went well. So well that my second brother, Henri, also came to Paris, because alone . . .

As in Salonika, Papou N. was going to take a wife from the rediscovered or reconstituted community.

In 1920, about March or April, I was going to the Sentier,[2] because I went to the Sentier all the time to buy textiles for my customers. I meet Monsieur B.: "So, what are you doing here?" Hugs and all that. "You know it's our Passover?" "Yes, I know." "And you aren't going to your parents in Marseille?" "No, because I'm waiting for two customers from Yugoslavia and Rumania." "OK, listen, since you're not leaving, come to my house. Tomorrow night is Passover and it's our tradition to entertain friends and acquaintances. So, it would give me great pleasure to entertain you. I don't want you to stay alone in Paris on Passover night." So I accepted and we set a time. The next night, they introduced me around—there were two daughters—a very pleasant welcome. We sat down at the table, where there were ten or twelve people. Really, a very friendly,

2. The Sentier is the garment district in Paris.

very warm atmosphere. The father of my future wife—I didn't know she was my future wife—welcomed me very graciously. . . . And they had me for the next night too—another very pleasant welcome. They read the prayers. And meantime, I said: "Listen, you've invited me twice. It's my turn to invite you out." Then my father-in-law—my future father-in-law, that is—said to me: "Listen, that's very kind, but I don't go out at night. But if you like, invite my daughter and my son." And three days later, I invited the daughter and the son. I invited them to go to the Opéra Comique to see *Carmen*. They accepted. I came to pick them up and then had another invitation to their house. One thing led to another. I wrote my parents that I wanted to ask for her hand. I wanted them to give their consent. They told me: "How do you want us to give you our consent? We know the gentleman very well, but we don't know the daughter. If you think the girl suits you, pleases you . . . As for the family, that's fine, since we know the parents very well. But ask by yourself, saying that we agree."

Local endogamy continued to be practiced. What remained to be done was to appropriate a space. In the period between the two world wars, having given up the import-export business, those from Marseille and Paris congregate again in the Sentier and go into knitwear:

Before the European war of '14, all the people of Turkey, either from Istanbul or Salonika, who came to France to work started out in textiles. Textiles means cloth, hosiery, pullovers, etc. There were two centers: one near the Place Voltaire, which was of a lower class, for more ordinary things; and a center that was a little more stylish, which was the Sentier in Paris. The Sentier, as it was called, was known since Napoleon, ever since they made Rue Réaumur and all that. So they came and started by looking for a shop in the Sentier. It was Rue d'Aboukir. So, they were clustered together, so to speak. In 1920, for example, without exaggerating, of three hundred shops in the Sentier, about a hundred of them belonged to Salonikans. So you were in the same group, so to speak . . . you couldn't call it a family circle, but we were fellow countrymen.

This scenario is reproduced in many memories: parents and adult children decide together on migrations, economic initiatives, reorientations, matrimonial alliances. They celebrate Passover together as well as the New Year's Eve and other local holidays. They rediscover others in the Sentier. Enrique S. y B., who arrived in the 1910s, spent his whole life in the trade and manufacture of cloth along with his father-in-law. Ida O., whose husband managed two cinemas, a theater, and a dance hall in Salonika, started a cloth business in 1930 on Rue de Cléry in Paris. She also tells us that her son succeeded her. Married to a Salonikan, Laure A., from Istanbul, was not in the Sentier, but her husband owned several clothing shops in Paris between 1930 and 1970. Several levels lower, Gabriel D., who came after the war, sold knitwear in open markets. M. M., an upholsterer in Salonika and an upholsterer in Paris between 1922 and 1938, finally went into the knitwear business with a Salonikan brother-in-law and Salonikan friends.

SUCCESSFUL EMANCIPATION

Was it a successful route? This is the impression left by the story of Papou N., as animated when he spoke of his homeland as when he talked of his life in France. Many people would not have anything to say about their life in France, as if it were the natural outcome of a movement started in Greece or Turkey, an "emancipation," as they call it, which could only lead to France.

M. M., whose whole family remained in Salonika and was annihilated in the deportations, measures the road he has covered with satisfaction. For him, he found material and professional security; for the children, upward mobility through the schools: the host country generously filled the aspirations that could not have been satisfied in Greece. "Back home," however, still indicates Salonika in his speech.

Of our stay—it's not our stay anymore, it's *our lives* that we have led in France, from every perspective, although it was very hard for work and everything—we have a very good memory. Of the work, of the constitution of France that allowed us to do what we wanted, to educate the children. It's an enormous advantage we couldn't have had back home except by paying. And God knows if you could pay. That's something. The social laws are very, very good in France.

. . . On the whole, I repeat, I have been very satisfied with my stay and my life in France, and I think that the country has done well by everybody, by all foreigners.

Coming from Egypt, Gioia A. also preserves a dazzling memory of her marriage with France. It's a dream she realized in 1933. In Paris, she found a brother who had preceded her, an architect cousin. Did she know any French people? Yes, she still sees them in the spotlights.

When I went to apply for naturalization, the police inspector said to me: "Why, Madame, do you want to become French?" I said: "Monsieur, it's your fault." "My fault?" He was a poor soul, a police inspector who didn't know Bécon-les-Bruyères.[3] I said to him: "Here, Monsieur, I had a papa who spoke to us in French; my mother tongue, in spite of my accent, is French. I nursed on French milk; all the lullabies were French. I was in a Jewish school where I learned French; I was at the high school where I learned French; I passed the baccalaureate exams in French. And when we were little, they told us: 'France, France, France.' So I wanted only one thing: to come to France." And that was true. Besides, I'm going to tell you, my older brother came to France before us; he came in '18 [*he died shortly after*].

I always dreamed of coming to Paris. And when I married a man who lived in Paris, I don't know if I married him for himself or to come to Paris. I really don't remember.

I lived on the Champs-Élysées, the Lido. Because when he came to Paris, my husband said: "Nothing is too good for my wife." So we lived in the Lido, no more and no less. He had an office in the Sentier, since he imported fabrics from Lyon and worked in silk manufacture. When he was a bachelor, he went to all the cafés on the Champs-Élysées. But that really didn't interest me. I didn't come to Paris to sit in a café. He said to me: "Tell me what you want." "I want to go to the the-ater."[4] So we went to the theater. I knew it very well. It was the time of Sacha Guitry, Louis Jouvet, Charles Dullin. The first

3. Equivalent of "nowhere, France."
4. A literary echo of this representation of France is found in the autobio-graphical novel of Nine Moatti, *Mon enfant, ma mère.*

time I saw *Le Faiseur,* it was with Charles Dullin and it was the theater of the *Oeuvre.* And we went to Deauville for weekends, for Easter, for vacations.

Z., born in 1900 and living in Paris since early childhood, considers that he left behind the darkness of the confined, fanatic atmosphere of the community of Istanbul at the beginning of the century. He is so opposed to every form of segregation, believes so strongly in the improvement of the entire human race that he coins a word, assimilization.

[*Against fanaticism*] I myself am for complete civilization of the races, I am for assimilation. I don't know "Jew," "Catholic," "Buddhist." [*I don't want*] any constraints.

He is an agnostic and a Freemason and calls himself "assimilated." I asked him what led him to freemasonry.

My personal ideas, the ideas of assimilation of the races, of freedom, of the improvement of man, brotherhood, mutual help, right. To make an abstraction of religion. And no nationalism. In discussions, we weren't afraid of anything, in . . . [*masonry*]. But during the war, it was closed down. I went to Rue Cadet every day. I saw the posters that it was closed. They also threw us [*Jews*] out of the club, not out of maliciousness but because they were forced to. The authorities said Jews couldn't join the club.

But does not this adherence to a universalist ideal reveal a form of Marranism? For Monsieur Z. wanted to blend into freemasonry so as not to be identified as a Jew. Recalling his childhood in Paris, in the communal school, he declared that he was "French without being French, while being French," and he concluded our conversation in a choked voice: "France is hospitable, but not the French."

"FRANCE IS HOSPITABLE
BUT NOT THE FRENCH"

There is a gap here between the desire for integration and the reality of a new exclusion. Was segregation desired or imposed? Desired, if one is to believe the many testimonies, for France did not live up to the image people had of it.

Claire C., Z.'s sister-in-law, pictured Paris as a fashion magazine.

I made a first trip to Europe. We crossed Italy. We came to Paris and stayed at a hotel. I was a bit of a Parisian for a while and was very disappointed. I thought, you know, that it would be like in the fashion magazines, that all Parisian women were like that. And I saw people in worn-down shoes. That surprised me very much.

Ida O., who made her first trip to France at the same time, in the 1920s, suffered the same disillusion.

I got married and I came here. Not to live. I came with my husband to visit. There was his family, who were here since before '18. Some of them lived in Reims, the brother, who had two jewelry stores. He was married to a Catholic down there. She was the daughter of the mayor of Reims. Another part was here in Paris. The year I came, I was really young. It was in July, and the weather was awful. I said: "This is France? No, I don't want it. I'm going back to my own country. I want to go where it's warm and see my girlfriends again, all that." So his whole family, who had come before—I didn't know them, I met them here—they said: "You're wrong to go. You'll see, France is good."

My sister was here. She said to me: "France! France, it's terrific!" [*The brothers-in-law suggest buying for her*] "a wine shop, a Nicolas." "Me, a wine merchant!"

"No, no, no, no, no. I'm going back to Greece," I told my husband. "I don't like it. I'm going to Greece. That's where I was born. This is not for me." The proof is that I stayed Greek.

I went back to Salonika. What could I tell you, it was a good life down there.

[*Five years later*], we said: "Let's go away. It's beginning to look fishy." They wouldn't leave the Jews in peace anymore. My parents and my husband sold everything down there.

In the community of the past, Jews became slowly estranged from the local population. In France in turn, they kept the indelible mark—accent, tastes, memory—of another place. One lived between two worlds, without belonging to either. Monsieur M. (Sousse, 1900), says: "We were on the border." Claire C., again, who returned to Paris and got married there, speaks of the unhappiness of being a "hybrid."

That, in a nutshell, was our misfortune. I'm a hybrid. I was born in Turkey. If I wanted to work for the French, not being French, they said: "Oh, she's a foreigner, with her accent . . . " Being in Turkey, I didn't know a word of Turkish, since Ataturk[5] wasn't still there in my generation. So Turkish wasn't compulsory; nobody knew Turkish.

Finally, did one ever leave? Claire C. says she found "all of Istanbul" in Paris, by which she means the Jewish population. She also observes that "there is a very big Jewish colony here," that is, solely of Istanbul. After half a century in France, Claire admits to finally "bridging" the gap that separated her from the "authentic French" environment—by means of the game of bridge.

In France, I had many girlfriends from Constantinople. Not many Frenchwomen, so to speak, no. But since I've been playing bridge, I've met Frenchwomen. I have a group of French-women I entertain and who invite me to their homes. We are very friendly with them.

You mustn't forget, there's a very big Jewish colony here. All my girlfriends are from Istanbul. I found them here. We used to say "all Istanbul is here," all my girlfriends. I continued with friends and relatives from Istanbul here in France. It hasn't been all that long—only a few years—that I've had French friends: when I took up bridge. A lady introduced me and then I got to know authentic French circles.

Exclusion was also imposed on these immigrants. They thought they were leaving the ghetto for an open society, exchanging the intensity (but narrowness) of communications in the Jewish environment for the diversity of relations with the French. The latter emerge as polite individuals who seem to greet you only to avoid any meaningful ex-

5. Ataturk was president of the first (1923) republic of Turkey.

change. They are discreet, do not ask questions, and do not gossip. But doesn't that mean that they ignore you and don't care about you? They look at you without seeing you and kill you by a kind of slow death. Exchanging neither words nor looks, they don't share bread and wine either. The same image recurs in several narratives: that of the individual piece of steak, a symbol of food that can't be shared. Reserved, this is finally the common quality of the French: reserved, hence on guard; reserved as a seat is reserved and consequently not available; reserved, hence exclusive, all complicity being suspect. In France, one is not invited to come in, but to reserve his seat and to stay in it.

As for me, coming from Istanbul to France, the first thing that shocked me was this: with us, in Istanbul, as soon as a person came in, you gave him coffee, jam, a glass of water. You had to. The maid came with the tray. You didn't have to ask: "Do you want?" When I came here, they didn't give anything. Here, I went upstairs—my upstairs neighbor is a very, very French lady. She didn't say: "Come in," whereas in my house, I always say: "Come in." It's something that shocked me tremendously.

Onc shouldn't generalize, but one thing did shock me—that they didn't offer anything. After my neighbor's husband dicd, I used to pay a little visit from time to time and stayed to chat for a little while. Never did she say: "Can I get you something?" That's just to tell you: as a Turk, I was shocked.

Edmond H. (Cairo, 1909) uses the same words to denounce the absence of spontaneous conviviality.

Here in France, if you come to my house at one o'clock and I'm eating, I won't so much as offer you a drink. When I buy two steaks, it's for me and my wife. If you want to come, you have to tell me in advance so I can buy a third steak. Back home, It wasn't like that. It drives me crazy.

We were used to living in common, living together, that was life. Now, I have an Algerian neighbor. With him, it's like living back in Egypt. But when we were downstairs, there was a French woman. With her, you opened the door: "Good morning," "Good evening." You could drop dead in your apartment and nobody would come say to you: "What's wrong with you?" And for me, that's appalling. Upstairs we had an old French lady. By chance, I saw her dragging along. She wanted to come down to call her doctor. I said: "Madame, why are you going downstairs? Come into my house to call." "How, do you allow me to come to your house to call?" She called her doctor. She wanted to pay me for the telephone call.

That hurts. We're not used to that kind of life. We're used to a life much closer to the heart . . .

It's not that I've got anything against France. It's a country like any other; maybe it's even worse in other countries. But the difference between what I imagined in my mind and what I found was between heaven and earth.

Like many Jews of Egypt, Edmond H. came to France in the great wave of expulsions following the Franco-Anglo-Israeli campaign of 1956. About 30,000 Jews left Egypt at that time. For Edmond H., the beginning of the 1950s had already been darkened by economic reverses, which he attributed to the arbitrariness of the political system. The revolution of 1952, which ousted the monarchy and brought Nasser to power, was not reported in the spontaneous flow of his memories. But he does recall the revolution that was taking place before his departure from Egypt, in which the Egyptians in general and the lower classes in particular were granted the power the old regime had withheld from them, while people like him lost the more favorable positions they had enjoyed.

The irony is that Edmond H., like other Jews who immigrated at the same time, suffered in France the very downfall he had tried to escape in Egypt.

With the Treasury on my back, which ruined me completely, I was able to leave Egypt at the end of '56 saying *hamdulallah* [*thank God*], I have nothing to lose. I had everything to gain. I was making a new life. Because, after me, after '56, there were people who stayed in Egypt, people who couldn't liquidate their property. They couldn't liquidate it: if they had liquidated, they would have lost everything. And believe me, to lose everything quietly like that, that really hurts. My son-in-law's father, G. F., was manager of the national spinning mill of Egypt, a fabulous job. He had to leave a large sum of money in Egypt. He just couldn't manage to get it out—in spite of court trials, in spite of anything you want. He had real estate, land and buildings. He came here: he, who had been a managing director in charge of two thousand workers, was forced to work like a bump in a publishing company where the young people made fun of him. He was seated at a little table where he was not even a clerk; he did the kind of paperwork you give to a child. And his boss, who wasn't even as old as his son, would tell him: "What, Monsieur F., you haven't finished your work?" That embittered him. He had a heart attack and died. And there were more just like him, dozens of them!

I myself—I came to France, I prostituted myself. I did all trades: I was a house painter; I was a carpenter . . . [*In Marseille, when I came*] the secretary of the Jewish Council said to me: "You know a lot, we'll keep you." To do what? *Shamash* [*beadle*] of the synagogue, not even shamash, assistant shamash. But I wanted to work. They gave me an apartment, for which I was very grateful. OK, there was the shamash. I said to him: "What does a shamash do?" He said to me (putting on airs): "You have no idea. Here, you can make yourself a lot of money being the shamash in the synagogue." "You make money for yourself?" "Yes. First, every Saturday, people come to synagogue or to the *sefer*. They make donations for the *hazan* and for the shamash and that's yours to keep. And there's *better* than that! When somebody dies, we go wash the corpse. The dead person's family gives us clothes and sheets and money."

My God, my God, my God. . . . I came to France to wash corpses? It can't be.

Edmond H. finally found less degrading employment. As with Monsieur M. just previously, the difficulties experienced by the immigrant generation were compensated in his eyes by the success and eventual integration of the children.

The children really did well. There are scholars, doctors, accountants, engineers. And that really gives you satisfaction. On the whole, the Jews of Egypt have succeeded in France.

Suzanne T. tells:

One day, the second or third day of Passover, after lunch, I lay down. I wasn't sleeping. I saw an old man dressed in the old-fashioned way, that is, in a white *gandoura*,[6] a burnoose and a white turban, looking at me. He said to me: "You don't know me. I am your husband's grandfather. You are going to have a boy and you will give him my name, Rahmin." So I sat up and wondered whether I had been dreaming. When my husband came home to have his coffee at four o'clock, I described his grandfather to him. He couldn't get over it. He said to me: "You never knew my grandfather. How did you do that?" So I told him, and his grandfather had died at least three years before.

Eight months later, I had my son, December 7, 1931, at four o'clock in the afternoon. It was the nicest day of my life. We called our son Pierre Rahmin, the grandfather's name.

A dream is the expression of the individual's most private wishes, and this one clearly articulated what Suzanne aspired to most. But this dream is also the almost transparent product of a cultural tradition. It says that life is constructed on the foundation built by our ancestors; that one need not have seen and known them to receive and transmit their heritage. It says that to give life is to guarantee the continuation of the name, the first name, in a kind of resurrection of the dead. But is it not God who brings the dead back to life? That is indeed what it is, for God expresses himself through that white-draped figure whom He thus wants to reincarnate.

Suzanne gives a minute description of three episodes—and only three—in her son's life: his circumcision, his bar mitzvah, and his death in the French army during the Algerian war of liberation. The end of his life signals a break in history, the rupture of a tradition dating from time immemorial. In France, men wrapped in a big white burnoose no longer appear in visions. Here is what T., born between the wars, dreams of.

6. Translator's note: A sleeveless garment worn by Arabs under a burnoose.

There is a row of houses lined up facing the sea. Now, between that line and the sea, another row of houses has been torn down, and only one of them remains, mine. I turn to the women surrounding me and get angry that people have torn down all those houses, cut down the landscape, transformed an inhabited space into a wasteland. I turn to those women, who had lived in those destroyed houses. Huddled together, they form a circle and are engaged in lively conversation. They don't seem in the least troubled. They seem to say: "Well, what can we do, that's how it is!" But I suddenly observe that each one has a bandage in the middle of her face. They explain to me, one of them at any rate, Berthe, a cousin, that they had to change their noses because, in France, you know . . .

The seashore, I know it, it's between Carthage and La Goulette. The two components of society, the Arabs and the Jews, form the two rows of houses and the second has to be torn down, to the last cabin. When I turn around, we are in France, and the lively conversation of the women says that life continues but you have to change your identity, hide that Jewish nose, which is viewed with disdain here. That's it. A strange dream, isn't it?

Memory of a destroyed town, memory of exile: that is Jewish memory.

THE GREAT DEPARTURE OF THE
JEWS OF NORTH AFRICA

When Edmond H. came to France, the exodus of North African Jews was already in progress. It was when the three countries achieved their independence. Tunisia and Morocco, both French protectorates, regained full sovereignty in 1956. After a bloody war lasting from 1954 to 1962, Algeria was also freed. Several thousand Jews left the two former protectorates for Israel as soon as the State was created. The mass departures for France started with independence but were spread over several years, with each serious crisis in the country itself or in its relations with the former colonial power being followed by a new wave of emigration. In Algeria the Jews had been French citizens since

1870 (except for those of the Mzab, who were naturalized on the spot at the time of their departure). They left the country en masse, either during the war or—like most of the colonial population—in 1962. The balance sheet of this movement reads as follows: most of the Jewish communities of North Africa have disappeared; those that survive, in the big cities like Tunis or Casablanca, for example, are reduced in number and continue to decline. In France today, the immigrants and their descendants form the majority of the Jewish population.

In recalling this period, the Jews from Algeria still use the euphemism that was found in the French press, "the events," for nobody wanted to admit that these were movements of national liberation. But once the word is uttered, people assume you know what it means and do not give a historical account. Instead, the so-called events coalesce in one single event, which touched them more directly—the death of a relative. This is what provoked a hasty departure, surrounded by an atmosphere of fear: a collective fear of a collective adversary, "the Arabs."

Louise G. (Aïn Beïda, 1921) does not indicate the year of her departure:

How did I leave Constantine? I had a brother killed on July 14. On the 13th, at night, poor J., we looked for him everywhere. When we found him, he was lying in a pool of blood. That's why, less than a year later, we left Constantine.

Manou B., Aïn Beïda, born in 1926, left Algeria in 1956:

As soon as the events started, we came because I have a first cousin whose throat was slit. That scared me a lot, and that's what made me leave. I sent my children immediately and I came pretty soon after that. I stayed at my mother's.

Viviane B., born in 1929, left Algeria in 1956:

My husband moved down there in the Postal Service, installing lines, and there was that attack in Colo. They massacred quite a few people, the F.L.N. [*the National Liberation Front*]. But fortunately, he was out of Colo that day. That's how he was saved. We were so scared we asked for his transfer to Paris.

My father's family had already been established here for several years, since 1933 . . .

Suzanne T., whose son was killed in 1956, did not leave Algiers until 1961:

It got worse and worse in Algiers. On October 7, 1961, we left Algiers with five children. Three were married. Needless to say, we didn't take anything with us. The cabinets were full of linen, the buffets and the cupboards full of dishes. The washing machine, the refrigerator, the television, not to mention the furniture, the paintings, the new mattresses. To abandon everything, to leave everything you own and leave without knowing where—that's very hard. Not knowing what you're going to find somewhere else. It's a whole life you leave behind, it was wrenching for everybody. We had to leave. On October 7, we took the plane to Marseille.

Alice B., Aïn Beïda, born in 1913, left Algeria in 1962:

There we were. We were doing very well. We never expected to leave Algeria and come here. Indeed, we were the last ones still there. We were supposed to spend Passover there. But because of the killings. . . . You know that J. [*her brother*] was a policeman at that time. He couldn't leave without being transferred. One Friday morning, just like that, they killed some poor guy, a Jew, the poor soul, right on Rue de France. He went to the grocer to buy a candle and go up to the cemetery—look at the coincidence—early in the morning. J. was sleeping. All of a sudden, we heard shouts. You know, everything happened on Rue de France. They went up to Négrier Place to go to the hospital and the cemetery. Everybody came to the windows. We saw that poor soul. J. got dressed, and one-two-three, he went to his pal, the one who made shipping crates. We told them that we were never going to leave and what about money? And J. said to us: "Mama and Alice, what are you doing here? Go to E. in Paris and wait for us to come." Could we tell him that we don't have the wherewithal to go to France? And where do we go, to E.'s?

So, J. came down to his pal and said to him: "Come up right away." He looked over the apartment. He saw the furniture, everything that could be taken away, and he made us a crate. On February 2, 1962, we set out—we by airplane and J. by ship.

And that's how we got here. In Algeria, it was snowing something awful. So much so that we couldn't take the airplane near Constantine; we had to go to Phillippeville. We took a car without an escort, without anything, and snow all around like a wall. And us with the Arabs, we were sure our [last] hour had come. And we took the airplane.

Annette B., born about 1930, left Morocco in 1967, following the Six Day War:

I was scared, I was scared. I was scared of the Arabs. I said, I'm leaving Morocco. My husband said to me: "Go, move to France for a month, two, three, four months with the kids. Let me work." My husband was a good soul. He had a good job. He had confidence.

We left our house, everything, everything, everything. We left with two suitcases, without a cent. And we stayed in Marseille. A year later, I changed my mind. I said to my husband: "Let's go back." But the children didn't want to.

THE PAIN OF DEATH

The lag between past and present is especially felt by the Jews of North Africa, as is the disjunction between the ideal France, the France of the textbooks, and the ground on which they have landed. Themes and images that came up earlier in the biographies of Jews from the eastern Mediterranean saturate the memories of the Jews of North Africa as well. The parents' social fall, compensated for by the excellence of the children's schooling, the resistance—not hostile but silent—put up by the French to the desire for communication; a kind of social division of labor that makes you a public charge—infantilized, in sum— while the French, including French Jews, assume the role of overseers with whom you maintain an impersonal relation. The image of the closed door is contrasted with the free circulation that prevailed in the past, and the carefully rationed portions of meat are measured against the abundance of food that had been the rule.

Suzanne T. is asked if she has visitors:

Yes, the doctor, the nurse, but I especially wait for the mailman, who brings me news of those in Israel.

By an irony of history, the daily human contact that breaks her solitude comes from her neighbors, Tunisian Arabs:

I'm helpless. I don't have anybody to talk to. I read the newspaper. I listen to the radio. I look at TV. Fortunately, I have neighbors. Tunisian Arabs. It's their son Habib who runs errands for me every day, buys me my bread and the newspaper.

Sonia H., born in Morocco in 1954, speaks of her father and then of her whole family:

He had pride, the pride of a completely self-made man, who never asked anybody for anything. So, to work, to go back to work as a clerk, it wasn't possible. That was failure. He had only one solution, to escape into illness. Papa's illness spread, he was 100 percent disabled, that is, an invalid, and that's now his source of income.

We came directly to Paris. I was thirteen at that time. It was rather difficult for me to live through, insofar as it was difficult for all those around me: problems in adapting made themselves felt at all levels. At the level of material life, practical life. OK, I was privileged enough insofar as, at the age of thirteen, it's an age when you're forming your own personality. And I succeeded in finding around us relief from the internal family life. That is, I had a thirst for learning, I had reading, the completely intellectual escape. That is how I could escape from the anguish that prevailed in the house. Mama was very depressed. Papa lived really [*silence*]. . . . He sort of lost his identity, that is, he had lost his role of patriarch in the family. He really tried to find work and to rehabilitate himself socially. But it just wasn't possible. He had a heavy family burden with his seven children. And then the whole external world was perceived to be hostile.

That is, the weather was bad, the climate was different, and even the language. He had to learn all over again how to live in French, to speak French, there was the whole administrative mishmash, forms to fill out, registration for Social Security, in short, all those rather barbaric inhuman things.

We children did have a French culture, if you like, when we came. School wasn't a no man's land you never entered. We spoke French, we had studied in French. Altogether we did quite well in school. There was never a problem at that level. But there was a kind of guilt that my father put on us. That is, in moments of crisis, there was the overblown-melodramatic "I'm finished, it's because of you." Those years, I remember, really had two angles. Those two years we spent in Paris, from 1967 to 1969—when I was between thirteen and fifteen—there were two aspects that I felt: first, the external, because Papa experienced it in a hostile way, and then finally . . . a kind of contentment because I went to the public library and discovered all of French literature. Perhaps I didn't understand everything, perhaps I didn't understand everything I was reading, but I was always reading. And things went very well at school. The environment at school wasn't hostile, but I was nevertheless a foreigner and they often took me for an Arab [laughter]. They often asked me if I ate with a fork or if I used my fingers to eat couscous. They would put me in the category of pied-noir.

My parents felt we were growing apart from them. They felt that very much. We had friends who came to the house, pals. . . . While they were real hermits. Outside of the family, strictly speaking, which was rather dispersed anyway—we saw each other every seven years at a holiday or a Shabbat—they were really alone. So we, as far as we were concerned, we operated on two levels. At home, it was rather stressful. We were pretty crowded because there were only five rooms for nine people. I slept with my three sisters in a little room, a room of three by two meters. My brothers had a room for the three of them. My parents had a room. And in the dining room, we were really on top of one another. So for me school was essentially a piece of luck, in fact, because it got me out of the family milieu.

Mama was stuck in the kitchen as she'd always been. That's why I felt that Mama wasn't adapting: it's because we continued to eat as we had eaten in Morocco, that is, a lot of meat, a lot of vegetables. In short, really, she didn't adapt at all either to French prices or to the French way of life. Mama squandered considerable sums in making the food we threw away on Sunday morning because there was too much.

Claire A., Constantine, born in 1916. She came to Paris in 1948. "We were almost the only Jews in '50–'51." Clearly, she is referring to the Jews of Constantine, for other Jews were as foreign to her as the French population that surrounded her.

It was really poverty. At the time we came, you had to give a security deposit to have a house. So we didn't have a place to live. We lived in a hotel room, but we weren't allowed to make food, nothing at all. We had a very little room that we paid for by the day. It was gloomy, gloomy, gloomy, gloomy.

DIS–ORIENTED JEWS

Images associated with the confused experience of exile and mourning now clog the memory of Mediterranean Jews. Exile and mourning, in other words, loss, deprivation, nostalgia for someone absent, the cutting off of your own being: these wounds are expressed again in the most diverse forms. Coming to Marseille, Edmond H. was offered a job washing corpses. For Alice B. and her mother, the city itself was deadly, and they inaugurated their move into a Parisian apartment with tears. Images of darkness also figure to Claire A., who came at the end of the 1940s: Paris, city of light, was for her "gloomy." As for Manou B., the houses were "all dark, all ugly." The west really was the place where the sun sets.

Having left "a whole life behind," as Suzanne T. writes, in the country you have left, you are, once in France, left without a life. Your body is broken, inert, dis-located. Manou B. still surrounds herself with all her children for the holiday of Kippur, but they no longer fast. It is as if she was cut off by that break; she embodies the sick tradition.

I can't stand that they don't respect Kippur anymore. So much that I can't stand, I can't walk anymore. It made me very, very sick.

One is also cut off by the death of those who were close. In going through their memories, people count their dead rather than the living. For the dead had shared their life, whereas the new generations, born on foreign soil, belong to another world. They do not renew the pact that not only bound God to the Jewish people but one generation to another.

I've often regretted not having raised my children in Algeria, in that Jewish community where our parents didn't have any problems, not the problems we have today. I have four children, three boys and a girl. The problem is that I have three mixed marriages. Imagine, three out of four, that's a lot! [*Manou B., born in 1926.*]

Paradoxically, deaths put you together again, for every funeral provides an occasion for the family to recollect. Now, you meet in the cemetery:

We have family here in Paris, but they're far away in the suburbs so we don't see each other. I only see X., that's all. Either in the synagogue or I go see her or she comes to see me. Or when we visit someone, we make an appointment and go together.

"Who do you go see?"

Oh, we visit sick people or pay condolence calls. Never to the theater, no, never, and yet I adore the theater. Before, yes. The first years we lived in Paris, with X., what excursions we made! We went to the park of Vincennes together. We took along a snack and we had a nice time together. Now that's over. First, it's always cold, no sun, so the climate also affects us. So we don't go out anymore. [*Louise G., born in 1921. The rest of her narrative shows that she remains in daily touch with her children and grandchildren.*]

To lose the taste for life: the metaphor is realized in many testimonies. Not a single person talks of the delicacies of French cui-

sine. On the contrary, the food in France is less meat than carrion. The chicken, "we throw it away," one woman tells us (see p. 54), its wings are broken and its flesh is blue, writes another. The meat is spoiled, rotten, gangrenous, while "back home," it was healthful and clean.

Manou B., born in Aïn Beïda, in 1926:

I'm not missing anything by keeping kosher. First, I'm used to eating kosher, it's clean. There's nothing wrong with kosher meat, anyhow. Ham, even on television, they warn against it; they say that it's spoiled.

Suzanne T., born in Sétif, in 1910:

Poultry, we had to buy it from the Arab. He came with us to the rabbi to see if we could buy it. Only then did we pay. The chicken couldn't have even a tiniest bruise or the rabbi rejected it. Not like now. The butchers sell you chickens with broken wings or broken thighs, full of bruises. Since you don't have a choice, you have to throw away all the affected parts. At that price, it's very expensive. And you can't do anything about it. That's France. I'll never get used to it. It's too hard for me, especially at my age—I'm going to be seventy. I've felt lost ever since I lost my poor husband. We lived together for forty-eight years. It's hard for me to be all alone—if only I could join him.

A NEW EXILE

The fullness of the world gone by is expressed by the repeated use of "all," "everybody," "together"; by the coincidence of the I of individual fate and the we of the community and tradition. The community is remembered as a homogeneous, uniform, unanimous whole, closed to others. By contrast, solitude, confinement in a foreign, even hostile, world, absence—these recur in the memories of the present with the words nothing, no one, *and the constant use of the negative form.*

We came to live in Paris, and my husband didn't have any work. The children were all little. Fortunately, we were able to get an empty apartment, not even a chair or a table, nothing at all. Eventually, my husband found work. Instead of being the boss, he became a bookkeeper. We didn't have anything to eat. We came here, we had just enough to pay for the apartment and then we didn't have anything left. [*Louise G., 1921.*]

Even the clock of time is out of order and there is no time left. Yesterday, the living and the dead lived together in a friendly familiarity. Gabriel D. tells us that, in Salonika,

A week before New Year's day, our parents made a pilgrimage to the cemetery to invite the dead to come to the house for the coming New Year's day. It was a tradition. Then we went home to celebrate the holiday.

It is true that for all important rituals, the visit to the cemetery involved the dead of the family in the celebrations. Besides, the children received the first names of their dead grandparents, circumcision renewed the pact between God and His people. What is one to think today, when the cemeteries have remained in the countries left behind, when the first names are lost, when the circumcision of male children is no longer the rule if their mothers are not Jewish?

Today, time is a routine, measured by punching in while yesterday's time was geared to rituals and social exchanges.

Manou B., again:

I came to follow my mother, and my husband couldn't take it. Not at all. He said to me: "For me to go to work in the morning and come home at night, that's out of the question." He stayed for two months and returned to Bone. First of all, at the time (1948), there weren't any apartments. There wasn't all this construction. There were only old houses, in Paris, all dark, all ugly, and with down payments. My husband couldn't take it. When he wanted to go back, I was thrilled. Because I didn't like Paris at all. When I returned in 1956, I was a nervous wreck, two years of total depression.

The time of exile is a discontinuous time; it is full only during holidays. But these always underline something that is missing: you no longer see one another except at holidays, or you don't even see one

another at holidays anymore. Holidays aren't the same, for the whole-
ness is shattered, sometimes by the desertion of a family member, some-
times by distance. And a part of the rituals is abandoned. Then, if you
have to celebrate—how to do it? The maternal cuisine and the holiday
table remain the ultimate refuge for being "all together," even briefly,
and for doing "everything" as before.

Manou B.:

Every Friday I have my children, oh yes! Whether they married *goys* or not, they know that on Friday they all have to be
there. And there isn't one of them who doesn't come. They're
all there, and I have my brother too. It's my older one who says
the prayer. He married a little Jewish girl. He's the only one,
the oldest son.

Annette B., Mogador, born about 1930:

We always arrange to do what we did in Morocco. I, at least,
didn't leave out anything, because I would be afraid to. I say
to myself: "If I take away anything, something is going to happen to my children, to my husband." As much as I can, I do.
Sometimes, I want to simplify life, but later, I have a dreadoubt,
I say no, I'd better not. I always did it.

Sometimes, now, I think it's stupid, really, to follow all those
things. I tell myself, really, it's not the old days anymore . . .

Doubts about the validity of traditions mix with fears of breaking
them: Annette B. coins a word to signify this tension: dreadoubt, *fear*
and doubt, which is exorcised only by respect for tradition.

Passover celebrates the Exodus from Egypt, the liberation from
exile. What to do when you yourself are deep in the solitude of exile?
Keep the tradition of the past in order to assure yourself a future.

Annette B., again:

We were far away, we were in Chatillon-sous-Bagneux, in
a suburb. I said to my husband: "I don't have a sister, I don't
have any family. Who is there?" He said: "Listen, do whatever you want." I said I won't prepare anything. I stayed like
that . . . and later on, I said to myself: "But even so. . . . Ever

since I got married, I've always set a nice table and I've always had people over. Even if there weren't people, there were my children, my husband." So I set a nice table that day. In half a day, I made more than I would have made in two whole days. And I made a nice spread. And we were there and, all of a sudden, my nephew—who was in Paris and whom I hadn't seen for quite some time—came. He came, he brought some pals with him. We didn't know where to put them. And we spent quite an evening! He really livened things up for us! He sang in Arabic, French, and Hebrew. There was another boy who sang. We spent an evening, really, with an atmosphere like I never spent in Morocco. If I hadn't prepared anything, how would I have met those people? My husband said to me: "You see, you must never lose hope." And we had a wonderful evening.

The memory of places and the people who populated them coincide when you recall the world gone by. The house, the street, the neighborhood formed so many familiar ghettos where communication was immediate. The space of exile is monumental and impersonal, populated and yet deserted since you don't recognize anyone there, inhabited but uninhabitable since you don't have access to dwellings that are too expensive. Displaced, you were disoriented, you still are.[7]

Alice B., born in 1913:

The first months were really terrible for us who had always been down there. We were uprooted from our home. Then, little by little, we adapted. But even now, it's already nineteen years that we've lived here, I don't like it as much as down there in my own home, that is, at home, in my own country, with all those people, there, all those friends. I did get used to it, but never completely. I'm not happy. It all boils down to that.

7. In his most autobiographical book, *La Terre intérieure,* Albert Memmi expresses his nostalgia for the ghetto of Tunis and he adds: "And I go on dreaming of a universe where things would be in their proper place" (p. 14), explaining further on: "In the ghetto, you play a game, you accept the laws, human, familial, social, and divine; you submit but you find in that submission a great rest, a great comfort, great joys. . . . That was the ghetto, at least in my memory . . . or in my imagination, I no longer know" (pp. 15–16).

Especially now when everybody is far away. My poor R. is gone [*deceased*]. My mother's gone. There's nobody anymore in the Place de la République,[8] and you can't even go there now.

Since we've been here, it's always been exactly the same routine. It's always the same closed doors in the tenants' apartments. You never see anybody on the stairs. You can't say hello here and there and nobody says to you: "Alice, you want to have a cup of coffee with me?"—like they did down there in Algeria.

Having moved into a new apartment, Alice B. wept: the neighbors kept their doors closed, her brothers had gone away—"everybody's gone." In France, space separates instead of uniting.

When we came here, if you only knew how much we cried, my mother and me, seeing ourselves all alone like that. And you know that Sunday here, it's deadly in Paris.

We came in here Feburary 17, 1963, and our neighbors told us there was a Jewish woman on the same floor as us, Madame S. But S., he said to his wife: "Listen, it seems they're Algerians." He didn't believe we were Jews. He thought that Algerian is Arab. "Listen to me: close the door, don't open it, because Algerians, they play with knives." So when we came there, everybody shut himself in, and we didn't see a soul.

Space of exile, space of dispersion: Sonia H., who lived successively in Paris, Strasbourg, and again in Paris, explains eloquently her being deprived of the Orient, her being dis-Oriented.[9]

I still encounter problems at the level of everyday life. I don't identify completely with French life; I don't identify with Moroccan life—I'm badly in need of some sort of identity. OK, I think that will last as long as I do and will end when I die. [*laughter*]. That is, places slip away, places never really tally with what you expect from them. I'm not really from Morocco; I'm

8. Place de la République is one of the most crowded piazzas in Paris.

9. Among the many literary expressions of this loss is the partly autobiographical novel of Albert Bensoussan, *Frimal-djezar* (Paris: Calmann-Lévy, 1976), which talks about the "love of the territory" (p. 200). He also writes: "You were my town and I owned you" (p. 171).

not really from France. Casa [*Casablanca*], it's not that it was the be all and end all, but we had it good there. In my opinion, it's not a problem of dimensions. It's a problem of knowing the town. That is, when I look at Paris like that and I try to locate places where I have somebody—you see, it's a rather sentimental measure—where I have someone I love and would like to visit, just like that, one afternoon, to knock on his door and say: "Hi, I've come to have a cup of tea." Well, there just isn't anybody in Paris like that. There are friends who work, so I have to call and say I'm coming. Whereas, when I was a child in Casablanca, it didn't seem especially big, even for a little one like me. My aunt lived two streets away. We lived in the western part of the city, and two of Mama's sisters were there. It was a place to which I was emotionally attached, because everywhere, there were people I knew.

In fact, it's not the city that's foreign, it's the people who live in it. Because Strasbourg, after all, never gave me the impression of being a foreign city, simply because Dad's family lived there. There were Dad's sisters and brothers, so there was a structure, and the streets were much more familiar. You went to see X, who lived on such and such a street. And that's how the city shrank, if you like, it looked like the . . . the ghetto. There, it was tamed.

And to demonstrate her present uneasiness, she turns to spatial references that indicate both what has been lost and what has been dismembered by this new Diaspora:

It's this dispersion in space. . . . That's it, it's a dispersion.

10
Genocide

"LEBN VI GOT in Frankraykh," "Happy as God in France?" Then came the French capitulation of June 1940, the Vichy regime, the German occupation. In everyone's memories, whatever the individual's age (adults as well as children), World War II is a point of convergence and defines the structure of the narrative. Often, before approaching the black years, there is a silence, then the tone of voice changes. They recount their trials and tribulations, their tragedies, the twists and turns of their personal histories. In the unfolding of memories, when they finally get to the end of the war and the Liberation, it seems that there is nothing left to tell. The tale has reached its conclusion: "What more is there to tell you?" In the time of memory, even for the survivors, the end of the war marks the end of life, of a certain life, that of the world before: afterward, a different life, an afterlife begins.

In fact, we generally had to press our informants to get them to talk about the postwar years; they then quickly skimmed over the course of a "normal" life, somehow without history, reduced to a curriculum vitae: stages of professional life, marriages, births. They dwelt more on the development of their political or religious convictions in a general way. Their memories turn into a reflection on the inevitable problem of Jewish identity. This reflection then brings them back to the war, and it is that which remains at the center of their memory: recollections of those who disappeared, of waiting for those who never returned, more stories of survivors, or sometimes even ghosts. For the trauma that sundered their lives is genocide. It is, for the survivors, the torment of mourning, an impossible mourning.

THREAT OF DEATH

Under the German occupation, difference came to be experienced as the threat of death: one was aware of an absolute and irrational otherness that questioned the very essence of the individual's being. Moreover, the permanent threat was inscribed in material signs, the "Jew" stamped on the identity card, and especially the yellow star, which stigmatized those who wore it in the eyes of everyone. Mathilde R. (psychoanalyst) accompanies her memories with almost professional commentaries (which might no doubt apply to many other cases), while intensely reliving the anguish of those days. The yellow star seems like the external and literally unbearable manifestation of a secret blemish, a blemish buried in the unconscious and then ignominiously revealed to expose the truth about the person.

I also remember the star I wore, which was sewn on a jacket, a jacket I carried on my arm. Always with the idea that if someone said to me "You're a Jew. Why aren't you wearing the star?"— I could show that everything was in order. What did I do with the jacket during class? Damn, I don't know; I think I never let anyone in school see that I had that star, but I did have it with me.

I also remember that the word "Jew" was written on the star with somewhat strange letters, shaped like Hebrew letters, and I found them terrifying. It was a stigma that revealed something scandalous about me, something I might analyze today, almost in psychoanalytical terms. Something scandalous not only in the eyes of others but also in my own eyes; something unknown, hidden from me yet manifest to others. And, indeed, I couldn't bear to show myself with that because it was a display of something . . . absolutely scandalous, ignoble, shameful, dark . . .

Does the knowledge of the outcome inflect the tone of memories? The danger of death was not clearly perceived at the beginning of the Occupation, either by French Jews (who could consider themselves protected by the Vichy government) or by immigrant Jews. Up to the middle of 1941, German policy was still limited to effecting the expulsion of the Jews from Germany and the territories she controlled.[1] In the

1. Michael R. Marrus and Robert O. Paxton, *Vichy France and the Jews.*

census required by the regulation of September 27, 1940, in the occupied zone, and by the law of June 2, 1941, in the free zone, most
(about 90 percent) declared themselves to the authorities:[2] indicative of
naïveté, fear, obsession for legality, of course, but also testimony to a
certain trust. The most urgent problems for most of them at that time
were practical and material: exclusion from public jobs and the liberal professions, and Aryanization (i.e., confiscation) of businesses
or workshops forced them to seek new means of existence.

Foreign Jews were threatened most directly. The Vichy government
promulgated a decree on October 4, 1940, declaring them liable to house
arrest or internment. It is estimated that at the beginning of 1941, forty
thousand of them were held in various camps in the free zone (Gurs,
Rivesaltes, Le Vernet, Les Milles, etc.).[3] Foreign Jews were also victims of the first waves of arrests in Paris, on May 14 and August 20,
1941: close to eight thousand were interned in the camps of Pithiviers,
Beaune-la-Rolande, and then Drancy (under French administration).[4]
They remained there for several months under increasingly intolerable
conditions, but their families still harbored hopes of seeing them freed.
However, on December 13 and 14, 1941, the arrests in Paris extended
to seven hundred distinguished Jews of French stock. And we now know
that the Nazi leaders decided in January 1942 on the means of the Final
Solution. Its execution began in France during the spring and summer
of 1942, which marks the "great turning point" in the history of
genocide.[5] The first convoy of deportation left Drancy on March 27
for Auschwitz, followed in May by convoys from Pithiviers and
Beaune-la-Rolande.[6] Then came the infamous roundup of the Vel
d'Hiv, on July 16 and 17, 1942, when French police arrested more
than twelve thousand people, sparing neither women nor children nor
old people. From August 14 on, Jewish children were also deported.

2. Ibid., pp. 99–100; Serge Klarsfeld, *Vichy-Auschwitz: Le rôle de Vichy dans
la solution finale de la question juive en France, 1942* [Vichy-Auschwitz: The Role
of Vichy in the Final Solution of the Jewish Question in France, 1942] (Paris:
Fayard, 1983), pp. 24–25.

3. Marrus and Paxton, *Vichy France*, p. 158.

4. Jacques Adler, *Face à la persécution: Les organisations juives à Paris de 1940
à 1944* [Confronting Persecution: Jewish Organizations in Paris from 1940 to
1944] (Paris: Calmann-Lévy, 1985), pp. 57, 63.

5. Marrus and Paxton, *Vichy France*, pp. 203ff.

6. Klarsfeld, *Vichy-Auschwitz*, Vol. I., pp. 59–60, 191; Marrus and Paxton,
Vichy France, p. 212; Adler, *Face à la persécution*, p. 20.

Why were they taking so many people unfit for work? The situation was such as to arouse the worst suspicions.

But how could one imagine the Final Solution? The official version—that they were being transferred to "labor camps" in Poland—seemed plausible. When information filtering out of Auschwitz began to appear in France and was circulated by the underground press at the end of 1942, it generally encountered only skepticism and disbelief.[7] If not pure propaganda, was it not at least exaggerated rumor? People certainly suspected that terrible things were taking place in "Pichipoi"; but what? Surely not the systematic extermination of all the Jews! Despite the anguish, people could not, did not want to believe it, even though they knew "in a certain way": reality surpassed understanding.

Mathilde R.:

You know, if I go back to that time, I have the impression finally (I can't speak for my parents or my aunt), I have the impression that somewhere we knew that the horror was there. In a certain way, we always knew it, from the time the Germans first came. But in each instance, we didn't quite want to know.

TRIBULATIONS

If our witnesses often violently denounce the scandal of the laws of Vichy in the country of the Rights of Man as well as the participation in genocide of the French police and administration, they also pay emotional homage to those sympathetic French people who sheltered them, helped them, saved them. These judgments are mixed with the memory of the ever-recurring, sadly banal tribulations: exodus, roundups, camps, flights, clandestine shelters, false identities, failed arrests, more flights, final arrest. As the rhythm of the episodes accelerates, the intensity of the reexperienced dramas and the very surge of memories slow down the time of the narrative: once again (even more than for the period of arrival in France), memory dwells on details and follows events day by day, hour by hour, restoring with amazing precision

7. Ibid., pp. 194–195. On the first publication of information from Auschwitz, see the narrative of Adam Rayski in his memoirs, *Nos illusions perdues* [Our Lost Illusions] (Paris: Balland, 1985), pp. 124–125.

the schedules, places, vicissitudes, dialogues, and even emotions of the moment.

We return to Charles and Hélène H. They met at school in Nancy and finished their medical studies in Paris. Charles H. was naturalized in 1931, and they were married. After Charles H. did his military service, they moved to a little town in Brie (between Meaux and Melun). In 1941, with the promulgation of the statute of the Jews, they were forbidden to practice medicine. In November, they decided to escape to the "free" zone.

Charles H.: I stayed in hiding for a week. I had given up my office, but there were still a few things to do. We decided to leave separately, I, by one route, she, by another; and we sent Guy [*their son*] by yet another road.

Hélène H.: We had a friend, Doctor V. One of his relatives was an official of Vichy. It was agreed that when he would take the train to go across the line of demarcation,[8] he would ask the German officer if the child could go see his grandmother. I accompanied them and I left Guy in Vierzon. He asked his question; [*the German officer answered*]: "Yes, why not?" Guy was five years old and he was terribly upset by this business, leaving with a gentleman he didn't know at all. Doctor V. had warned his mother, a lady of seventy-five. This lady wasn't informed at all, she didn't know what a Jew was; she didn't know why these people were hiding. So she smelled something fishy. Finally, since it was a child who was coming, she agreed. Guy kept on crying nonstop for twenty-four hours. They told him he would see his father there; but my husband hadn't come.

Charles H.: So I decided to go across. My contact was the address of a pharmacist in Beaune who knew a network that worked for prisoners of war. I took the train; I saw the pharmacist. The contact was very simple: he was a gentleman who lived on the line of demarcation and had stone quarries on the other side.

8. The line that separated the northern part of France, then occupied by the German army, from the southern "free" zone. After the armistice of June 1940, Pétain set up his government in Vichy.

[. . .] In the end the pharmacist couldn't get confirmation [*from the network*]. When I left, he did give me the name, but he didn't know if it would work. But I was in a hurry because I knew that Guy was waiting for me at Chateauroux. I had to rush.

I left Beaune by train to get to that little town on the line of demarcation, near Chalon-sur-Saône. I chatted with the people in the train. I was scared of an inspection when I got off the train. That was very dangerous. So somebody proposed a car that was waiting at the station before Chalon-sur-Saône. I was going to Buxy. Normally, you went to Chalon and then you took the train for Buxy. I decided to get off at the station before Chalon, about fifteen kilometers earlier, in order to avoid the inspection.

The people I met had a car waiting for them at the station and they took me to a crossroads a few miles from Buxy. From there, I went on foot. I already had a winter overcoat (it was November), a briefcase with some sandwiches the pharmacist's wife had generously made for me in Beaune, and a Chaix, a railroad timetable. There was a fog you could cut with a knife, which suited me just fine. It was between five and six o'clock in the morning, and you couldn't see six feet in front of you.

I was almost two kilometers from Buxy, when all of a sudden, the fog lifted and I found myself face-to-face with two Germans on a bike! They stopped me: "What are you doing here?" I gestured to them that I didn't understand any German and I explained:

"I'm building a house and I'm going to buy stones. I need materials and they told me there's somebody who has quarries over there." "No, you're going to cross the line of demarcation!" "Of course not; I would have asked for an *Ausweiss* and I would have sat quietly on the train. No, somebody put me down there (I pointed to the Chaix): this way I save a day." In fact, it would save a day if I were going round trip; my answers were plausible. And he repeated: "Comrade, shoot, comrade shoot, if you go over the line of demarcation."

He had my papers. I had a card without the Jewish stamp but with my name. The boss read: "Holzberg" and he said: "Ah, these French names, it's a real pain!" The other one said to him in German: "We're going to take him to the station; the officer will get it out of him." As for me, I told my story in gibberish. The one who couldn't read my name finally said: *"Lass ihn laufen!"* (Let him go!) When I heard that, I didn't react at all. There was a great silence: "You still need my papers?" He gave them back to me and repeated: "Good, but comrade shoot!" I kept wondering: I don't know if he thought I was a Jew, but he certainly suspected that I was going to the other side. From the fact that he repeated: "Comrade shoot," with the gesture.

OK, I left again. The village was at the end of the road I was taking. Before entering the village, I saw a kind of hut in the corner. That's the gentleman I was looking for. I went into his house, into the office. There were people there, and I waited for them to leave. Then I got straight to the point! "It's to cross the line of demarcation." "Just to go and come back next week?" "No, for good!"

I had the impression he was going to do something. In fact, he said to me:

"This contact isn't working anymore; it's finished. I'm under surveillance myself, to such an extent that if a German were to come in now and find you here, he'd ship you off."

You could see the road through the window.

"You see the line of demarcation—that's the road in front of us, the one that passes under the window. All you've got to do is jump over the ditch. The Germans never cross to the other side, but they do shoot."

From his house the width of the road was almost thirty feet, maybe twenty-five feet, and then the ditch. The house was on a rise, and the road was on the side of a hill. There were fields, since we were on the edge of the village. At the end of the road, there was a steep drop.

"You'll be exposed for two hundred yards. Once you're on the sloping ground, it's all over."

He proposed that he go his own way into the fields toward the hills.

"Go along with the story you told. Pretend you're returning to take the train to Chalon. Go almost two hundred yards. I'll be up above. I'm going to go in front of you. You'll see me on top. And I'll start pissing; that will be the sign that there's no patrol in sight, that you can go. Then jump."

Fine. You see, the fields were bordered with hedges of haw-thorns, which go down. I went, I can't say how far, maybe I walked too fast or maybe he was arrested, I don't have any idea. Or maybe he got cold feet. I don't know. I never saw that man again. I went about a hundred fifty yards. Nothing in front of me. No gentleman pissing, nothing at all. I didn't see anybody. He had told me: "Most important, don't look around. That would be suspicious." I did it anyway. I didn't see anything in front of me. The road was straight. I looked to the left, the right, in back, and didn't see anybody. So, without hesitating, hop, I jumped, and I started running along a hedge, like that, bent over, telling myself they didn't see me on the other side.

And then I heard shots. I didn't know if it was for me. I didn't look behind me. I didn't hear the whistling. Were they hunting a rabbit in back, or was I the rabbit? The hedge was to my left as I ran. I am telling you they couldn't see me on the other side, but they could have seen me if someone was on top or to my right. I had my overcoat on my arm. It was a hedge of hawthorns. While I was running I threw my coat onto the hawthorns, lengthwise. I let myself roll over to the other side on my coat. I grabbed my coat and ran to the other side.

I heard another shot. There were two to three hundred yards, once I reached the slope. I was out of the woods. He had told me that, at the bottom, at the edge of the river, I would find a farm where they would give me directions to the road. I reached that farm through the fields. My hands were full of thorns. There was a little girl. Her parents weren't there. She asked me if I wanted something. There was a basin with water. I washed my hands. I started pulling out the thorns. She said to me: "Your hands are shaking!" I still remember the child's comment.

Inducted into the French army, Robert S. was taken prisoner in the Vosges in June 1940. With the other prisoners, he was held in a barracks in Strasbourg. Thanks to his commander—a Frenchman—he

succeeded in concealing the fact that he was a Jew and then in get-
ting free. A dentist, he managed to work in Clermont-Ferrand at the
beginning of 1941.

I worked for B., as an assistant. He was a bachelor and a liber-
tine. He lived at night and rested during the day. It suited him
to have an assistant. He admitted he never had an assistant like
me because he had more customers than ever before. Moreover,
there were customers from the prefecture, who had good positions. We agreed that if there was ever any danger, he would
warn me by telephone and tell me: "Get out, there's danger."

I worked for a year and a half until '42, and then, things
started heating up because it seemed that the Germans were
invading the free zone. The situation was becoming dangerous.
I had to leave B., and I found another dentist, K., who had
a friend who was a district attorney in Riom. So he was covered and I was too, indirectly. But, one day, at ten o'clock in
the morning, two delegates of the Jewish Commissariat[9] came
looking for me. The nurse called me, and I found myself facing
two gentlemen, one old and one young. The old one asked me:
"Monsieur, you're a Jew. Don't you know you don't have the
right to work?" So I played my last card: "Monsieur, I am the
head of a household. I have a wife and a child to feed. And I
am a Jew. You've found me out. My fate is in your hands." So
the young one—a piece of filth, the Nazi type in the French
militia—interjected: "So, do we ship him off?" The other one
said: "Leave him alone!" And to me: "I'm going, but you,
disappear."

That meant: Don't stay in Clermont. He left. I went and got
my wife and child, and we left for Giat, where I knew a dentist
who had a skin disease on his hands. He had to work with
gloves, something that's hardly practical for the mouth. He
kept a place for me as prosthesis technician. It wasn't far from
Clermont, but it was in the country, and the Germans couldn't
be everywhere. Moreover, the Resistance was well established.
And that was a land of milk and honey. There was no lack of

9. In March 1941, the Vichy government organized the *Commissariat Géné-
ral aux Questions Juives,* a commission to deal with Jewish affairs.

bread or meat or milk. There were other problems, however, and I still had to be careful.

One day at the dentist's, the police sergeant, a swindler who was trying to make money on the backs of the Jews, came to have a gold bridge made. I quickly understood that he had no intention of paying for it. Blackmail, but done subtly—you had to understand it and not expose yourself to something that could have been disastrous. I saw who I was dealing with; I did the work and explained to the dentist that it was at my own expense. I met that police sergeant later on, after the Liberation. He trembled when he saw me.

A few months later, the dentist didn't need me anymore. He fired me. We had to eat. So I took a bike, put my instruments in the saddlebags, and played the traveling dentist, doing sixty miles a day on my bike. Every day, I went to take care of the peasants in their houses, which suited them because they didn't have to go anywhere. You know that you have to wait at the dentist's. For the peasant, that was a day lost. I didn't ask for payment in money, I didn't care about that. It was for food supplies.

When I made my rounds on the bike, I couldn't tell people what I was doing. It was a very risky business. People began to gossip, saying that I was doing black market business in my saddlebags. A Jew doing black market. There was always anti-Semitism. You had to be on guard. One Sunday, the village priest said this in his sermon: "If the Jewish people are suffering, they deserve it. It's because they are the people who committed deicide!" In Giat, there was also an aviation officer who asked the mayor one day: "How come that kike is there?"—meaning me. The mayor made it clear to him that he was interfering in things that were none of his business and that, if he made a move, the Resistance would intervene.

[. . .] We really weren't in danger because, in that section of Auvergne, with the forests, the Resistance was well established. Every time it looked like danger, we were warned: "Get out to the fields, scatter, the Germans are coming to Giat!" We were warned—my wife who was pregnant with Dany—we ran like crazy people into the fields.

When I told the head of the Resistance that I wanted to participate actively, he told me: "We don't have enough weapons, and you can help us as a dentist. First because when we have guys who are in pain, we really can't take them to the dentist. And you know Russian, Polish, and, most important, German." So I served as an intelligence agent.

Georges F.:

I left Paris after the roundup in the XI arrondissement in September '41. There was the big roundup and, just by chance, I don't know how it happened, at noon, they stopped. There were maybe three houses they hadn't gotten to. I left the next day, with a woman, a Frenchwoman, who took charge of me and got me into the free zone. She didn't take a cent. She just did it for her personal glory.

Georges F. went to Lyon, where he was joined in July 1942 by his wife, Martha, his three-year-old daughter, and his mother-in-law.

In Lyon, we were also pursued, worse than in Paris. I continued to work illegally, hiding, hugging the wall to go to work. I lived near the railroad station of Perrache, and I went to work on the other side, at the Croix Rousse. I had to take the trolley and try to get through the nets. Sometimes there were roundups. I couldn't get back home again; I had to stay there. The boss knew who I was. He let me stay one night when there was danger. Then, leaving, I took the trolley with another worker; and the Gestapo stopped the trolley to check if there were any Jews inside. He got scared. He jumped off the train, and they killed him. They shot overhead and he died, in front of me. Then, they had to deal with the corpse. They let the trolley go on, and I got through like that, without being touched.

[. . .] So I lived on that Rue des Trois-Maries, in Lyon, with my wife and my mother-in-law, in the house of an old Frenchwoman. When I came to her house, I introduced myself as an escaped prisoner. Maybe she knew I was a Jew, but she never said anything. From time to time, when she knew there were roundups, she told us: "If anybody knocks during the night, don't open the door. I'll get it."

And once, there was a very big roundup. She wasn't there. The area was surrounded, in old Lyon. It was very easy for them when they took up their positions. There was no way to escape them. It was over. It's a city of bridges, Lyon. There are a lot of bridges. Our daughter was placed in the country. We put an iron bed in front of the door, and we said: "If they knock, we won't open the door. Let them do what they want, but we won't open the door. If they break down the door, we'll play it by ear." They came. They went from one house to another on Rue des Trois-Maries. Our house was the only one that wasn't broken into. There was no exit on the other side. Across from us, they deported a family with maybe ten children. We never saw a trace of them. No one came back. And when they came to our house, they thought they had already done it on the other side. They stopped there and it was over.

There was a whistle. They left, and we were saved just like that, without doing anything at all. That's how we escaped [*laughter*].

Then we started that terrible life again. It can't be described. We lived like moles.

Martha F.: And then there was my mother, who went on talking Yiddish as if nothing was happening.

Georges F.: She couldn't speak anything else. It was terrible.

Martha F.: There was no use begging her. There was nothing to do.

Georges F.: Most of the Jews who came from Paris met on a commercial square, the Place des Terreaux. It was a place like the Pletzel, full of Jews, who managed to do a bit of business to survive. I never went to that square. That's why I escaped.

One day, my wife sent someone to me to tell me not to come back, that there were Gestapo in the little square.

Martha F.: When I saw that, I was scared. We had a prostitute in the house, who lived right upstairs. She was very nice, very devoted, very decent. I went up and I said to her: "Listen, Georges isn't back yet. He's going to come any minute, and, look, there are Gestapo downstairs"—still on the pretext that he was an escaped prisoner, but everybody knew. So she said to me: "Don't worry, I'm going to go ahead of him and I'll tell him what's happening." She did, in fact, meet him on the bridge, and he went back to his boss.

Georges F.: I went back and slept there that night. Another time, it was a really unbelievable story. In that house on Rue des Trois-Maries, there was an old maid who had cats. I don't know what got into her. One of her cats climbed up onto the roof. He fell and died. And she thought it was the Jews who cast a spell over him. She went out howling that the Jews cast a spell over him. Just that echo, that "the Jews cast a spell over him," that forced us to leave and go sleep at the Croix Rousse.

Martha F.: It sounds like a novel, this stuff.

Mathilde R.:

Finally the war came. It was obvious that we had to leave. We were part of the exodus like everybody else. What I can tell you first is that (including also schools before the war), I went to eleven schools up to the university, which represents a certain number of moves. We left the Parisian region in '40. We went to Normandy, where my parents had a little house. Then we really left on the exodus: we wound up in Bordeaux and then in the Tarn. As for school, I don't know, I must have spent a month or two in each one and then we came back to Paris.

So I entered the Lycée Racine in the seventh grade. Then we lived in Paris until the roundup of the Vel d'Hiv', doing all the absurd things Jews did, that is, declaring yourself, having a stamp put on your identity card, bringing your radio to the police station. For reasons of provisions, penury, and economy, we went to live with my doctor aunt, the one I just talked about, who lived on Avenue Carnot, one of the avenues of the Étoile. We were right in the heart of the occupation. When I read Patrick Modiano's *La Place de l'Étoile*,[10] it really struck me: the at-

10. Patrick Modiano, *La Place de l'Étoile* (Paris, 1968), is a novel about German occupation in Paris. There is an obvious double meaning to the word *Étoile* [Star] in the title.

mosphere he describes is what I saw at that time. I was twelve years old in '40. You couldn't help but feel the mood of things: I saw German soldiers marching every day at noon; the cinemas of the Champs Élysées, which were forbidden to Jews, the cafés, the restaurants. It wasn't always obligatory, but some of the French people did it zealously and put up: "Jews Forbidden." I also remember when they showed *Jud Süss,* because of those terrifying posters in the subway. In short, that very special and yet very familiar atmosphere, very familiar for me because of that sense of proximity to danger: you were in the wolf's maw. At the same time, at school, I hid the fact that I was a Jew. That's what's so crazy about the whole thing. Because, obviously, I had a name that aroused all sorts of suspicion . . .

I also remember one moment. . . . There were some moments that shone like little lights in that world where Jews quaked every time the doorbell rang at an unseemly hour. One day I saw my father coming out of the Gare du Nord or the Gare de l'Est, I don't know anymore, he must have made a trip—perhaps he simply went to a suburb—I think in fact that I was with him. In any case, I saw him coming out of the railroad station and a plainclothes policeman asked to see his papers. My father took out the identity card with the stamp, and the guy—and I'll never know if he was French or German—put his finger on the stamp and let my father go. And he was there for a roundup. I also remember how naïve we could be; namely, with my father we said: "It's really extraordinary—he put his finger on the stamp, and he didn't see it!"

I think they must have made us wear the star a little while before the roundup of the Vel d'Hiv'. And I remember the bizarre tricks we did, really bizarre tricks. We had the absurd idea that the men were threatened and not the women. And the children, obviously, even less. So my aunt [*whose specialty was tuberculosis*] walked in front, with her star. She walked as some sort of courier, in front of my father, who walked a few meters behind her. My father didn't wear the star. She looked to see if they were arresting people. And my father took the subway every morning. But why the devil did he take the subway? He wasn't working. I think that by that time he was hiding from the neighbors that he wasn't working. We lived for some time like that. It seems completely absurd because my aunt could have been taken—she was arrested later on . . . There.

After the roundup of the Vel d'Hiv', Mathilde R.'s family escaped first to a village of the Cher, and then they went to Toulouse, in the southwest of France.

Why Toulouse? Because my father had gone to school in Toulouse and he still had very fond memories of his landlady. Such tenuous things. The landlady, meantime, had aged a lot. She had started listening to Vichy radio and found that the Jews and the terrorists (what they called "terrorists" on the radio)[11] were awful.

I was put in boarding school. It was strange, at school. The atmosphere was different from Paris before the Germans had invaded the zone. There were a lot of girls who were Jewish. Most of them hid it. I hid it too. There was one girl named Markestein and, one day, a school monitor said to her: "People of your race—we can't expect anything of them!" There was also a girl named Dreyfus, who really looked as Jewish as a synagogue, and she didn't admit it either. Then another one, named Barque, yes, that's Jewish, she was from Bordeaux, and everybody thought she was Catholic. One day, she came in tears. She hadn't gotten any letters from her parents for some time, and that's when she told us her father was a Jew. It was a big surprise for me. She played the French girl like nobody's business. Another girl was called Ciezanowska—what names!— but for me, that was a Polish name; she was a pretty blond girl with ringlets, big blue eyes, absolutely adored by everybody. One day, she came in tears, saying: "They arrested my parents!" They had been arrested in Paris. They were leatherworkers. And that's when she told us she was a Jew. It was a surprise for all of us, for me as much as for the others. There too, there was a kind of process of blacking things out: it had happened to them; was it going to happen to me? It wasn't obvious that

11. The Resistance movements were labeled "terrorist" by the Vichy press and radio.

there was a connection. It's hard to resituate yourself in that kind of double situation in which we lived.

Mathilde R.'s family continued its wandering and escaped to a village of the Cantal in the center of France. The father left on a bicycle every morning, pretending to go to work, while the daughter went to the convent school.

Again, I went to a school run by nuns, what was called a convent. Thanks to my Catholic education—a partial education, but it had some impact—I didn't have any trouble reciting the prayers. I must say that my parents, while having funny ideas, had nevertheless been good for something. So I could do the prayers. Moreover, I had presence of mind, which seemed to surprise only the adults. It is, after all, a fact that children got through this period with much more craftiness in general than grown-ups. Anyway, I was no longer a child. This must have been at the end of '43; I was fourteen years old. For example, when the priest who taught us Latin and Greek asked me: "Ah, you're from Paris. What parish?"—I answered immediately, like this, smartly, which really wasn't obvious (my parents wouldn't have known if I had asked them): "The parish of Saint Ferdinand-des-Ternes." Fortunately, he didn't know the priest. That would have caused me trouble.

The suspicion was there nevertheless, I must say, because my parents had an accent. Maybe I could have passed, but with my parents it was harder. OK, we were in the Cantal. The atmosphere was strange, very anti-Semitic, openly anti-Semitic.

Marc B.:

I enlisted as a volunteer. I went but they sent me away, saying that the quota had been filled. Twice like that, I don't know, they didn't want me.

Later, when the exodus started, I wanted to leave. Only, I had the feeling that I wouldn't get far and that they would catch me on the way. So I said to myself: It's better to stay home. I returned home. Little by little, we started organizing ourselves. That is, even during the war, at least at the beginning, you could get books at the library. Later on, they closed it.

To earn a living, we started making little purses at home for a person who gave us work.

Later, on May 14, 1941, all foreigners received a summons to appear. We didn't know what to do. We got the summons at seven or eight o'clock at night, to appear the next day at eight o'clock in the morning. We didn't even know who to ask for advice, what to do, if we should go or not. I said to myself: "I'm not going." I had my wife and daughter to worry about. "Maybe they'd take it out on them. But where could we hide?" At that time, we didn't have so many contacts with French people. Today it's different. So I went. It was too late to get away. They told my wife to go gather the necessary things. They didn't tell us where we were going, and they sent us to Beaune-la-Rolande.

Down there, the first week, we learned what it meant to be hungry. Later, we could receive little packages. What kind of food did we get? Twice a day, a soup of white beets. And one loaf of bread for eight of us. To divide it, what did we do? A little scale with pieces of wood and string; if there was an extra piece of bread for one person, they took it away to give to somebody else. Later, they sent us to Sologne, supposedly to work on the abandoned farms. I was miserable, because they had started allowing visits from wives, families, and me, it was just my turn to have a visit when, without notice, they send me to Sologne. We were guarded by French policemen. They let us buy food from the peasants. We were able to write, and when the wives found out where we were, they came, they were allowed in. Once my wife came to visit with my daughter. We were afraid because we knew at that time: roundups, other roundups, had already started. The police rotated every month, and they too were trying to get food to send packages to their families. So we had a certain freedom of movement. We took them to the farms and they could buy food to send.

There were guards in front of the farms. The policemen laughed if someone escaped. But not the guard, because he was punished or fired. In short, we saw that the situation couldn't go on like that. I escaped. I was lucky, because only a week after my escape, all of those from Beaune-la-Rolande were deported.

How did I escape? I went to this farm, several miles away, to get food. I struck up an acquaintance with a gamekeeper. We started talking. He needed shirts, he didn't have enough fabric; because, at that time, to buy a shirt or something else, you needed coupons. So I wrote to my wife, she bought some shirts, sent them, and he got me some food.

[. . .] To escape, you had to go to Orléans to take the train to Paris. But the train went through Orléans at nine o'clock in the morning and roll call for us was at eight; if anyone was missing, they would call Orléans. Someone explained how to do it. I don't remember the name of the station, but you had to walk all night to get there. I left with a friend at ten o'clock at night. We got to the station about five in the morning. At 5:30, there was a train, and, when they made the roll call down there, we were already in Paris.

"LET US AVENGE OUR JEWISH BROTHERS"

The struggles of the Resistance left a deep trace in memories: despite a certain myth to the contrary, the Jews in fact did not submit passively to genocide. From the outset of the German occupation, mutual aid organs were set up: in Paris, the Committee of the Rue Amelot, established by the leading community workers, Bundists and Left and Right Labor Zionists functioning in semisecrecy, providing solidarity and assistance (canteens, clinics, financial help, contacts, false papers, etc.).[12] As for the Jewish Communists, by the summer of 1940, they too organized neighborhood committees, groups of women and young people, gathered in the Solidarity movement. They would supply the Resistance with some of its first fighters the following year.[13] And despite the silence of the "official" versions, we now know that the activists of the M.O.I. (Immigrant Labor), composed mostly of Jewish Communists from eastern Europe, especially Poland (along with Spanish, Italian, and Armenian activists), formed the vanguard of the armed

12. Adler, *Face à la persécution*, p. 158.
13. Ibid., pp. 161ff.; Maurice Rajsfus, *L'An prochain la révolution: Les communistes juifs immigrés dans la tourmente stalinienne, 1930–1945* [Next Year the Revolution: Immigrant Jewish Communists in Stalinist Torment, 1930–1945] (Paris: Mazarine, 1985), pp. 125ff.

struggle against the Nazis, in Paris as well as in Lyon, Grenoble, Marseille, and Toulouse.[14]

Politically and geographically, Bernard P. and Maurice N. followed analogous itineraries: their troubles first took them to the Lyon suburb, where they found each other, in the summer of 1942, in the same networks. First they belonged to Jewish youth groups affiliated with the Communist party and naturally went from the U.J.J. (Union of Jewish Youth, one of the components of the Solidarity movement) to the U.J.R.E. (Union of Jews for Resistance and Mutual Aid), when the latter was formed in the summer of 1943 to provide a wider, united base for Jewish resistance. Henceforth, the new organization gave priority to specifically Jewish problems and led to the formation of a big "national" movement.[15] *In his memories, Bernard P. speaks very lucidly of a "kind of excitement of the special activity of each group. Because the U.J.R.E. corresponded to a return to nationalism. Though not Zionism, it was nevertheless an assertion to the effect: let us avenge our Jewish brothers. A mobilization, as the Soviet Union mobilized Yiddish writers."*

I had an education that was both Zionist and Marxist, since, in Poland, I had been active for many years in the Hashomer HaZa'ir movement. I read a lot as soon as I started reading French. This was in '40 and '41. I read a lot of books on the French Revolution, which led me to discern parallels with the Bolshevik Revolution. The German-Soviet pact had already occurred, but that didn't keep me from reexamining my assumptions. It was a purely intellectual process that led me to try to get close to the Communists.

To get close to the Communists, in Roanne, there wasn't much choice. I didn't have much, three or four Communist Jews, so they were reputed to be, who kept their distance from the community. I must say from afar they didn't seem to be such sterling Communists. You mustn't forget that the Communist party was outlawed, so that was the only contact I could have. So I made contact with those Jews, all of whose activity

14. Adler, *Face à la persécution,* pp. 203–204; Rajsfus, *L'an prochain la révolution,* pp. 142ff., 176ff.

15. Ibid., p. 149; Adler, *Face à la persécution,* pp. 201–211.

consisted of a cautious wait-and-see. I must say that that corresponded to the general wait-and-see attitude of the majority of the Party at that time, between the Pact and '41.

I was looking for a chance to act, but I didn't find any immediate opportunities with those Jewish Communists of Roanne. So I started on my own. Anyway, *act* is a very grand word. I wrote a little newspaper and produced twenty copies by hand. I must have put out three or four issues, which were probably full of mistakes. I distributed them in mailboxes, and I think I gave a copy to one of the Jewish Communists I was in touch with. Because of this "initiative," he put me in touch with one of his authorities in Lyon.

"You took the initiative alone?"

Alone, absolutely alone. This wait-and-see attitude didn't satisfy me. It was about March or April of '41. There was in particular the watchword of making peace with the German people by going over the heads of the leaders. Let's say that I never expressed an opinion, but I never quite understood what that meant in practice.

I have an excellent memory. I am telling you this because it left a mark on me. I can't forget it. It was June 21, the date of the German invasion of Russia. It was a Sunday. We were together with a comrade from Lyon, I can tell you his name, he's well known, R. He was there to try to explain to us what making peace with the German people over the heads of the leaders was all about. And Paulette came in. Paulette was the wife of the Communist in whose house we were gathered. And she said: "The Germans have attacked the Soviet Union!" That ended that: the meeting was adjourned. He was a bit sheepish. He explained that the world is dialectic. Dialectic explains a lot of things. In short, the business of making peace was over.

I don't remember very well anymore what I was doing between '41 and August of '42. Comrades from Lyon came to Roanne. The watchword was no longer the same: it was war against the occupier. But we still weren't doing anything. During that time, I was working as a farmer because I didn't have any papers.

I went underground in July of '42. I had my first forged identity card made. At that time, you could buy cards in every to-bacco shop. I filled it out as an Alsatian and used a false stamp I made with a child's printing set. Alsatian for my accent, of course. I got in touch with the first groups of young Jews attached to the Jewish organization, the O.J.J. which later became the U.J.R.E. A while later, I found myself appointed to lead that group of young Jews. It wasn't yet the Southern Zone; it was only Lyon. We printed tracts, and we distributed them. We wrote graffiti with chalk. They were already beginning to look for the first recruits to go into the combat groups, for armed struggle. A fellow like Simon Fried, who was guillotined in Lyon in '43, I think, came from that first group. It wasn't a very heroic act, but a useful act. He was caught stealing food ration cards in city halls. And he was guillotined.

In that first group, there was L., who is still around; there was Simon Fried. You could say that was the leadership. There was Fred, a zoot-suiter, a terrific guy, who joined the F.T.P.[16] very quickly. He stupidly got himself killed in the fights for the Liberation of Paris. There was C., who joined the F.T.P. He's alive. I think he's still a Communist. There was N., who also went to the fighting groups and the F.T.P. Yes, they were all Jews.

As for me, I still had political work, publishing tracts and then publishing a newspaper, *Young Combat*. The newspaper began publishing in '43, I think, the same time the U.J.J. became the U.J.R.E. I think there was a connection with the dissolution of the *Komintern* and with that kind of excitement for the special activity of each group. [. . .]

We recruited especially, though not exclusively, among Jews. During '42 and the beginning of '43, we spread rapidly, and we had groups of young Jews throughout Lyon and its environs. From the beginning of '43, I started traveling to organize groups in Grenoble, Marseille, Nice, Toulouse, Perigueux, and Limoges.

From '43 on, I can't say precisely when, there were changes in the leadership of the U.J.J. With the big downfalls in Paris,

16. F.T.P: Franc-Tireur et Partisan, the Resistance movement led by the Communists.

and the danger for the leadership of remaining in Paris, the most celebrated members of the Jewish organization came to the Southern Zone. A whole team came with Rayski. Kowalski was one who came. I think he's living in Israel now. Earlier he had gone to Poland. Then he left there at the time of the outbreak of anti-Semitism.[17] At the same time, I had a chance to meet once or twice with the person in charge of M.O.I., who was Rayski's superior.

So, with the arrival of the Parisian group, the whole structure of our organization was changed in the direction of greater vigilance. Vigilance as regards security. We were an underground organization, pursued by the Germans. That's one thing. But also vigilance over ideological purity. That was copied from the party's organization. They appointed people responsible for the cells. They started checking peoples' personal biographies. That vigilance went too far, extending even to family and origins. It was political vigilance. For example, if people started in the A.J.,[18] you couldn't give them responsibilities because they were considered to be under Trotskyite influence. In short, what I mean is that it went beyond the question of security.

I had a hard time swallowing that. In short, we had some points of disagreement. We didn't really click with Feld. At any rate, my main activity was editing *Young Combat,* traveling, liaison with the provinces. Besides, at the beginning of '44, I was removed from Lyon and sent to Marseille. That was after the American landing in Italy, after the landing in Corsica, I believe. They predicted there would be a landing in the south before the landing in the north, and we had to strengthen the leadership of the movements, that is, of the Party, in the zones where the Americans would appear first.

In Marseille, I got in touch with the adult Jewish organizations, perhaps it was the M.O.I., to coordinate activities. And

17. Most of the leaders of the M.O.I. (Main d'Oeuvre Immigrée, a Communist organization for migrant workers), did indeed return to their homeland after the Liberation and then came back to France, especially in the wake of the wave of anti-Semitism in 1968 in Poland. But Edouard Kowalski did in fact remain in Poland, according to the testimony of Louis Gronowski-Brunot, collected by Rajsfus, *L'An prochain la révolution,* pp. 345–347.

18. Youth organization.

in June, right after the landing, they told us: "You're going back to Lyon." I was then with my wife. She wasn't yet my wife, but we were living together. She had come to Lyon in December of '43. She was my liaison and quite naturally. . . . Anyway, we went back together on June 7. I almost got myself arrested by the Gestapo when I arrived in Lyon.

I was arrested in a roundup while getting off the train. I was usually quite careful. I looked around but didn't see anything. Then a guy in civilian clothes came up to me, a Frenchman of the P.P.F., I don't know. He said to me: "Please follow me." I had papers as a liberal arts student or some such gimmick. It was at the railroad station of Brotteaux. My wife was with me. She started grumbling. He said: "Listen, it's an identity check." Finally he saw her—I tell you this because it's important for what comes later. It was three in the afternoon. He took me to a Red Cross hut, toward Brotteaux. There were about fifty of us there, guarded with submachine guns. Since morning, they had been making roundups because some guy, I don't know who, had thrown a grenade. It was the day after the landing, don't forget. They took my papers. The first thing, I went to the bathroom to eat all the little papers on me that might have been at all compromising. What are we waiting for? The arrival of the doctor for the medical checkup. I took that to mean deportation. There had been roundups at all the railroad stations and especially at Perrache. Therefore the doctor was late. During this time, I started talking with the fellow who had arrested me, this guy who worked for the Gestapo. He gave me some advice: "If you want quiet, come with us to Doriot, you'll be fine." OK, I went along with the game: I listened to what he said, how they could win. . . . And the time passed. In the meantime the doctor still hadn't showed up because he was busy in Perrache. And there was only one doctor, but I guess I was just lucky. They decided: "You're going to spend the night in the depot of Saint-Jean." So they phoned for the Lyonnais buses to take us to the depot. I don't know if it was sabotage or bad will, another hour, hour and a half, passed before the bus came. It came from Perrache half full, so there wasn't room for everybody.

I was already in the car to be taken to the depot of Saint-Jean. They were beginning to release certain categories, people who worked for the railroad factories, who had certificates and therefore worked for the Germans, or heads of large families. I had nothing to lose. I went to the window of the car. There was the boss who had all the papers. I said to him: "Listen, my wife is pregnant and if I don't come back, she's going to be sick." And on the side, thirty feet away from him, was the fellow who had arrested me and who had seen my wife. He said: "Yes." And the other man understood that he saw she was pregnant. So then, listen to this, he took my papers, which were of course forged; they weren't the papers I had made myself, they were a little better than that. And he said to me: "You're what? You do what?" "I'm a student." "Student of what?" "Liberal arts." "What arts?" I shrugged my shoulders. "You're French at least?" Imagine that, given my accent. I just shrugged my shoulders again. And he had my card, on which my life depended. He says: "Get out!"

I got out of the car and took back my papers. Then I took to my heels because there was a curfew. I caught a trolley that went to Décines, for the workers on the night shift. A worker gave me a ticket because you had to have special tickets. In short, an hour after the curfew, I arrived at Décines, to Gabriel, whose only concern was to know whether I had been followed. He was right, of course.

Anyway, I had enormous luck. I had enormous luck because, as I think about it today, I should have been dead for forty years already.

Maurice N.:

Yes, the census was taken in '41, before the Germans attacked Russia. We didn't know how to react. We discussed Marxism, we liked to be together, we engaged in propaganda against the imperialist war, but we didn't know how to react against the occupier. So we went to be recorded and once you had the stamp . . .

Things went on like that until June of '41, when Russia entered the war, at which time the whole policy, our policy, changed. Work started completely different—instead of just talking, we started acting. That was in the Communist party. We were in a cell organized by four, five, six—all Jews. It was deliberate because, in general, they always formed separate cells. When Jews entered the youth movement or the Party, you know, they didn't speak French very well. They did much better among themselves. At that time, I didn't know of any other cell than the Jewish cells. We tried to work; we started distributing tracts. That was a completely different work. There weren't any Frenchmen in the first groups.

[. . .] In February of '42, we left for Lyon. I had been summoned to the prefecture, and they wanted to take away my naturalization. My wife pushed me to leave and so did my parents. I left for Lyon, in the free zone. In the free zone, I remained French.

In Paris, my mother, my two sisters, and my brother were deported on July 16, 1942. All that remained was my father, who left on July 14 or 15 to come to me in Décines, near Lyon. He came to join me. In Décines, we lived together, in the same house, with my father, my in-laws, and my wife's two brothers. My mother was deported in '42 with my brother and two sisters. I remained alone with my father.

In Lyon, we continued to work. I got in touch with P., then with Charles L., who was called Émile. He was a very skillful speaker; he was very capable. There was Henri L., Charles B., Henriette, Ernest. That was the first group. They started organizing the youth in Lyon. I was assigned Décines. We printed pamphlets ourselves, at Fred's house. Our work consisted mainly of propaganda and military training. They were preparing people to join the F.T.P. There are many people like Charles who joined the F.T.P. We had one woman friend, Pierrine, yes. We didn't even know if that was her real name. There was P.—he became the leader of the whole Southern Region. He also lived in Décines. They knew I was in Décines, but they didn't know where he lived.

Then, right on the eve of the Liberation, I was denounced and they took my father, my mother-in-law, and my two brothers-in-law from our house. One of them came back, the younger one. At the age of eleven, he was the youngest deportee from France.

[. . .] There were cases when the police helped us. For example, a police sergeant was in front of the trolley and when he saw a Jew get off, he told him to go back. Moreover, I have an interesting case to tell regarding that police sergeant. It was the last year of the war, right before the Liberation of Décines. There was a woman who lived with the Germans, and the Maquisards,[19] friends, came and threatened the woman. She started shouting: "Help, stop, thief!" The police sergeant came. He ordered them to stop. They didn't stop and he drew his revolver and killed one of them. Subsequently, at the Liberation, the same Maquisards came and arrested him. I thought that police sergeant had done a lot to help Jews and others so I owed him something. I went to free him. I went to a lot of trouble; I had to fight to get his freedom. I thought I owed him something, not for myself, but as a Jew and as a man.

A month before the Allies entered Lyon, there was the uprising at Villeurbanne. That must have been the end of August '44. We occupied the skyscrapers. We fought. And, as the German army was retreating after the landing at Marseille, we were obliged to give way to the Germans. We were the ones who liberated Décines.

MIRACLES

How did the survivors escape persecution? They are still amazed at it today. If they express their gratitude for French friends who generously agreed to help them, often at great peril, almost all the survivors ultimately reckon that they owed their salvation to chance, to luck, luck bordering on the miraculous. On such and such a day, some policeman came to warn them that it was better not to stay home in the next few hours, since there was going to be a roundup: "Look, I have an order to arrest you. I'll say I didn't find anybody!" Or (as Mathilde R. tells) some policeman, apparently inadvertently, covered over the "Jew" on the identity card with his finger; or even some German soldier, to whom

19. Translator's note: French Resistance fighters.

you had dared to speak German, took pity; or you managed to trick
some French militiaman (like Bernard P.). So many survivals, so many
miracles.

Here is how Mathilde R., who hid in a village of the Cantal, es-
caped arrest. As she recalls the episode, she truly relives the events,
the gestures, the words, the thoughts, and even the perception of the
landscape in a time that becomes almost unmoving, suspended.

One day, they arrested all the Jews of the village, right in the
middle of the morning. One of the daughters of a collaborator
came to school saying to somebody: "This morning, they arrested all the Jews of the village" or "They're going to arrest
all the Jews of the village." And then it's the intensity of . . . I
don't know what. This mechanism, I really want to call it denial, but really you mustn't show anything. I didn't show anything, but more than that, I didn't feel anything—consciously
felt nothing. That didn't bother me. And I knew that, in the
morning, my father was supposed to come get my bicycle either
to pretend to go to work or to get cheese. I left school, and the
bicycle was in front of the door. I didn't realize what might have
happened to me. I took my bicycle and went home. And as
usual, I stopped at all the farms along the way, to ask if there
were eggs, milk, cheese, whatever you could imagine finding
and never did find, but which you did find nevertheless from
time to time.

And I stopped. While I was asking a woman if she had any
eggs, I was aware that I had the handlebars of my bicycle in
my hands and that I shouldn't have had them, that my father
should have come to get the bicycle. And while I was asking
her if she had any eggs, I was thinking: "Well, my parents have
been arrested, obviously, since the girl said to the other one that
they arrested all the Jews this morning. So, I'm alone. What am
I going to do?" Really, in a flash: "What am I going to do? I'm
going to try to go find my aunt in the Vaucluse. So, I've got
to shift for myself to find some money for the trip." My mind
was working to figure out how to get money for the trip.
Absolutely no emotion. Nothing. Up until the moment when,
approaching the house, I saw my father, and then and there I

started crying. Up until then, I hadn't felt anything. Nothing but practical things.

Later, they told me that the owner of the house where we were living, a marvelous house in an absolutely spendid landscape overlooking the distant mountains of the Cantal—it was very beautiful, there was a green meadow—so, the owner had gone to get the police to tell them: "I don't understand, you arrested all the Jews but you didn't arrest mine!" And among those policemen was one whose little girl my mother had taken for a walk just by chance. He answered: "You tell me that those are Jews, but I don't know anything about it. I don't have any proof."

MOURNING

The miracle, alas, didn't always take place. We know the figures today, thanks to the labors of Serge Klarsfeld: of the 300,000–330,000 Jews in France just before the war (190,000–200,000 French Jews, 130,000–140,000 foreign Jews), close to 80,000, that is, 25 percent, perished. Those who disappeared include 56,500 foreign Jews and 24,500 French Jews. The latter included 8,000 children of foreign parents and 8,000 naturalized French citizens.[20] In other words, 10 percent of French Jews and 40 percent of immigrant Jews were victims of genocide.[21]

Memories indicate an immeasurable void. There is practically no family that was untouched: almost always, several close relatives died, plus all those who stayed in Poland and the other homelands. The survivors suffered a trauma that cut their lives in two: when memory of the catastrophe, of the arrest of loved ones returns, it is once again stupor, the sense of a rupture, a tearing apart, something unfinished. Likewise, the children of deportees who could talk to Claudine Vegh after forty years of silence and confess their private break constantly repeat the same lament, like a tragic refrain: "I didn't say good-bye."[22]

20. Serge Klarsfeld, *Vichy-Auschwitz: Le rôle de Vichy dans la solution finale de la question juive en France, 1943–1944* [Vichy-Auschwitz: The Role of Vichy in the Final Solution of the Jewish Question in France] (Paris: Fayard, 1985), pp. 179–181.

21. Ibid.; and Adler, *Face à la persécution*, p. 29.

22. Claudine Vegh, *I Didn't Say Goodbye.* [*Je ne lui ai pas dit au revoir*]. Postface Introduction by Bruno Bettelheim (London: Caliban Books, 1984).

It's the same laceration that Golda R. recounts at the time of her husband's arrest:

You had to register at the commander's office. I didn't let my husband go. I took his identity card and I went with mine and his. I come to Rouen. They registered me and that was that. Then they couldn't find my card. They looked and didn't find it.

So they sent police to Elbeuf to arrest me and take me to the commander's office. The police were my husband's best friends. They used to eat and drink in my house. They came in the morning, very early. I was still sleeping. My husband went out. Two policemen came.

"We have to examine your wife's identity card."

I threw on my dressing gown. They said to me:

"Unfortunately, Madame R., we didn't come to get the identity card, we came to get you."

And my husband cried out:

"You came to get my wife? What has she done? They're not taking women yet! Why are they taking you? Did you do something in Poland? Were you a Communist?"

They forced me to go. I got dressed. I wanted to take the child (Madeleine was six months old at the time), but my husband didn't want me to. The two boys had already left for school. I asked permission to go say good-bye to the children. My husband went to get them at school. They were crying. All the people who saw the police taking me insulted them: "What do you want with that woman? She never hurt anybody!" I said to the policeman: "You ate with my husband, you drank with my husband, I set the table for you."

That was in '40. They weren't yet taking women at that time. I came to the commander's office. My husband telephoned to ask them to release his wife. He said that he wanted to go in her place. They answered him that his wife was going to return and that when they needed him, they would take him.

[. . .] We had a dog. He'd bark when a child passed by. But when the police showed up at the door, he didn't budge. He remained silent. There were two exits. When the dog barked,

I said: "Avrom, go out the back and go to Suzanne's house." I didn't know they were police, and my husband was at home.

"Unfortunately, R., it's you we've come to get. You telephoned that we should release your wife and take you."

I begged;

"Listen, you're my husband's best friends. You ate and drank in my house. You know he's sick. You can say he wasn't there."

"You want them to shoot us instead of your husband?"

My husband got dressed, and they took him away. That was in 1942. They took him to Drancy . . .

The days of the Liberation brought with them an indescribable burst of joy in August and September of 1944—short-lived joy that would be shattered when the survivors, along with the rest of the world, discovered the horror of the Nazi camps. In truth it was but a half-revelation, for, more or less consciously, they suspected, they knew, that horror. But then the emaciated skeletons of survivors returned and told of it, and the photos were published, and the films showing the heaps of corpses at Auschwitz, the piles of shoes and eyeglasses, the crematoria. And there was the waiting, the long, interminable, desperately futile waiting, the pitiful lines at the Hotel Lutetia[23] in search of news of those who had disappeared. Nothing, no one. You waited, however; you kept on waiting, stubbornly, silently clinging to a futile (though unspeakable) hope. You watched for the mailman, the sound of footsteps on the stairs; in the street, you rushed toward a stranger because you thought, in the distance, you recognized a profile. Mute grief that you didn't talk about even with those who were close to you because you knew that the hope was mad, that the return of those who disappeared was unlikely, more and more mad, more and more unlikely with the passing of the months and the years. But you still waited, you waited incessantly, for the rest of your life. This "unspeakable secret," this waiting, never failed to disappoint and inevitably recurred. It gave rise to uncannily similar formulations.

Mathilde R.:

I dreamed of that aunt I loved so much, who was a very important figure for me in my childhood. I dreamed for years and

23. A large hotel in Paris where the survivors of concentration camps were gathered after their return in the spring of 1945.

years, and, every now and then, it still comes back to me. It's a recurring dream: I enter her apartment and she's there (that apartment where I lived with her during the war). She's there, yet, at the same time, I know it can't be. In the dream, there's something of a doubt about that possibility, so that it won't be so hopeless on waking.

Mourning was impossible, for it was denied in its proper time. In a way, the survivors continue to live in an extension of the moment when they couldn't say good-bye. How could the process of mourning be done without knowing when and how loved ones died, when there is no tomb, no body, and no traditional funeral rites? Hence, one encounters a fixation on the past, the perception of the present "through a special prism,"[24] and this interminable waiting mixed with a sense of guilt. Of what are these victims of Nazi crimes guilty? Simply put, of living or, rather, of surviving. The uneasiness is especially strong in those who were children at the time and lost their parents: they have a sense of owing their lives to them a second time, of having survived only at the cost of their parents' sacrifice. Similar feelings are expressed by those who remember the family they left behind, in Poland—family who were trapped by the genocide.

Mathilde R.:

We had to go back to Paris in October [1944]. Returning to Paris was also something wonderful. To return to Paris was another July 14, another landing. It was wonderful, except that my aunt, meanwhile, had been deported.

She was deported under truly senseless conditions. First, she stayed in Paris longer than we did. She didn't want to leave. In retrospect, I understood why. I understood later on that my aunt was involved in the Resistance. She had a friend who lived downstairs from her, a doctor and a Communist. I understood because my aunt used to type things all day long on the typewriter. I guess she must have been making pamphlets. Then, at a certain moment, they crossed the line of demarcation and went to the free zone. And the people whose house they were hiding in were denounced, or they were denounced themselves.

24. Vegh, *I Didn't Say Goodbye,* p. 171.

She stayed in Drancy for several months—I know the date she arrived and I saw in Klarsfeld's book the date the convoy that took her to Drancy left. She wasn't very old, fifty some, but she had dyed her hair. I think that her hair turned white during those months in Drancy, and I suppose she was put into the gas chamber almost immediately because of that.

OK, when we returned, she wasn't there anymore, and we knew that she had been deported. We harbored vague hopes; I must say that I never really mourned for that aunt. I think, besides, that nothing is harder than to mourn for someone whose body you haven't seen.

What more can I tell you?

Reaching the end of her memories, Mathilde R. returns to her parents from Poland. Their story had inspired the opening of her narrative, but they had almost been forgotten since. And this return takes the form of a funeral litany, a monotonous enumeration of the dead: memory itself becomes a memorial.

My family in Poland was entirely. . . . My grandfather, my grandmother, ninety years old, were . . . according to different versions, either deported to Treblinka or shot. That uncle I talked about just now, who was a doctor in the Warsaw ghetto; his son who was half-Jewish was also shot in the ghetto. His wife, who was a Christian Armenian, went mad as a result of those two deaths. She threw herself into the Vistula. . . . So it goes, pathetic stories, but that's reality. Several of my father's sisters were killed by the Germans, one in Treblinka, the other, no one knows where. She was in Bialystok; she had returned to Judaism.

Really, it's a family that was snuffed out. On my mother's side, I talked about that uncle with bright yellow gloves and a cane with a knob: he and his wife died in the Warsaw Ghetto.

With Robert S., we find the same morbid preoccupation, tinged with a sense of uneasiness at the idea that he couldn't get all the members of his family out in time. At the same time, this man, who evinced such admirable moral rigor and humanist ideals in the course of his memories, questions himself in anguish: Can we, must we, forgive?

Not forget, but forgive? This problem of the relationship between ethics and memory still gnaws away.

When the war was over, I wanted to know what had become of my parents in Poland. So I wrote a letter to the Polish embassy, and they confirmed that my parents died in the crematorium, at Auschwitz. This happened on a Thursday morning, at ten o'clock. The postman brought me the letter, and tears ran down my face as I read it. At the same moment—you'd say the devil plays these tricks, unthinkable tricks, on you—there was a German prisoner who was working on a farm who just showed up with a bad tooth. He came in, sat down. I had just read the letter, and my first impulse was to take the forceps and, without giving him a shot, pull the tooth so he'd cry out in pain. Telling it makes it endure, but the thought passed quickly. I said to myself: Brute, what do you blame him for? Being a Nazi? It may hurt you that he killed your parents, but if you commit the barbarism of pulling the tooth without a shot, you're a barbarian like him. You are no better than he. I pulled myself together. I gave him a shot, then did the operation. I wouldn't have done it better for my own father.

And when I finished, I said to him in German: "You see, I got a letter that confirms the death of my parents, dead in the crematorium." I waited. If he had said something to try to clear himself, I would have punched him in the face. I was absolutely sure of that. Fortunately, he was prudent; he bowed his head and left. I never saw him again [*long silence*].

I asked myself the question: If I had seen my parents die, would I have been able to forgive so easily? Because I bear forgiveness inside me, but not forgetting. You can forgive; you can never forget those things. But I wonder: If I had witnessed my parents' death, would I have had the strength to forgive? I admit that, even now, I don't have the answer, and I think that I'll die without answering the question.

GHOSTS

As the narrative draws to a close, when there is nothing more to say because their previous lives really seem finished, they go back again, to another comeback: that of survivors who helped them uncover some traces of those who disappeared (a date, a meeting, some information about the way they died) or told the tragedy they went through. Survivors emerge as ghosts from another world.

The one Yacob-Jacques L. met right after the war revealed strange coincidences to him. His memories unfold with episodes embedded within other episodes, and shift from third person narratives to first person identification with those recalled.

One day, I had a client at Sèvres–Babylone—you know? There's the Hotel Lutetia. It was right after the Liberation. I was passing by the Hotel Lutetia, and a girl was staring at me. She asked me: "Do you speak Polish?" "Yes." "Oh, I'm saved, I'm saved." "What's going on?"

We went into a café and she told me a story like this. Her father lived on a main street in Warsaw, not in the ghetto. They had a clock shop, a big one. I was the only daughter, and I was already in my last year of law school when the war broke out. On the first day the Germans sent planes to bomb Warsaw, my mother happened to be in the street; she was killed. I don't have a mother anymore, she said to me, and she stopped. She couldn't talk anymore.

"Easy," I said to her.

So the day came when we had to go to the ghetto. We had a little money but the merchandise—we hadn't hidden it—the Germans took everything. We found a hole with some other Jews. I didn't speak Yiddish, very little anyway. What could we do? They thought and thought, and they found out that you could get forged papers, identity cards with certificates of baptism, all that, but it was very expensive. My father said to me: "Listen, my child, I won't survive the war but I want to save you. Take this money. You're to go to this place I know. They'll make you an identity card and a certificate of baptism, and you'll go to work. I don't know how, but you'll survive the war."

I didn't want to, I didn't want to. Then my father died too. I was alone, all alone. I took the money I had. They made papers for me; that wasn't easy. Now, what did I do? I looked for work. As a housekeeper. She found it right away. They sent her to a Polish lady. A big woman with three or four children. I didn't see the husband there. In the morning I started working, but the woman looked at me suspiciously. She never did that, you understand? At night, she was already sure I wasn't Polish: "Come, my dear, you're—(she says the Polish name, I don't remember anymore) like I'm a ballerina at the Warsaw Opera! You think I'm going to keep Jewish blood in my house? Get out at once!"

It was already night, eight o'clock. What could I do? I left. In the main entrance, there was a guard, a caretaker: she opened her door and then she closed it. And all of a sudden, a Polish policeman passed in the street, and she cried out: "Come here, there's a Jewish woman who wants to hide in my house!"

OK, she went with the policeman. In the middle of the street, the policeman stopped and said: "My God, just like my daughter, just like my daughter. She was killed in a bombing two days ago!" "So, Monsieur, that being the case, how can you turn me over to the Gestapo?" "No, I won't give you to the Gestapo. We have to think something up. Here's what I'm going to say: I was passing by, there was a scuffle, there was shouting and crying. I went back to ask what was going on. And the woman said to me: she stole a watch, something. And then one of her children came and said: here, Mama, I found the watch! I have to take you to the police station. I'll tell that story."

He went with her to the station. He told this story. So the chief said: "But why did you bring her here?" "Why? Because there's a curfew. She's a proud Polish woman. As soon as she was suspected of a theft, she didn't want to stay with her boss anymore. Since there's a curfew, I thought she could spend the night here, and tomorrow, she can go wherever she wants."

On the way again, he had said to her: "Mademoiselle, do you have any money?" "No." "I'll give you some. I don't know how much, but something. When you survive the war. . . . I'm going to tell you why: among your own people, you'll tell them you found a Pole, a policeman, who was a decent person. My sister lives about fifty kilometers from Warsaw. She is a greengrocer. You tell her everything, the whole truth, and she'll look after you."

So, she spent the night in the police station, and, in the morning, she went to the railroad station. She bought a ticket, and she went to the policeman's sister. She told her everything. "Mademoiselle, I have to hide you in my house for three days. I'll tell all my neighbors I'm expecting a niece." She stayed hidden for three days, until the fourth day. She helped sell all the time, throughout the war. That's how she was saved.

Later on, I couldn't stay there. My father was dead; my mother was dead. I had a brother in Australia. I wrote to him, and he answered me. I'm waiting for the papers he's supposed to send me.

There were other cases like that, but very few, very few. After the war, I wrote to the city hall there to ask what had become of my brothers and sisters. They answered kindly: "They were taken on October 10 or 20, 1942, and, unfortunately, have not been seen since. But you have a cousin who lived in Lublin. He left us an address in case someone asked for him." I wrote right away: "What do you need?" He answered me right away. He didn't want money. "Send me papers." And he came.

Wait, that't not all. What a small world it is! I was in Menton on vacation. There was a big park and Jews there with whom I could discuss Talmud, Bible—who still knew. This couple came and sat down. They were speaking Polish. I was curious: Polish in Menton? So I was bold: "Monsieur, you're speaking a language I understand very well." He told me: his wife was Jewish, he wasn't. They had known each other before the war, but not well enough to get married. In Warsaw, during the war, she hid in some hole. She stayed there for months. And then, before the ghetto uprising, he (her husband now) helped her run away. It was very difficult. He had to pay off the guards. She stayed with his family throughout the war, and after the war, they got married. They live in Mexico now. He's an engineer.

When I heard that she had hidden in a hole. . . . My cousin I just mentioned, he also was hidden in a hole. "Madame, can you tell me who you hid with?" "Oh, yes, wait. There was

Monsieur Z. and another man with a thirteen- or fourteen-year-old son. He was called . . . oh, yes, F.L." That was my cousin! In the same hole, you realize? What a world . . .

We listen now to the voice of another "ghost" who tells her own story. Of all the people from central Europe whose memories we have gathered, she is the only one who came to France after the war. With her, we find ourselves in the very heart of the genocide, in Poland.

Anna D.:

Hitler had already started. From '38 on, the Poles stood in front of stores to keep people from going in. They said: "You mustn't buy from the Jews." The pogroms had already started.

When Hitler entered, in the early days, they took the men to work. Once, a German came to my house, in the courtyard. He went to all the apartments and took all the men. My husband didn't move fast enough so the German kicked him. The next day, he escaped. He came back, saying: "I don't want to work there anymore. I'm going away. Come if you want. If not, I'll go by myself. If I stay, I'll resist, and they'll shoot me."

At that time, my children were very little: two, four, six years old. It was cold, 27 or 28 degrees below zero. I didn't want to go with him because I had heard people say that they couldn't get through, that they had to stay on the border. Many children didn't have anything to eat, were frozen. I said to myself: "Where am I going to go? I'm going to lose my children." So I stayed. In my house, there were twenty-seven Jewish tenants. There were women with children; one of them was pregnant. The men all left together. We women stayed. What could we do?

A week later, they announced that if you had family outside of Lodz, in the country or in another city, you should go to them because they didn't know what was going to happen in three days.

What to do? If you had seen what was going on in the street! Everybody was wailing, crying in the street, with children. It was terrible to hear that. There is no good God. I wondered what to do, all alone with three children. I went up to my aunt's house and asked her: "Where are you going? What should we do?" So my aunt started crying over me: "What did you do? Why did you let your husband go? You're left with three children, all by yourself. We don't know what's going to happen." She was yelling at me, I didn't know what to do. I left.

I didn't have a lot of money. We dealt in wholesale goods. There were seasons, and we bought inventory for the whole season. So we didn't have much money left. I suggested to a neighbor to leave with me, to go to my in-laws outside of Lodz, about a hundred miles away. The Germans weren't there yet. I thought that would be good and I wouldn't be all alone.

It was Friday, the last day. There was a Pole who lived outside of Lodz, in the suburb. He had a cart with two horses. I put everything I could on it—linen, blankets; the neighbor did too. We set out. A while later, the owner of the cart said: "We have to go through customs. Thousands of people are waiting to go through. It's cold, the children are cold. Let's go back to my house. We'll spend the night and leave tomorrow."

The children were crying. They were freezing. Even the birds were dropping dead. He took everything I had put in the cart back to his house, the children went to bed, and I stood off to the side. Then he talked with the neighbors and saw that he had taken less money than the others. About midnight, one in the morning, he went to bed, and I stretched out next to the children to spend the few hours until the next morning. After getting the children ready to leave, I knocked on his door: "It's light already, we have to leave." No answer, I knocked three times, four times: "We have to leave, I can't stay here!" "I'm not leaving." "What? I paid you, I gave you what you wanted and you don't want to leave? It can't be." "No, I'm not leaving."

What could I do? I went out to the road. There were people who were going back to Lodz because things had been extended to three months. So I went back to his house and asked him to take me back to Lodz.

"No. I'm not going anywhere."

I went back out to the road and asked some people to take me. Someone had pity—the children were crying, it was cold.

I went back to get my things. He kept everything. Some of his neighbors treated him like a murderer: "You see a woman alone with three children and you do that?" Since he was ashamed, he left me some blankets and linens and he kept all the rest. I said "My tough luck!" and I returned to Lodz. I met a neighbor, who took my packages. Another person I knew took the youngest child home to warm him up. All of a sudden, about ten German soldiers arrived. They started knocking people on the head, everywhere, with their rifles. Fortunately, we had just reached the house. He gave me tea to warm me up. Then I went to get the child who was warmed up and had slept.

Then I went home, to my house. When I came, there was already somebody inside. I couldn't get back in. It was all over. I didn't have a home anymore. Where could I go in this terrible cold with my children? There was a neighbor to whom I explained:

"I don't have a place to live. I can't go back."

"I have a neighbor's key. If you want, go in there."

She gave me the key of the neighbor, who had left with five children. There was a bed, a cupboard, a little stove. I found some coal, a little wood, and I lit a fire. There was a bucket of water—it was a piece of ice. It was night. I put the children to bed and I went to bed, crying.

The next day, I asked the neighbor to watch the children so I could try to earn a few cents to be able to feed the children. I washed laundry. I washed the ground. I was happy to have found that. On the fourth day, the neighbor said to me:

"A Polish gentleman sent by your father-in-law came to look for you."

At that time, Jews couldn't leave anymore. They didn't give them tickets; only Poles were allowed. Knowing that, that I was alone, my father-in-law had paid a Pole to come get us and take us there, to them. I was happy. I wept with joy. I had to be ready to leave the next morning.

Very early, it was still dark, he brought me the tickets, helped me put the bundles in the droshky, and we left for the railroad station. I thought he was going to accompany me all the way.

No. He gave me the tickets and said: "You're on your own."
With the children, and it was so cold! I came to the railroad station. There were Germans, inspections. A German woman felt
my bag, searched, and let me go through. I was happy. Behind
me she kept a woman with a big bundle from going through.
I got to the platform and what did I see? Thousands and
thousands of people. They were on the roof of the train, in the
doorways, on the steps. Impossible to get on. The train left and
I was all alone with the children.

Someone who worked on the trains came up to me, took the
bundles, and asked me to follow him. He took me to the last
train, and I got on. We left, but not for long. The tracks were
broken. We had to walk three kilometers to the other station.
I couldn't get there with all the children and the bundles. I rented
a cart for a few pennies; I went through three stations like that.
It was cold. The Poles took pity. They took each of the children
to warm up in a little cafeteria. They ran with them, they were
very nice. One of them helped me climb up onto the roof of
the train.

I still had fourteen kilometers to go, and I had to change
trains. I got off; the platforms were crawling with Germans. We
had to wait all night until the next day to take another train,
and we couldn't stay on the platform. What to do? I had an aunt
who lived in that town, so I decided to go find her. Seeing children, outside, people wouldn't say anything: I left the two
younger ones with the bundles, and I took the oldest one with
me.

It was dark. It was midnight or one in the morning. Winter.
I knew she lived in a new house. I walked, I walked. I saw one
house. It wasn't finished. I went back and fell into a hole. The
child remained on the side. How I got out of it I don't know.
I got out and looked around. There was still a long way to go.
I searched some more and found the house. I found it because
he was a shoemaker and there was a little sign outside. Only I
didn't know which door. I went into the courtyard, and I heard
Germans talking and singing. "That's it, it's all over. If anybody
comes out, he'll take me." I hid in a corner and waited. Some
lights went on, and somebody came down the stairs. "If it's a

German, I'm finished. Whatever he'll do he'll do." It was my cousin:

"What are you doing here?"

"Don't say anything. Let me in."

I went in, she woke everybody up. I explained. Her two sons, who were fifteen and thirteen, went with me to get the children at the railroad station, all alone among the Germans. I brought the children back, I put them to bed on chairs, and I stayed next to them. The next morning, the two boys took me to the railroad station and put me on the train.

I arrived. It was Shabbat, but at that time, nobody cared. Pious or not, this was war. They knew I was coming. They were glad about it, and so was I. That lasted for a week or two, no more.

My husband had two younger brothers, one fifteen, the other twenty, who worked with his father, a tailor for the peasants. One day, he said:

"I don't want to work for strangers' children."

"They're not strangers, they're your brother's children."

What could I do? I tried to earn a few cents. I offered to help a dressmaker. She agreed. I was pleased. I could buy the children something to eat.

Some time went by like that. The Germans started deporting people for labor. The brothers left. I did dressmaking in exchange for a sack of potatoes. But I didn't want to stay there. I felt unwanted. There were three rooms and a kitchen. They closed the door of the kitchen. They didn't heat it. My iron bed was next to the door. It was so cold there was ice on the walls. The parents were in a heated room, and their married daughter with a child in the other room. I was in the kitchen. It was so cold!

Badly received by her family, Anna D. did piecework for the Polish peasants:

By then, we weren't allowed to go more than a mile outside the town. The last peasant where I worked lived near the railroad station. There were two Germans who came to eat in his house. The first day, when they came in, they shook my hand.

They didn't see that I wasn't Polish because I wore a scarf on my head, a long skirt with an apron, like the other women. The second day, the German asked: "Who is that woman with the child?" My son had black curly hair, not like the Poles, who are blond. The peasant had enough sense to answer: "It's my daughter-in-law, who came to rest here for a few days." Later, he told me to leave because he was scared for me and for himself. He could be shot. I took the child and left.

Later, we weren't allowed to go out. The police were guarding the street. There was no work. It was lousy. There were roundups all the time. One day, I decided to go to the market to buy some potatoes. A German arrested me. I started shouting. My father-in-law told me not to get upset, that I would only get two weeks and would then return. But it didn't turn out like that.

They put me in the police station. It was full of people, women, girls, men. A military truck, covered with a tarpaulin, came to get us. They forced us to get in. The police were guarding us with rifles. When I saw that, I started crying, shouting that they should let me go. Everybody said: "Stop it! They're going to shoot all of us because of you!" Because of me? I stopped.

They took us to a camp, at Skarzysko, almost ten miles away, and they separated us. There was my mother-in-law's cousin on one side and me on the other. So I said to myself: "I'm going to go with her. That way we'll be together." And I went over to her, to her side. And on her side, everybody said to me: "Why did you come here? Over there, they're sending people home, but us they're taking for labor." When I heard that, I wanted to go back to the other side but there was a soldier who prevented me. So I stayed. And the next day, they told me: "You know what happened with the others, where you were? They deported them all. They're going to the ovens."

They put us in camps. We were maybe four hundred women, separated from the men, not in the same camp. We slept on boards put on top of one another, without anything at all, only on the boards. They took us to work, you had to walk two, three miles every day to go work. Soldiers guarded us with rifles, on all sides. By now, it was winter. There was a lot of snow. We had wooden clogs, open in back. Those who couldn't walk were shot.

Later on, they built huts. By then, there were fewer people, maybe thirty, forty women in a hut. Every day, we got up at six o'clock to go to work. One week we worked during the day, one week at night. Everybody had a number. Those who tended the machines were on their feet all night long. When you were tired, when you closed your eyes, you were beaten. That went on for three and a half years. For food, they gave us soup that smelled bad, dry beets. You couldn't eat it. A lot of people got sick, they had diarrhea and were taken to the hospital. That was the end. From the hospital, they were deported.

I was lucky, I had seven machines. There were big barrels. You had to fill them with fourteen thousand pounds of stuff a day. The others had four or six. I had seven! One day, the boss made a cross on a barrel, and that meant sabotage. I really didn't pay attention at the time. There was a German inspector who spoke Polish. When she saw that, she told the Pole that I had committed sabotage. (With us, there were some Poles who were mechanics.) The Pole took me to the manager, to his office, thinking he was going to beat me on the spot. He wasn't there. We waited and waited. He didn't come. The Pole was so hysterical that he took a very hard belt and beat me, shouting: "Dirty Jew, you call that work?" That hurt. I didn't say anything, I cried. Then the boss came, and the Pole pointed to me and said: "There, she's the one. Sabotage, sabotage!" He thought the boss would take me out and kill me on the spot. But the boss didn't say anything because he knew how I worked. The Pole was furious. A few days later, the top brass— commanders of the camps—came and beat the Pole. All the Jews were happy. He had beaten me. Now it was his turn. Two days later, he disappeared.

At that time, the Russians were starting to advance. They selected people to send to Germany. I was in the last group. As the Russians advanced, the Germans got scared. All of a sudden, they were there—while the boss was reading the list of all the names, we saw Russian airplanes coming. When the boss saw them, he disappeared and we never saw him again. A soldier took us to another place. We had to cross a river, the Wartha. They put us in a kind of cellar. I don't know what it was. We went in there like animals. Men were praying, women were crying. We thought we were waiting for the train: "They're going to send us somewhere, we don't know where." It was dark; a German came: "Everybody has to get out; in five minutes, everyone must be outside!" Everybody started trampling over everyone else, over legs, over heads. They were scared of being shot; it was atrocious. We went out; we were put in groups of five. They took us in the direction of the bridge. We all looked at each other: "That's it, it's over. They're going to throw us in the water. This is the end."

But it wasn't that. They took us back to the camp. There were still bosses, police. They opened the door: "What's going on, everybody's coming back?" When we returned, everyone in his hut, it was already dark. The lights were out and every time you heard "zzz, zzz," it was airplanes passing, shrapnel whistling. We were all women; the men were separate. We said: "We're going to go to the men; we'll be safer." We weren't allowed to move. About four o'clock in the morning, all at once, everything stopped. We didn't hear anything anymore. It was calm. It was in January. Some men who weren't afraid said to each other: "This calm, it can't be, we've got to get out." To get out into the street, you had to pass through seven gates. One man went through a gate, where a soldier was lying. Nobody. Everything was open. He looked under the bed—he was afraid that somebody was hiding there. There was a rifle; he took it: "What's going on? There's no one here." He went through all the gates: nobody. So he went out into the street. "Come on, come on, we're free, nobody's here!" "Nobody? It can't be!" Everybody was scared. He came back and started shouting: "Come out, come out, we're free, free, nobody's here!" Some men came out and started shouting the same thing. Some of them went crazy with joy. They shouted, sang. They didn't know what to do. Joy!

The survivors of the camp of Skarzysko were liberated by the Russians and then put in other transit camps. Six months later, they were released.

Where to go? We had never gone out into the street. We didn't know where to go. Some of us women went out looking for a place to move into. We meet some Poles and we asked them: "Where are the Jews who came out of the camps?" They pointed to a house the Germans had left. We went there. What did we see? Jam-packed with women, maybe a hundred women, one on top of the other. It was so small. So we just lay down on the ground. There wasn't anything at all. What did we hear at night? Somebody knocking: "Open up or you'll all be shot!" One woman said: "Too bad, let them do what they want." She opened the door. There were two Russian soldiers with rifles. They came in, took two women, and went away with them. They brought them back the next morning. When I saw that, I said: "I don't care where I go, but I'm not staying here. Who's coming with me?"

The trains weren't back on schedule yet; everything had been destroyed. We left half on foot, half on the train. You had to jump onto the moving trains. We left anyway. We got to Czitloviesco, where my parents were. They were all deported; there wasn't anybody left. I said: "Let's go to the small town. There are people who came back." On the way, I recognized a woman I had worked for during the war. It was a Sunday. I stopped her: "Do you recognize me?" "No. Who are you?" "You remember your dressmaker who worked for you?" "It's you, it's you, you're . . . " "Yes, it's me." She knelt down and started praying right in front of me.

After much more wandering, Anna D. finally returned to Lodz.

We got to Lodz. I went out of the railroad station, into the street. I didn't recognize anything at all. Everything was changed. I didn't know where to go, although I knew the city. I showed the address. They pointed the way. I went up to that woman's house. She was very comfortable . . .

I went to look for work. I asked at the committee, and they

gave me an address. I got there and knocked. Nobody there. They gave me another address, nobody again. I tell myself, "I'm going to the ghetto, maybe I'll find someone." Who do I see? A gentleman next to a door. Is it him or not? How am I going to ask? It's a Pole, a neighbor who lived in the same house. I stood next to him, looking at him and said:

"You recognize me?"

"No. Who are you?"

I told him.

"Oh! You're. . . . It's you? There is a neighbor—if you want to go to her, I'll take you there."

It was the neighbor who had once given me the keys of the apartment. We go up, the door was closed. "She has a little bakeshop; we'll go there." We went down, she came out. I recognized her right away, but she didn't recognize me. He talked with her, I stood off to the side. I heard everything. When he saw that she didn't ask who I was, he asked her:

"Do you know this lady?"

"No, I don't."

He told her my name. She looked at me and started crying:

"You know, your husband was here, dressed as a soldier. He said that if he didn't find anybody, he wouldn't stay, but he would send word from wherever he was."

When I heard that, I couldn't believe it. What to do? Where to go? There was a Russian headquarters. I went there and asked if they knew the name, if it was possible to get information. They didn't know. What could I do? I'd have to wait, maybe he'd write. And, so, every day, I went to the ghetto.

Anna D. received help from a "Czechoslovakian caretaker," who got her a room and dressmaking work as well.

At that time, there were Russian women soldiers who had military coats. They brought them to me, and I made skirts and jackets out of them, whatever I could. They were happy to be able to change their clothes. When there was a piece of leftover fabric, they gave it to me. I made myself a little skirt. I earned a few cents. I went to the market and bought a pair of secondhand shoes, old shoes—I had still been wearing the clogs.

Later, I had another piece of cloth left over and made myself a jacket. I had a suit, a skirt, a jacket, shoes. I was a real lady . . .

Every day, I went to the committee to see if I might not find someone. One day, I saw a girl I had worked with in the camp, carrying a little sack on her back. She was crying her eyes out:

"Here I am, I don't know where to go, I don't have anything, I've been sleeping outside."

"That's silly. Come with me."

Once while I was working at the machine next to the window, I heard somebody calling me. I looked out and saw that neighbor with a piece of paper in her hand:

"You've got a letter from your husband!"

I don't know how I got down. Through the window, through the stairs! I don't remember anymore. There was no address, just a number.

"Go to the railroad station, they'll know."

I went to the railroad station. I showed them the letter and they gave me a ticket.

It was night when I arrived. There were a lot of Poles traveling, dealing on the black market. I sat on the ground with them, waiting for dawn. A Russian came by: "Come with me!" I looked at him. I didn't want to. He took me by the hand and pulled me. There was a Polish agent across from me: "Don't go. They're looking for women." When I heard that, I ran. I'm still running.

Day dawned, but where should I go? I saw a soldier, a colonel maybe:

"Do you know a hospital where there are wounded soldiers?"

He showed me the way. I got there. There was a wall around. I walked around. I saw a wounded man. He was wearing a bathrobe:

"Do you know this name?"

"I can't tell. There are a lot of them I don't know. Go to the office, you'll find out."

I went to the office. "What name?" She looked but didn't find anything. I asked her to try again. She was a Russian woman who spoke a little Polish. I looked too, and I saw the name way down at the bottom. "Go with him." I accompanied the soldier to the room and waited outside. He returned with a nurse. "He is wounded so bad that he can't come out. Go see him." I went in. There were three rows of beds. I looked, but I didn't see him. I looked again. He was way at the end, his head bandaged. He had been wounded eleven miles from Berlin. When I came in, he saw me. He didn't ask me anything. He knew everything. He didn't have to ask. I didn't tell him anything, he understood everything.

And what of the fates of our other characters? After the arrest of Golda R.'s husband, she fled to a sister-in-law, in Viry-Chatillon, where she remained hidden until the end of the war. At the Liberation, as soon as she returned to Paris, she met a returnee who, with brutal frankness, confirmed the death of her husband.

At the Liberation, the Resistance liberated Viry. All the Jews who had been in hiding rejoiced and danced. But I wept. "You're rejoicing. You have your children, your husbands. I'm still in the dark."

[. . .] Walking in the street, in Paris, I met one of our friends. He came up to me. His daughter had boarded in my house. He had returned. He said to me: "Golda, I can tell you that Avrom won't come back. He swelled up after two weeks in Auschwitz and died. I buried him myself. If you need a witness for your pension, you can quote me."

She also learned what happened to Chil, her former suitor. Chil, Golda's and Rosette's indecisive lover, Chil, who had finally married Rosette, also died in Auschwitz. He committed suicide by throwing himself against the barbed wire.

RETURNS

Are these evanescent traces in the memories of the survivors all that is left of the original world? To exist in memory is a form of existence after all, one that is nourished by nostalgia. Not a simple regret over the past or a romantic sense of the ephemeral, it is the stubborn quest for a destroyed world. This nostalgia permeates memories in various tones, from violent aspiration to modest melancholy. It is manifest throughout the narratives, sometimes in pathetic effusions, sometimes in a discreet remark or in a sigh or in silence.

Georges F.:

That was my life. Now, why do I want to go back there? It would certainly give me pleasure to see things again, to see how they turned out, how it is now. Yes, even without contact with people. I wouldn't have contact with people I don't know. I wouldn't even tell them I was born there. But I have an enormous desire to see the place where I spent my youth. Even if it doesn't exist anymore, I would recognize the place all the same. It could not have moved. Even if there's a house where there was once a courtyard, I would recognize precisely that place where my courtyard was. We lived there.

With this throbbing subject of return, the memories we have collected converge with the written memoirs that have multiplied in France over the last ten years: autobiographies, chronicles, testimonies. We will present a few examples of this abundant literature, as a comparison and to close our tour.

Return can be an obsession. For Ginette Hirtz, it is, first of all, the return to her hometown, in this case, Amiens, to be there to greet those who disappeared in case they came back: you really need an address, a familiar place where you can be found.[25] But fate can be ironic: she could not return home, for the door had been sealed shut by the English authorities. She had now to prove her identity after dissimulating it for months. When the door was finally opened, what horror she experienced at the spectacle of death and decay:

One image has survived in my memory—of a soup tureen filled with spaghetti swarming with worms, on a shelf in the kitchen. Broken cabinets, clothes strewn over the filthy, stained floor. I went forward as onto a stage set, without recognizing anything except minute absurd traces in some nook, staggering.[26] [*The narrator undertook to clean the house, to tidy it up, and*

25. Ginette Hirtz, *Les Hortillonnages sous la grêle: Histoire d'une famille juive en France sous l'Occupation* [Gardens under Hail: The History of a Jewish Family in France Under the Occupation] (Paris: Mercure de France, 1982), p. 128.
26. Ibid., p. 128.

even to reconstruct the decor she had known. For the idea is to re-create a "pretense of a home," while waiting for her parents, in the very place of the lost Paradise.] Hope riveted us to that encounter with those who disappeared: the address of 14 Rue Alberic-de-Calonne in Amiens.[27]

There is another original world, even older than the one where one was born: the Holy Land. After living under several false identities and even thinking of converting to Catholicism, Saul Friedländer decided to go to Palestine to find his true identity. For him that provided the sense of a definitive break with his past and his entry into a new era. On the ship, shortly before landing, he lost the only souvenir he had of his father, a watch, and he interpreted this loss as a symbolic rupture:

There was no way of recovering it. Thus the most beloved memento of my childhood disappeared at the moment that I was approaching Israel, at the dawn of a new life. Symbolically, what measured time past was no more: symbolically, everything was beginning all over again.[28]

However, in the extremely skillful composition of his book, Saul Friedländer constantly interweaves times. In a series of flashbacks and flash-forwards, he can move in a few pages from the account of his arrival in Israel (in 1947) to the analysis of his feelings at the moment he writes (June 5, 1977) to the memory of the Six Day War—then, finally, to return far, very far back, to that time with which he has not entirely broken (despite the symbol of the lost watch), that of his native land. Through the art of writing, he also attempts to realize the ambition of the famous Rabbi Loew, creator and then destroyer of the Golem: to abolish time, to achieve the fusion of past and present.[29] Indeed, what did he find in Israel, in his life barely begun again? Precisely "the way of life of the Jews of Prague," at the time of his childhood.

27. Ibid., p. 140.
28. Saul Friedländer, *When Memory Comes* (New York: Farrae, Straus & Giroux), p. 186.
29. Ibid., pp. 18–20.

It was in the evening, after long workdays in the sun, that the world of "yesterday" came to occupy its true place once again. Over their bridge game, surrounded by the few pieces of furniture and books that still belonged to "back home," our peasants took on their real nature once more and dropped their masks, so to speak. Heller, Fleishman, Prager, or Glaser seemed to forget the mosquito bites, the drone of the sprinklers, or the smell of orange blossom, and they must all have had the impression that they were back once again in those large, rather dark apartments that I had known for such a short time, but whose scent, that discreet charm made up of old things, wax-polished wood, and well-worn leather, I could still describe today. . . . The way of life of the Jews of Prague of my childhood was perhaps futile and "rootless," seen from a historical viewpoint. Yet this way of life was ours, the one we treasured.[30]

Some have attempted to rediscover the original world by going to look for it where it really was, returning to the very places where their ancestors had lived, by a pilgrimage, by returning to the shtetl. Maurice Rajsfus had made a first trip to Poland in 1935, at the age of seven, to Bledow, the village where his mother was born. He was accompanying his parents, who had themselves been away for ten years, on a visit to his maternal grandmother. His parents had already adapted to another way of life and he remembers with bitter irony that, during that first trip, in spite of their admonitions, he was an unbearably fresh kid. Forty-five years later, he refuses to think of himself as a Jew but he does feel the strange, almost "morbid" need to make the pilgrimage: "I've been haunted by this project for more than twenty years."[31]

So, in 1980, he made the second trip. Arriving in Warsaw, he didn't recognize any of the streets he had once known. But when someone told him that he was crossing the border of the former ghetto, he says: "I can't help trembling and, calmly, I explain: not that I'm of Jewish origin, as I often say when anyone questions me about that, but that I am a Jew. Quite simply."[32]

30. Ibid., pp. 8–9.
31. Rajsfus, *Quand j'étais juif* [When I Was a Jew], p. 209.
32. Ibid., p. 219.

Overwhelmed by emotion, Maurice Rajsfus becomes a Jew again in another place too: at the end of his quest, returning at last to the original place, Bledow, the former shtetl. At first, the village seems completely unfamiliar to him; on entering, he discovers a church which he had "thrown out of his memory," while the synagogue had remained "so present" to him. This unexpected landscape plunges him into a profound confusion until, led along by some reminiscence, he finds both his grandmother's house and the child he was:

Everything was clear in my memory. I remembered perfectly the baker's house and the bakery, the smell of good bread that drifted into the street. All of a sudden, I remembered the pond where the Polish children had pushed me after throwing stones at me. I remembered the carts and the horses, the peasant women with scarves on their heads and you could have sworn they were the same ones who were strolling in the church square where Tadeusz had parked his car. I felt lost near that church, a complete intruder into that landscape. . . . I was helpless, already thinking I had made that trip for nothing. To have come so far and to find an unexpected landscape, what an atrocious deception. . . . Despite my friends who explain to me that they are going to inquire since they felt my confusion, I walk away, practically escape from them and here I am, in the street. That can only be the sidewalk on the right. Where is the house? I don't have time to reflect. Almost a half century disappears in a fraction of a second. I stagger and lean against the wall. Suddenly I burst into sobs. I'm crying like a baby, more nervously perhaps, but almost without tears. It hurts so much to rediscover the traces of a happy past. All those old stones that knew my mother. . . . I no longer control myself and I cry.[33]

To return to the shtetl: it isn't necessary to pick up physically and go look for it in space; it is enough to journey in time and rediscover it in imagination. Such is the return, or pilgrimage, of Regine Robin, into the past: "I remember a Kaluszyn that I never knew."[34] She starts by retracing family legends, reproducing tales she heard from her father,

33. Ibid., pp. 225–226.
34. Regine Robin, *Le Cheval blanc de Lenine, ou l'histoire autre* [Lenin's White Horse or Different History] (Brussels: Complexe, 1979), p. 19.

enriching them with scenes she reinvents. History goes back to the ancestor Moshe who, during the massacres of 1648, had an epic dialogue with Bogdan Chmielnicki; his son Junkle, a disciple of the false messiah Sabbatai Zevi, was sold to Berber pirates in Constantinople; Shlomo, Junkle's great-grandson, one of the three hundred disciples of the Baal Shem Tov, was a sage who lived for a hundred and twenty years; Schmil, the great-grandfather of Regine Robin's grandfather, was the musician of the family, who once played the violin for Napoleon. As for the author's father, he had met Lenin in 1920, leading the Bolshevik army "on a beautiful white horse," and had conducted his own epic dialogue with him on the meaning of the Revolution. Then, in the course of her journey through the centuries, Regine Robin stops at a certain moment. More precisely, she stops time in the year 1931, to re-create a day in Kaluszyn. "Yes, a day in Kaluszyn, in my mother's house."[35] She is truly present in another world, in a period when she wasn't yet born:

More precisely, a summer night. It is very heavy. A storm is threatening. The whole day has been nothing but a slow incandescence. We're stifling. . . . My mother's grandfather, Avram Zuker, born in 1857 (so he was seventy-four years old in 1931) barely works anymore. . . . Tonight he hurries. . . . Farther away on the Warshawa Gass, my grandfather Raime Mortre closes his candy shop. Business hasn't been good. He thinks more and more seriously of going to Warsaw where two of his sons have already moved. . . . Yes, of leaving Kaluszyn. Tonight, he almost makes the decision. . . . My father is far from having finished with his shaving brushes. What heat. The day has been rough. The police broke into the cell meeting. True, once again, they could pretend that the comrades were waiting for a haircut. . . . My mother rocks my brother. He's only a year old. She sings an old Yiddish lullaby to him. "Happy is he who has a mother and a little cradle." Ten years later, I too will hear this refrain. She opens the window. No wind . . . [36]

And there is more. At the end of her pilgrimage, Regine Robin reinvents history, or at least her own history, and forges a new fate for

35. Ibid., p. 67.
36. Ibid., pp. 67–71.

herself: she too is born in Kaluszyn (some twenty years before her real date of birth) and, from then on, lives the life of a shtetl girl. This then is the opposite of the survival of those who lived through the genocide since the issue here is a previous life, a pre-life, whose end is none other than Treblinka, where "everything is finished."[37]

There remains one last form of return: the narrator abolishes time not by going backward, from the present to the past, but by keeping that past so alive inside himself that it truly lives in the present. After the disappearance of her parents, Ginette Hirtz feels herself to be "their free and voluntary extension, moved by them."[38] *When she returned to Amiens right after the Liberation, it was her father who made decisions for her: "It was still him, dead, who dictated that behavior to me."*[39] *And Ginette Hirtz, born in France to an assimilated family, herself a professor of literature whose whole mode of thought is rationalist, uses the metaphor of the dybbuk: it is as if she is inhabited, possessed by the spirit of her father. Again at the Liberation, when she returns to the little woods he had bought before the war and notes that the oaks have been cut down, she is gripped by rage and despair: "My father howled in me like a dybbuk, and he breathed scornful attitudes into me, fierce words for which the appraisor had no use."*[40] *At the end of her narrative, meditating on her life and her profession, she realizes that it is the spirit of her parents she has attempted to instill into her role as a mother and her work as a professor: "Into all the young people that I have loved, educated, accompanied for a long or short period of time: my brother, my children, some of my students, the dybbuk of my parents has passed without my even knowing it rationally."*[41] *And Ginette Hirtz ends her memoirs as she had begun, by going quite naturally, without any transitions, from the dybbuk of her parents to the Winterreise, adding a few small details: she lies on the ground and listens to one of her son's favorite pieces of music. Thus the chain of the generations is reconstructed to the sound of Schubert's lieder. "I listen to that singing blended with the piano and I curl up in my father's arms, protected from the danger that threatens, over there."*[42]

37. Ibid., pp. 133–134.
38. Hirtz, *Les Hortillonnages*, p. 104.
39. Ibid., p. 124.
40. Ibid., p. 146.
41. Ibid., p. 173.
42. Ibid.

| *Remember* | FROM EASTERN EUROPE to the Mediterranean countries, Jewish memories echo one another. Despite the diversity of paths and the irreducible uniqueness of each experience lived, individual memories relate basically the same trials: uprooting, migrations, persecutions, impossible mourning, exile. Shared memories, single and multiple, memories of memories: each individual, a spokesman for the others, both |

transmits and contributes to shape the collective memory. Is it accidental that all memories are arranged according to similar structures, oriented toward the final catastrophe? The setting changes, the scene shifts over immense distances, but it is actors in the same play exchanging their lines. And the theater is history.

These mutual relays between the individual and the collective underlie not only oral memories but also written memories as indicated by two very different and independent literary genres that developed since World War II. One is the monumental enterprise of editing the *Yisker-biher,* "Books of Memory," dedicated to several hundred disappeared communities; the other is the amazing efflorescence of autobiographies, chronicles, and narratives of authors who lived through the drama of Nazi persecutions or exile.

The fashioning of books of memory by the survivors of genocide constitutes an event that, although widely unrecognized, is in itself historic:[1] the more than five hundred works cataloged to date form an immense library of tombstones. It is a memory that is largely spontaneous, not supported by any official or state institution. Rather, it is the members of the associations of emigrants from the same community (the *Landmanshaften*) who have set up editorial committees responsible for the preparation and publication of each work. The role of these associations is indicated by the geography of the *Yisherbiher*: the enormous majority (85 percent) correspond to what Poland was between the two world wars. Most often, the authors of the contributions are not professional writers but are either survivors who offer their testimony or simply emigrants who recall the lost world. More than about ten thousand contributors have taken up their pens.[2] These books of memory are not only a collective Kaddish. They wish to recall not only the death of the martyrs but their lives as well. Hence, they recount narratives, memories, and anecdotes in order to resurrect those who disappeared in their environment, their customs, their daily activities, their faith, their hopes. We have in these works a genuine literary genre: it imposes on each of these books a plan that follows regular rules, both thematically and chronologically, and that confers coherence and unity on them. At the same time, the authors, freely following their personal inspiration, themes, and periods, overlap in the successive chapters. Editors mix different types of texts (historical sketches, old press cuttings, first person memories), so that the collective memory draws its substance from individual memoirs and adopts their rhythms and movements.

Recently, works coming from the Mediterranean communities and designed for their descendants have also been published. Without presenting the tragic and necrological character of the memory books—rather than tombstones they are portable territories—they store up in a single volume images, remarkable

1. Two recent works, dedicated to the *Yisker-Buher,* present convenient, brief anthologies: Annette Wieviorka and Itzhok Niborski, *Les Livres du souvenir*; Jack Kugelmass and Jonathan Boyarin, *From a Ruined Garden: The Memorial Books of Polish Jewry* (New York: Schocken Books), 1983.

2. Zachery Baker, "Bibliography of Eastern European Memorial Books, updated and revised," *Toledot,* Fall 1979–Winter 1980; the same author completed that bibliography in Appendix I of Jack Kugelmass and Jonathan Boyarin, pp. 223–264.

individuals, and events which are present in the memory, and transmit a collective identity.

Yet another phenomenon has developed over these last years, the multiplication of autobiographies. As in oral memoirs, the recurrent themes echo from one work to the other. They tell of nostalgia for the lost world, of tribulations crossing borders, of persecutions and exile. A chronological gap, however, separates the *Yizkor-biher* from the published autobiographies. The production of the books of memory began right after the genocide, reaching its peak between 1965 and 1975, while the big wave of autobiographies appeared later. But both are literatures of testimony and mourning: the *Yizkor-biher* record the history of the martyrs for posterity; similarly, most of the autobiographies are dedicated to the memory of parents or to the education of children and present the same obituary tones.[3] However, the memory books form a self-enclosed genre. Their distribution extends only to the network of organizations formed by those who came from the former communities, and their language (Hebrew or Yiddish) usually makes them inaccessible to new generations. Other forms of expression were therefore necessary. Perhaps, some of the autobiographies bear witness to a generational phenomenon: those who were marked by the traumas of their wartime childhood (like Claudine Vegh's orphans) have reached maturity. Thirty or forty years after the tragedy, they are the age their parents were at the time, and their own children are as old as they themselves had been. Hence, a double process is operating, one of identification and a re-animation of the past and one of the irrepressible need to transmit their testimony along the chain of the generations. No doubt it was necessary to wait all these years for the work of memory—in this case, of mourning—to be accomplished.

One may ask: Why are there so many correspondences between the memories of the Jews of eastern Europe and those of the Mediterranean Jews when their original milieus and their paths seem so different? All of them left their native land and

3. Cf. Lucette Valensi, "From Sacred History . . . ," and Nathan Wachtel, "Remember . . . ," in *History and Anthropology,* 1986.

knew exile, but the former also suffered, directly, the shock of genocide. If exile seems commonplace, genocide is a unique event in history and the memories of those who have survived are marked by tragic tones and by the imprint of impossible mourning. But those who were not touched by the Nazi threat also incorporate the *Shoah* into their memory and inscribe it in their own past just as (and even more than) the Spanish Expulsion at the dawn of the modern age became a theme of reference for Jewish collective memory. Thus, multiple memories, Ashkenazic and Sepharadic, converge to form, with nuances and variations, a single collective memory. For the Jews, whether from the east or the west, share a common historical experience: an exile distinct from all other exiles. Already in their countries of origin, from the Baltic to the Mediterranean, they were in a state of exile. Thus their present exile is an exile of the second order, an exile within an exile. Nostalgia for lost Andalusias is grafted onto the initial dispersion and takes up the relay of nostalgia for Jerusalem, so tenaciously proclaimed throughout the centuries.

Profound memory, founding memory—it is no less. Before they migrated, these Jews belonged to cultural minorities where they were immersed, despite internal diversities, as into a totality in which their being assumed meaning and confronted the dominant societies. So often hostile, those societies fostered Jewish difference and the Jews' sense of their own identity. Beyond the attachment to the native land, this identity was based on the identification with a shared historical fate, that of the Jewish Diaspora, and on the millennial loyalty to the same religious faith. Loyalty here coincided with memory, which the Bible commands as an absolute duty: *zakhor,* remember.[4] Most Jewish holidays—it has often been mentioned—are most essentially the commemoration of great events of sacred history: the Exodus from Egypt, the giving of the Torah at Mount Sinai. These "basic experiences of Judaism" are defined as manifestations of God in history; by replicating them in the present,

4. Cf. Yosef Hayim Yerushalmi, *Zakhor* (New York: Schocken Books, 1989).

memory is converted into faith and hope.[5] Jewish theological thought has consistently maintained the tensions entailed in belief in the divine presence—which is both prescriptive and saving—by orienting them toward a future in which the omnipotence and transcendence of God on the one hand and manifestations of divine power and human freedom on the other, would be reconciled. Within the totality of Judaism, the awareness of the incompleteness of history leads to the requirement of redemption and messianic expectation.

Is it accidental that the recurrent themes (Paradise Lost, Exile, Return) that supply the basic frameworks of oral as well as written memories coincide with eminently biblical themes? Must we interpret them as the expression of a collective unconscious? This unconscious would be nothing else but the internalization of a culture: the witnesses whose voices we have listened to, although often detached from religion, are more or less permeated with a tradition of which biblical teaching is an essential component. Even when this culture has weakened or combined with that of another language (German, Russian, or French), something remains of it, transcending acculturation and assimilation. And this ultimate remnant is memory. A memory composed insolubly of unique memories of particular private details and the general categories that subsume them and give them meaning. Individual memory is embedded in a long history from which it derives structures and intelligibility. Conversely, collective memory is fed by individual memories, even following their wanderings and internal rhythms. These overlapping exchanges generate a multiple memory that gives to Jewish identity in our time a foundation that is both ancient and renewed.

This memory, henceforth marked by the trauma of genocide, emerges from the most tragic event in secular history. How does it fit in with traditional Jewish memory, defined by the faithfully renewed reactualization of the events of holy history? The memories we have heard belong to a secularized memory. They do culminate in a waiting and bear the imprint of nostalgia

5. Emil Fackenheim, *God's Presence in History: Jewish Affirmations and Philosophical Reflections* (New York: Harper Torchbooks, 1973).

but theirs is the banal nostalgia for the original world and the senseless waiting for those who have disappeared. No trace of a messianic hope remains in these narratives—except, for some, in the equally secular form of the return to the Land of Israel. Of course, the secularization of Jewish memory is the result of an already ancient process, which was widely developed in the country of origin before the departure into exile. But, in the history of Jewish memory, it is clearly genocide that catalyzes a radical break: How can theology account for Auschwitz? How can the presence of God in history be reconciled with that absolute evil, the Shoah? "It is not strange," notes Emil Fackenheim, "that, until recent years, Jewish theological thinking observed an almost total silence on the question of the Holocaust."[6] If Auschwitz is an unprecedented event, evil in history is not new, and catastrophes have not been lacking in the fate of the Jewish people: at least the victims of Worms and Mayence or those of the Inquisition had the choice between conversion and death and could hope that their martyrdom testified to their faith. "In Auschwitz, on the contrary, there was no choice, young and old, believers and non-believers were massacred without discrimination. Can there be a martyr where there is no choice?"[7] In Auschwitz, God was no longer present in history, and, for the Messiah, it was too late.[8]

Are we abandoned then in theological silence? Perhaps. But genocide makes memory—even secularized memory—into a duty more sacred than ever. The Nazis reduced their victims to anonymous numbers, transformed their corpses into smoke, did their best to wipe out all traces of their existence, even their memory: as if they had never been. Conversely, with the will of survival, the denial of Auschwitz is the safeguard of memory. The witnesses we have heard piously recall what was—all that was—with obsessive care, so that we too can transmit the echo

6. Ibid., pp. 125–126.
7. Ibid., p. 130.
8. Cf. Ibid., pp. 138, 152, commenting on Élie Wiesel, *Les Portes de la forêt* [The Gates of the Forest] (Paris: Editions du Seuil, 1964).

of their voices to the sentinels who will come after us. And what those voices repeat over and over, stubbornly, indefatigably, is the biblical imperative, the essential and ever-present obligation: *zakhor,* remember.

designer: Seventeenth Street Studios
compositor: Prestige Typography   **text and display:** Bembo
printer: Thomson-Shore, Inc.   **binder:** Thomson-Shore, Inc.